D0880068

THE CLASSICS OF WESTERN SPIRITUALITY

THE CLASSICS OF WESTERN SPIRITUALITY
A Library of the Great Spiritual Masters

Apocalyptic Spirituality

TREATISES AND LETTERS OF
LACTANTIUS, ADSO OF MONTIER-EN-DER,
JOACHIM OF FIORE, THE FRANCISCAN SPIRITUALS, SAVONAROLA

TRANSLATION AND INTRODUCTION
BY
BERNARD McGINN

PREFACE
BY
MARJORIE REEVES

PAULIST PRESS

Covert Art
YISROEL TUVIA HELLER'S etchings, photographs, watercolors, sculptures, and paintings are in several public and private collections. His pictures have been used by the major New York City publishing companies for a wide range of books dealing with subjects from accounting to astronomy. Articles on his works have appeared in *Popular Photography, Petersen's Photographic, Art News, N.Y. Arts Journal,* and *Hadassah Magazine.* He is founder and chairman of the Jewish Visual Artists' Association.

Having had no formal art training, he says his pictures are the result of dreams and experiences resulting from dreams. Of the image on this cover, he says, "One night an angel with wings of light came to me and carried me high above the apocalypse."

Design: Barbini, Pesce & Noble, Inc.

Library of Congress
Catalog Card Number: 79-90834

ISBN: 0-8091-2242-1

Published by Paulist Press
997 Macarthur Boulevard
Mahwah, New Jersey 07430

Printed and bound in the
United States of America

Contents

CONTENTS

Author of the Preface

Marjorie Reeves received an M.A. from St. Hugh's College, Oxford, and a Ph.D. from the University of London. A Fellow of St. Anne's College, Oxford, from 1938 to 1972, she also served as Vice-Principal there for many years. Her honors include a D.Litt. from Oxford, a Fellowship in the Royal Historical Society, and membership in many of the most prestigious educational commissions of the United Kingdom. In recent years she has taught and lectured at a number of American universities. Although she has written widely in the areas of education and general medieval history, Miss Reeves is best known for her work in the history of medieval apocalypticism. A series of ground-breaking articles and her collaboration with L. Tondelli and B. Hirsch-Reich on the critical edition of Joachim of Fiore's *Book of Figures* (1953) culminated in the publication of two major books on Joachim and his role in later medieval apocalypticism—*The Influence of Prophecy in the Later Middle Ages: A Study in Joachimism* (1969), and *The Figurae of Joachim of Fiore* (1972, with B. Hirsch-Reich).

Foreword

"Amen. Come, Lord Jesus" (Apoc. 22:20). The significance of these closing words of the New Testament for later Christian spirituality is the subject of this volume. Biblical scholars of the past generation have emphasized the importance of apocalyptic beliefs for the origins of Christianity, and the studies of patristic experts and medievalists have shown that expectations of the imminent end of the current age and the return of the Lord did not die out in the second century.

The relation of apocalyptic traditions to religious, social and political change during the centuries between A. D. 200 and 1500 were extraordinarily complex. This selection of texts does not try to illustrate the full range of transformations that apocalypticism underwent during the patristic and medieval periods. Its purpose is rather to show how apocalyptic beliefs continued to serve as the basis for distinctive forms of piety over these centuries.

Although they speak to particular times and situations, the texts translated here, many for the first time available in English, are part of a continuous tradition. The Seventh Book of the *Divine Institutes* of Lactantius was written at the time of Constantine's recognition of the Church. It is both a summary of early Christian beliefs about the Antichrist and the millennial age, as well as a witness to the changes brought about in Christian apocalypticism through contact with other religions. The monk Adso, whose treatise dates from the middle of the bleak tenth century, provides a classic account of Antichrist's career and shows how the Roman empire and her ruler had come to play an important role in Christian hopes for the end of history.

Joachim of Fiore (died 1202) was the most important apocalyptic author of the middle ages. This devout monk's complex historical symbolism, an original appropriation of the pessimism and optimism which always characterize apocalyticism, centered on hopes for the coming purification of the Church. Joachim's thought is illustrated here by four brief texts and a key excerpt from one of his major works. Much influenced by the thought of Joachim, especially by his hopes for a future order of "spiritual men," the radical wing of the Franciscan order developed a special form of apocalyptic piety during the thirteenth century. Letters from two of the leaders of this "Spiritual" party among the Franciscans, Peter Olivi and Angelo of Clareno, illustrate their suffering and dedication.

The fiery Dominican Girolamo Savonarola (1452-98) was the most noted apocalyptic preacher of the end of the middle ages. The friar's *Compendium of Revelations*, a defense of his prophetic career and an allegorical account of a heavenly dream vision, provides an exemplary illustration of the continuing importance of apocalypticism in Renaissance society.

Preface

The history of Christian Apocalyptic reveals one thing very clearly: the desire of the human soul to find a significant place for itself in the time process. This is rooted in the Judaeo-Christian lineal concept of history, and belief in the soul's immortality is intimately linked with the place of the human personality in an ongoing historical process which has two terminals—an individual one in death and a universal one in the end of the world. This sense of "place" and of "end" is one of the chief roots of morality, and in all generations Christian writers have exhorted themselves and others to be "watchful servants," each playing his allotted role responsibly, "for the end cometh."

> Ye servants of the Lord,
> Each in his office, wait,
> Observant of his heavenly word,
> And watchful at his gate.
>
> Watch! 'tis your Lord's command,
> And while we speak he's near;
> Mark the first signal of his hand,
> And ready all appear.
> (P. Doddridge)

This eighteenth-century hymn echoes the exhortations of Lactantius in the early fourth century. There is also an element of "waiting" here which is, indeed, common to all human experience, since everything must have an end and we are always waiting for it. Because Christian Apocalyptic writings set the life of the human soul in the context of a time process begun, and to be ended, by God, they speak to both individuals and societies in terms of watchful duty and patient waiting. All the writings in this selection sound these notes in one way or another. The term "Apocalyptic" is, of course, used in different ways, but if, in this context, we think of it, in the editor's words, as centering "on the relation between time and eternity, between man's life in history and the heavenly realm," it is clear that much Christian spirituality is apocalyptic, for the soul's meditation on its own meaning and destiny cannot escape this dimension.

Characteristically, such meditation swings between terror and hope. Humanity was blighted by the Fall. An ineluctable law decrees that it must be purged before it can be redeemed, and this process must be cosmic as well as individual. The concept of the End imposes a sense of climax which dictates that, beyond the daily lot of human sorrow and punishment, tribulation must rise into a dramatic final act. Expectation loads the imagination with portentous and horrifying images. Antichrist, collective and individual, stalks through the history of the imagination from earliest Christian times, the "historical" embodiment of Evil, and when he finds his biographer in Abbot Adso in the tenth century, this becomes a best seller.

The message of redemption beyond the dreadful flood remains the one sustaining hope. Here we perceive that apocalyptic spirituality bifurcates into two forms—social and individual. Christianity inherited from Judaism not only the idea of the chosen people but also that of a God involved in his creation at both the material and the socio-political levels. St. Paul saw the whole creation in travail along with man, and St. John saw the New Jerusalem coming down from heaven to earth. Thus it was natural that in early Christian centuries hope took the form of a redeemed and recreated society in a redeemed creation. We find this vision and the dreams of millennialists such as Irenaeus, Commodian and Lactantius himself: if the tribulation of Antichrist was to be cosmic, redemption must

also be cosmic. In more limited form we meet it in the seventh
century in the Syriac pseudo-Methodius where consolation in
face of the political onslaught of Islam is sought in the political
dream of a Christian Last World Emperor. But millennial visions raised so many problems in terms of fantastic materialist
hopes of imminent millennium, which undermined the sober
morality of waiting, that we see developing the counter view
that the only important climax in history had already occurred
in the incarnation, that the only redemption within the time
process was that of the individual soul, and that the redeemed
society belonged essentially to the blessedness of eternity. The
pilgrim Church, marching toward the end of time, did, indeed,
already taste of its redemption, but could not be relieved from
tribulation until translated into its supra-temporal state. Thus
St. Augustine, in the early fifth century, sought to block the
road to hopes of any blessed age within history, and his view
dominated much medieval thinking. Emphasis was laid on the
spiritual duty of individual souls to watch and wait devoutly
for the End, for the world was growing old, the world was slip-
ping downhill, the hopes of the world were collapsing.

Nothing, however, could stifle speculation. "It is not for
you to know the times or the seasons which the Father hath put
in his own power" was the oft-quoted warning to Christ's disciples, but the Old Testament prophetic tradition affirmed
God's revelation of his purposes in history to his chosen servants in the past, and men in the Christian Dispensation felt
themselves permitted to seek, under God's guidance, the signs
of the future. The collection of signs—pagan, Jewish, Christian—became an absorbing preoccupation. Sibylline oracles
were interwoven with scriptural texts, both canonical and
apocryphal. Lactantius in his day and Adso in his represent
this concern, and Adso has already picked up the optimistic
"sign" of the Last World Emperor prophecy, thus reviving in
the West hopes which the Augustinian view sought to quench.
But it is in the twelfth century that we really begin to detect a
new interest in the process of history itself and especially in the
Church's history since the incarnation. There is a new awareness of change as a factor in the Church's experience: the truths

of the faith are timeless, but spirituality expresses itself in different historical forms in different ages. If these developments are the work of the Holy Spirit, through what stages is the Church being led and toward what end? The image of the Book with Seven Seals is seen as a figure of the Church's history: the six stages can be mapped out with confidence, but where is the opening of the seventh seal, always associated with the idea of the Sabbath Age, to take place? Still following the Augustinian view, Anselm of Havelberg places it beyond time. Yet an optimistic note of some further achievement within history is now creeping in and finds expression in the belief that after the death of Antichrist a "space" will be given before the End, not only for the "refreshment of the saints" but for the conversion of the nations, Jewish and pagan. The universal triumph of Christianity would, after all, be the triumph of history.

These lines of expectation prepared the way for Joachim of Fiore's break with the Augustinian tradition in his great affirmation that before the end of time, but after the greatest tribulation, men would attain a further spiritual illumination in the Age of the Spirit, the Third Age or *Status*. Joachim denied himself the title of prophet but claimed to read the signs which God had set in history by the divine gift of spiritual intelligence bestowed upon him. These signs were, of course, enshrined in the sacred history of the Scriptures, but were also to be sought in the history of the Church and in secular history. Through these signs the ceaseless activity of the Trinity manifested itself in historical happenings, charting, as it were, the great sweep of progress through the three stages of human development associated with Father, Son and Spirit. Joachim was a true spiritual father, exhorting his brethren and disciples by preaching and by writing to be watchful and waiting as faithful servants of the Lord. Like other biblical exegetes of his time he used the fourfold senses of Scripture (which he extended to five) to edify the individual soul, leading it finally to the anagogical sense, the anticipation of the heavenly life. But he also read the signs in terms of the total meaning of history and developed his method of concords or parallels between the first two stages of history from which he attempted very tentatively to extrapolate the pattern into the future third stage into which he thought the Church was just entering. At its most elaborate this method became his *sensus typicus* significantly divided into seven modes which represented the seven ways in which the inner relationships of the Trinity were expressed in history.[1] Thus Joachim's sense of apocalyptic led him to write, not only for the comfort of individual souls, but also in order to prepare them for the *transitus* into the new society of the third age, partially delineated in the figure of the New People of the Third *Status*. His originality lies particularly in his affirmation of a further turning point in history and a further stage of spiritual illumination, yet he does not wholly break with Augustinian teaching: the third stage must itself deteriorate and end in tribulation; there is no human perfection this side of Judgment Day.

Nevertheless, Joachim's legacy to the succeeding generations was an exhilarating prospect of "something more to come" before history was to be wound up. The *transitus* through tribulation—figuratively the crossing of Jordan— might be severe, but to be assigned a place among the "New People" of the future lifted the eyes to the Promised Land beyond. In the thirteenth century Franciscan spirituality was infused with an urgent sense of mission *in novissimis diebus* and running through this was the conviction that St. Francis had embodied in his life a new "advent" of Christ, thus initiating the further stage of spiritual understanding. This probably had Joachimist roots, since Joachim saw the work of Christ as being completed in his Mystical Body of the Third *Status*. Those who clung passionately to St. Francis' Rule and Testament saw absolute poverty as the key to this last stage of history and read the signs as a vindication of their belief. Sevenfold tribulations must be heaped upon them, but beyond Antichrist the future would be theirs. The dynamism which springs from the total belief that history is on your side infused many of the early Franciscans and inspired the passionate obstinacy with which

1. On the fives and sevens in Joachim's hermeneutics, see M. Reeves, "The Abbot Joachim's Sense of History," *1274. Année charnière. Mutations et continuités* (Paris, 1977), 787–95.

Clareno and his group, for instance, endured persecution and wrestled with the cruel dilemma between obedience and a sense of utter rightness. In the end such a belief, under persecution, produces the mentality of the "saving remnant": the powers that be have become the instruments of Antichrist and the true Church now resides solely in the faithful few gathered in the Ark. This was the final fate of the pathetic Fraticelli and Beguin groups, battered and drowned by waves of persecution in the fourteenth century.

Extremes of hope and terror in anticipation of the last age still swept through Renaissance Italy in the fifteenth century. It is a mistake to suppose that the calm steady light of humanist scholarship left no dark corners in the imagination. The Florentine Platonists were open to mystical as well as rational approaches to knowledge, and the prophets of note who appeared sporadically in Italian cities were not treated with scorn. The sources of Savonarola's prophetic preaching were medieval and in many respects Joachimist, but his words did not strike an anachronistic note or fall on alienated ears. Some members of Marsilio Ficino's Platonic Academy could join Savonarola's disciples, the *Piagnoni,* and Botticelli could paint two apocalyptic pictures under his inspiration. The program of the greatest tribulation and the highest human blessedness beyond it continued to dominate the prophetic future to which most people paid attention in Western Europe during the fifteenth and sixteenth centuries. In particular, the Joachimist idea of a new age before the end of time could be transformed by Renaissance aspirations into a vision in which medieval and Renaissance elements are combined: the universalization of Christendom by its extension to all the new worlds, the ecumenical and peaceful rule of a benevolent Emperor and spiritual Pope, the steady spread of enlightenment through the new learning and the printing press. Apocalyptic spirituality was still a universal form of experience in the sixteenth century and was to remain so, in much the same forms, for at least another century.

Marjorie Reeves
St. Anne's College
Oxford

Introduction

APOCALYPTIC SPIRITUALITY

"To prophesy is extremely difficult—especially about the future." [1]

Many may think that all apocalyptic literature deserves to be received with cool irony. The modern frame of mind with its scientific and rationalistic outlook surely has little sympathy with traditional prophecy about the end of history based on divine revelation. Even among believing Christians, the demythologizing of the scriptural message would seem to leave small viability for biblical apocalyptic. Is there anything more mythological in the whole of scripture than the Book of Daniel and the Apocalypse of John with their bizarre visions and luxuriant symbols? Is there anything more ludicrous in the history of Christianity than the stream of apocalyptic prophets and publicists whose announcements of the proximity of the end of history have long since been overtaken by its course?

Anyone who surveys the full range of present-day Christian beliefs, of course, would be forced to admit that there are still strong elements of literal apocalypticism found in many fundamentalist and charismatic groups. The success of the works of Hal Lindsey is evidence enough of how many mil-

1

lions of readers still are convinced by literal applications of biblical prophecies to events present and soon to come.[2] (One presumes that at least some of Lindsey's readers go to him for enlightenment and not for entertainment.)

It might be argued that all this proves is that in some less-respectable circles strange ideas will always abound. But the hunger for apocalypse is far more widespread. The case has been advanced that like so many of the traditional modes of religious discourse, apocalypticism has not so much disappeared from the scene as it has adopted a variety of secular disguises.[3] Considerable ingenuity and no little effort would be needed to trace the history of these disguises, though the result would make a fascinating study. J.V. Schall may well be right, however, in his observation that at the present time "apocalypse has become pre-eminently a scientific rather than a religious phenomenon."[4] We are, in fact, surrounded by prophets of approaching doom who base their reading of the times on scientific revelations at times as obscure and controversial as the religious showings of old. Population expansion, the atomic threat, potential atmospheric changes, depletion of essential resources, and a host of other scientific projections can and are being used to predict imminent destruction for the human race and the world. It is not so much the empirical data, correct or incorrect, that is being used as the form and style of the message proclaimed and the way in which action is invoked that mark off such books as Robert Heilbroner's *An Inquiry into the Human Prospect* as a type of secular apocalypse.[5]

Fundamentalist literalism and secular scientific prophetism are not the only existing forms of apocalypticism alive in the modern world. Over the past few decades there have been serious attempts to understand the theological significance of apocalypticism in Jewish and Christian thought. One could point first of all to the studies of the biblical and intertestamental origins of apocalypticism, which have enriched us with new and better editions of texts, a wealth of detailed investigations, and a number of broad treatments that attempt to define the essence of the genre "apocalypse" and to determine the content of apocalypticism. Although there is still considerable disagreement over central issues, the increase in knowledge and interest over the past few decades has been considerable.

These same past years have also seen a renewal of interest in the role of apocalypticism in contemporary theology. German theologians like Ernst Käsemann, Wolfhart Pannenberg, Karl Rahner, and Jürgen Moltmann have devoted much thought to the theological significance of apocalypticism.[6] Swiss theologian H. Mottu has recently studied the implications for contemporary theology of Joachim of Fiore, the foremost medieval apocalyptic author.[7] Without attempting to describe or evaluate these critical retrievals of apocalypticism, their very existence should be enough to make our point: Apocalypticism remains a serious concern for contemporary Christianity.

The bulk of the studies devoted to apocalypticism in recent years has focused on apocalyptic theology, the coherence and claims of the various apocalyptic systems of thought. Though the most work has been done on the intertestamental and New Testament periods, various studies of later Christian apocalypticism have also been produced.[8] Among the areas less touched on in the recent wealth of investigation has been what we will here call apocalyptic spirituality, that is, the ways in which apocalypticism affects the believer and his actions.

This book is designed to be a contribution to wider knowledge of apocalyptic spirituality in the patristic and medieval periods—well over half the time that apocalypticism has been a part of Christian belief. My subject is not apocalyptic thought or theology as such, and hence there is no attempt here to present a general historical sketch, nor to solve any of the hotly disputed questions about the nature and development of apocalyptic thought. If one wishes to learn more about the details of the developing scenario of the last events, there are many texts more essential than those translated here. These treatises and letters have been chosen because of the way in which they manifest how beliefs about the imminent end affected the lives of their adherents. They reveal the particular sense of the divine present in the apocalyptic publicist, the awareness of mission or calling that moved him to his efforts, and above all the outlook and actions that he was trying to encourage in his audience.

Our works span almost twelve centuries and were the products of diverse authors and circumstances. For these reasons individual introductions to the five sections seem necessary to set the stage for each. But two more general questions are better suited to treatment in a general introduction. The first concerns the notion of apocalypticism (or apocalyptic as some would call it in imitation of the German *Apokalyptik*) as it is here employed. How are we to judge which works may be called apocalyptic and which not? The second question revolves around the notion of apocalyptic spirituality itself. Is there really a distinctive apocalyptic spirituality that spans the centuries or is this too broad a category to be useful? So little work has been done in this area that my remarks are meant to be guides to further investigation and debate, not fixed conclusions. The purpose of these selections, indeed, is to present some of the evidence for the answer to this question to a wider audience and thus to stimulate further discussion.

THE NOTION OF APOCALYPTICISM

Apocalypticism, etymologically based on the Greek word for revelation, has usually been understood as indicating a divine message of the imminent end of the world, or at least the end of the present form of the world.[9] However, this dictionary commonplace masks considerable scholarly debate and no little popular confusion of terms.

The confusion of terms results from the relation of apocalypticism to such kindred words as eschatology, prophecy (prophetism), millenarianism, chiliasm, messianism, and the like. We need not ask everyone to agree on the meaning of these terms, but we might at least expect authors to provide us with some preliminary explanation of their own use. Failure to do so, or more frequently the interpretation of another's use of a term according to our own preconceived ideas, has been the source of unnecessary confusion. Briefly put, I take apocalypti-

INTRODUCTION

cism to be a particular form of eschatology, a species of a broader genus that covers any type of belief that looks forward to the end of history as that which gives structure and meaning to the whole. Thus in the Old Testament there is a prophetic eschatology that can be distinguished from an apocalyptic eschatology, as in later Christian history Augustinian eschatology (to give but one example) is decidedly antiapocalyptic in outlook. Prophecy also has a wider sense than apocalypticism. A prophet is any "inspired person who believes that he has been sent by his god with a message to tell."[10] According to this definition all apocalypticists would be prophets, but the reverse would not be true, because not all prophets announced the message distinctive to apocalypticism. What sets off apocalypticism from general eschatology is the sense of the proximity of the end. What makes the apocalypticist a particular kind of prophet is not only the specification of his message, but also the way in which he proclaims it, especially its learned, written, or "scribal" character.[11]

Millenarianism generally refers to beliefs in a coming more perfect terrestrial form of society. Jewish and Christian apocalyptic systems usually contained such hopes, the most noted example being the thousand-year reign of Christ and the saints on earth proclaimed in the twentieth chapter of the Apocalypse (the doctrine of chiliasm). Important as such expectations were to the history of apocalypticism, however, they do not exhaust the content of the apocalyptic message, but concentrate on its optimistic pole. Similarly, the apocalyptic message almost always involves the activity of the returning Christ and various other divine agents, and thus always has elements of messianism; but these too are aspects of the whole, not the thing itself.

If scholars could agree, at least in broad fashion, about what constitutes the core of apocalypticism, these nominalistic problems would probably not bulk as large as they do. But debate about the best way to understand the content of apocalypticism, whether found in a work that is formally an apocalypse or present in some other literary genre, still continues. There is more agreement about what constitutes the genre apocalypse than about what is distinctively apocalyptic, at least in English-speaking scholarship.

Most of the attempts to list the essential components of apocalypticism have directed their attention to the Jewish apocalypses of the period between 200 B.C. and A.D 100. The variety among these lists serves to warn us at the outset that apocalypticism is a complex notion that is difficult, perhaps impossible, to reduce to one single formula. This is particularly true when we attempt to broaden the definition to include later Jewish and Christian beliefs about the imminent end. I would suggest that instead of searching for one essential component or a single list of characteristics based only on the early Jewish examples,[12] we should attempt to work out a structure of interrelated concerns and motifs, not all of which need to be present in any single case and which do not always need to be related in the same way, but which will be broad and flexible enough to do justice to a variety of related traditions over a range of many centuries. We are only at the beginning of such a task, as the following remarks will show.

I believe that the issues and interests of apocalypticism center on the relation between time and eternity, between man's life in history and the heavenly realm that is the home of God's eternal plan. Through the book of the apocalyptic seer a message from the heavenly realm is revealed that proclaims a three-act historical drama of present trial, imminent judgment, and future salvation. This triple pattern is implicitly or explicitly put within the framework of a sense of the total structure of history, frequently a survey of the ages of the world or the succession of empires.[13] A hope for the coming salvation of the just both individually and collectively provides the prime motive for endurance of present trials. For the apocalypticist, death is about to be overcome.

All of these themes are present in varying ways in the Jewish apocalypses of the formative period of 200 B.C. to A.D. 100. They contribute to the evolution of apocalypticism in Christian circles both directly and indirectly over many centuries. Christian apocalypticism, rarely expressed in the formal

INTRODUCTION

genre apocalypse after about A.D. 300, shows similar motifs: the drive toward a universal view of history as a divinely ordered structure; a profound pessimism about the present that is seen as a time of crisis involving moral degeneration, persecution of the good, and the triumph of the wicked; and, finally, an optimism that is founded on a belief in an imminent divine judgment of the wicked and vindication of the just. Vindication was conceived of in many ways, frequently millenarian, but not necessarily so. From its origins, apocalypticism's hopes for the future have involved the transcendence of death. It should not surprise us that Jewish apocalyptic literature seems to have had a double offspring in later Christianity, for not only apocalyptic texts themselves but also the rich visionary literature on the fate of the soul after death have direct links with the Jewish apocalypses of the vital intertestamental period.

APOCALYPTIC SPIRITUALITY

On the basis of these broad themes some aspects of a tradition of apocalyptic spirituality that spans the centuries seem to appear. Though we must remain ever conscious of the significant differences in substance and in nuance (attempts to isolate a single "apocalyptic mentality" usually appear too rigid),[14] there still is good reason for speaking of apocalyptic spirituality as one of the important strands in the history of Christian striving toward God.

The observation that apocalyptic literature is a literature of consolation of those undergoing crisis, especially persecution for religious belief, is a commonplace. Like so many commonplaces, it can be initially helpful, but rapidly grows harmful if it becomes a roadblock to further thought. The relation between apocalyptic religious attitudes and shattering crises— from the persecution of the Jews under Antiochus IV Epiphanes that forms the background to the Book of Daniel up to the Armageddons of modern war—has been eloquently portrayed by Amos N. Wilder in his paper "The Rhetoric of Ancient and Modern Apocalyptic."[15] For Wilder, "the rheto-

7

rics of apocalyptic ... dramatize the group hierophany in a situation of broken continuities."[16] He sees apocalyptic as the product of a general crisis in which all seems forfeit to chaos, and in which revelation as an ecstatic disclosure gives renewed meaning to the historical process in the moment of greatest anomie.[17] It is true that almost every apocalyptic text can be related to some time of crisis, frequently one of persecution. It is also true that apocalyptic texts hold out hope for the suffering righteous. They are told to stand fast in the hour of trial because God will soon come to reward them and to punish their enemies. But we may well ask if crisis really is the cause of apocalypticism and if consolation forms its only message.

As Walter Schmithals has observed, apocalyptic "is always more than a reaction to causal structures in existing reality."[18] The crisis of the persecution of Antiochus Epiphanes did not "cause" the birth of apocalypticism in intertestamental Judaism any more than the crisis of the twelfth-century Church caused the new apocalyptic ideas of Joachim of Fiore. A sense of present crisis might be better described as the occasion or context rather than the motivating force in these cases. While it is true that some of the major stages in the history of apocalyptic traditions have arisen within situations of broken continuities, or of serious social anomie, many others have not. One person's sense of what constitutes a trial or crisis need not coincide with the general judgment of his time or with the later views of historians. Thus the presence of messengers of doom in late Quattrocento Italy, the Age of Savonarola, need not be seen as either typical or anomalous of Renaissance society, but as illustrating one way of coming to terms with the conditions of a highly volatile era. Perhaps the apocalypticist might be better described as one on the lookout for crisis, rather than one who merely reacts to it when it happens. The apocalyptic mentality is a particular form of pre-understanding rather than a mere way of responding. More sensitive to change than the mass of their fellows, apocalypticists are more in need of a religious structure within which to absorb and give meaning to the anxieties that always accompany existence and change.

INTRODUCTION

This need moves them to shape their history and lives in distinctive and recognizable ways.

The purposes for which apocalyptic messages were spread abroad are far too complex to be exhausted under the rubric of consolation alone. The apocalypticist not only strives to console the believer with the hope of coming vindication, but he also tries to strengthen him to endure and to rouse him to resist. Because of its concern with the structure and meaning of history, apocalyptic literature has broad political implications in the root sense of politics as that which pertains to the government of the state. One author has described apocalyptic as a form of political rhetoric,[19] a description that is helpful provided that we do not forget the religious dimensions of the political.

In my book *Visions of the End* I have suggested that the dynamic range of uses to which apocalypticism has been put, in medieval history at least, can be understood on the basis of a distinction between a priori and a posteriori modes of apocalyptic discourse, each of which can be used in positive and negative ways. In the a priori mode the inherited apocalyptic drama with its various symbolic figures and conflicts is used to give meaning to current events. By fitting a present situation into the framework of an inherited prophetic message the believer is not only enlightened but also motivated to take a stand. The a priori mode is used positively when it is invoked to support the structures of Christian society at a time when they are challenged or threatened, or negatively when the symbols are used to provoke passive or active resistance to ruling powers who are viewed as the agents of the present evil age. The fact that apocalypticism originated at a time when the Jewish people lived under foreign domination and that it was adopted by Christianity when it too was a persecuted sect, first of all within the matrix of Judaism and subsequently within the wider Roman world, meant that the earliest stages of apocalypticism were generally of the negative a priori type.[20] This has tended to blind observers to the positive, sustaining uses of apocalyptic that become evident after the conversion of

the empire to Christianity. While apocalyptic traditions continued to be used in negative fashion, either to foster revolution,
as in the case of the Taborites of fifteenth-century Bohemia, or
as the basis for forms of passive resistance, such as with the
Fraticelli of the fourteenth century, it was more frequently
employed to encourage support of Christian society against
enemies, either external, like Islam or the Mongols, or internal,
especially heretics and wicked rulers. Although it was always
God and not man who was seen as bestowing the final victory
over evil in the drama of the end, one might well be called on to
take up arms and fight on God's side. There are numerous
examples of such summonses in the history of medieval apocalypticism.

Apocalyptic literature, at least after the fourth century,
also displays a posteriori functions, that is, expansions of the
inherited scenario of the last events to make room for transcen-
dentalized reflections of major changes and developments in
the history of Christian society. This function is an attempt to
make sense of drastic change (not always crisis in the negative
sense) in terms of the end, because it is the end that provides
history with meaning and structure.

The two major examples of the a posteriori mode of
apocalypticism are the ways in which the conversion of the
Roman Empire and the rise of the papacy to a position of
universal religious leadership gave birth to new actors and new
scenes in the drama of the end.[21] There is not the slightest hint
in scripture or in the early Christian tradition for such figures.
Their creation was the response of a series of apocalyptic
authors to changes that from the perspective of apocalyptic
beliefs could be grasped only on the basis of their transcendental projection into the end-time. If the Christian Roman Empire was the force restraining the Antichrist, and if the emperor himself was the highest source of divine authority on
earth, then it was inconceivable that the empire and its leader
would have no role in the last events. The myth of the Last
World Emperor, a belief that the empire would not totally fail
before a messianic emperor had vindicated its supremacy over

everyone but the dread last enemy himself, was fully developed by the late seventh century. If the papacy were indeed the supreme religious office of Christendom, how could it too lack a role in the last times?

The a posteriori uses of apocalypticism tended to support the institutions it apocalypticized. This is eminently true of the legends concerning the Last Emperor. Various individual Christian emperors and kings had been seen as the Antichrist or one of his predecessors (there was precedent in the Bible for this); some, like Nero and Frederick II, even managed to reach heights of infamy that gave them a transcendental role as returning Antichrists. But the Last Emperor himself in his many forms was always the summation of the dignity of the imperial office, the supreme rallying point for Christian allegiance. He was seen as a warrior and scourge, one who would wreak bloody vengeance on Christianity's enemies and purify the corrupt Church with fire and sword if necessary, but always as a positive messianic figure.

The apocalyptic role of the papacy was a bit more ambiguous. Hopes for a series of coming holy popes, or *pastores angelici*, were widespread in the later Middle Ages. They testified not only to belief in the significance of the papal office, but also to the criticism of current popes who did not seem to measure up to the high standards of their job. Making use of the scriptural notion of the Antichrist as a false teacher seated in the Temple (that is, the Church) some late medieval authors identified contemporary evil or heretical popes with the Antichrist himself. This is not to be seen as a rejection of the papacy (something that had to wait for the radical Hussites and later sixteenth-century Reformers), but as an appeal from an unworthy present to an imminent messianic restoration and reform of the glory of the Petrine office.

Apocalypticism then could be used for a variety of purposes, not only in criticism of the powers of this world, but also in their behalf. The message of the apocalypticists was one of consolation and promise of reward, but there were other dimensions that we must not forget, such as those of historical illumination and martial exhortation. To neglect the full range of uses is to misunderstand the meaning of apocalyptic spirituality.

Apocalyptic texts invite the reader to a decision between good and evil. Hence we should not be disturbed at the strong component of moralism built into most apocalyptic writings.[22] Steadfast perseverance in good, particularly in time of persecution, will be rewarded. Persistence in evil will be punished. This message is never far from the apocalypticist's mind. Lactantius's treatise on the last things found in the seventh book of his *Divine Institutes* is as much an analysis of the virtuous life as it is a description of the end-time. For the Christian Roman rhetorician, each necessarily implied the other. Authors like Joachim of Fiore and Savonarola also felt impelled to proclaim their messages of impending doom as a way of providing one last warning to sinners to forsake their evil ways while it was still possible. To hear this message and continue to reject it was to increase one's guilt in the face of coming judgment. The moralizing of apocalyptic authors may strike us as tedious at times, but it was a necessary corollary of their conviction that the final acts of history could contain no gray areas.

The other side of the at times self-righteous moralism of the apocalypticists is the emphasis that they give to the value of endurance and patience under trial and suffering. None of the texts translated here lacks this dimension; it shines out especially clearly in the letters of the monk Adso and of the Spiritual Franciscans. Angelo of Clareno's poignant account of the forty years of trials that he and his companions had undergone is an unforgettable lesson in patient suffering. Peter John Olivi's *Letter to the Sons of Charles II* is a carefully structured theological fugue on the same topic. These texts show that enduring until the end is not meant to be a merely passive state; it is considered a supremely active exercise of virtue.

In the midst of present trial and persecution the confidence of the believer in the imminent end is bouyed up in three ways. First of all, he rejoices in a basic security that flows from his sense of belonging in history, his ability to fit the present into the grand scheme of things that God had laid down from all eternity. Second, he is able to endure present evil precisely because he knows that its time is short. Third, his hope fills him with joy because he knows that the vindication that is at hand will be definitive—history's perfection or consummation and his own transcendence of death. Each of these three ways deserves some amplification.

Frank Kermode in his provoking work *The Sense of an Ending* has argued:

> Men, like poets, rush "into the middest," *in medias res*, when they are born; they also die *in mediis rebus*, and to make sense of their span they need fictive concords with origins and ends, such as give meaning to lives and to poems. The End they imagine will reflect their irreducibly intermediary preoccupations.[23]

To have one's life related to a beginning and an end, not only in individual terms, but also from the viewpoint of the whole, is one way of overcoming what Mircea Eliade has called the "terror of history."[24] The special strength of apocalyptic beliefs is the way in which they answer the desire for knowledge of past, present, and future that is certain and detailed, not merely tentative and general. This not only explains much of why they survive in disguised fashion today, but also why "Apocalypse can be disconfirmed without being discredited."[25] Most apocalyptic systems have survived disconfirmation again and again through adaptation, adjustment, and recalculation. The reason is that the human anxieties that apocalypticism alleviates are far too permanent and pressing to allow temporary disconfirmation ruinous power.

Even more important than the security afforded by a sense of the wholeness and purpose of history is the way in which apocalypticism gives particular meaning to the present. As W. Schmithals has said:

> The apocalypticist's thought is intensively *historical*. . . .
> This is demonstrated, not so much by the interest in history
> in general, which could in fact be a detached, curious,

13

speculative interest, as it often appears in modern times, but by the apocalypticist's concern about the hour which is striking for his generation.[26]

Above all, it is the relation of this hour to the imminent end, the decisive transformation of the world that involves the vindication of the just and the destruction of the wicked, that gives apocalyptic believers the courage to endure the brief evils they face.

There are, of course, many ways in which the imminence has been perceived, as is evident from the texts given here. Perhaps the distinction invoked by George Caird between the end beyond which nothing can take place in history and the end-time in which much will happen may be useful here.[27] Such a distinction was by no means foreign to our authors: Something similar appears in Joachim of Fiore's text on the figure of the seven-headed dragon.[28] Even authors like Lactantius, who believed that Christ's return lay perhaps as much as two hundred years in the future, still had an overwhelming conviction that the hour in which they were writing was witnessing the beginning of the end-time, that period in which the chain of events of the apocalyptic drama had already begun its inexorable course. The end-time could be short or long, and it could be thought of as spanning both the hour of trial and suffering and the terrestrial millennium of victory to come after it. What was distinctive of the traditional apocalypticist was his conviction that the present was a part of the end-time in which history was to achieve its purpose. The chronological imminence of the coming reward was less significant than its psychological imminence. The curtain had opened and the play had begun.

The vindication that the apocalypticist awaited so ardently was founded on a hope stronger than any suffering. According to John Collins:

The effect of apocalyptic is a perspective on human life. Physical death is not an ultimate disaster. There is a life, and there are values which go beyond, or transcend, death.

The purpose of apocalyptic is to foster the cherishing of
values which transcend death and thereby the experience of
transcendent life.[29]

For the apocalyptic authors the hope in the transcendence of
death involved individual and collective aspects in an inseparable way. A belief in individual survival after death in the
distinctive form of the resurrection of the flesh that guaranteed
the victory of the total human person has been counted as the
greatest achievement of the creators of apocalyptic spirituality.[30] In the presence of the critical hour each man was individually called to the decision that would be the basis for his
imminent reward or punishment, but the apocalypticist was
never a solipsist. The faithful remnant, the company of the
just, the true Church, was as much the object of coming vindication as was each believer. Man and his society were to be
transformed, a hope that is among the most precious contribu-
tions of apocalypticism to Western thought.

It may seem that apocalyptic spirituality is nothing more
than a species of wish fulfillment, a projection of human needs,
or, in a kinder vein, a stage in religious development that we
have been able to leave behind. Even so sympathetic an
investigator as Frank Kermode is convinced that the end must
now be conceived as immanent rather than imminent, that
realized eschatology must replace naive consistent eschatology,
and that apocalyptic must be swallowed up by tragedy and
finally by absurdity, however much certain of its patterns
persist.[31] The contemporary theological retrievals of apocalypticism by a Pannenberg, a Moltmann, or a Rahner also see no
return to outmoded historical patterns and naive predictions
for the future. So much seems agreed on, and I have no reason
to demur. I do think it worth a final warning, though, to note
that the destruction of the naive literal apocalypticisms of the
past can proceed too precipitously and pervasively to allow us
to understand the religious significance of this long tradition.
There is a wisdom and meaning in the symbols of apocalyptic
spirituality that can easily be lost by the ham-handed application of the critical method. Something like Paul Ricoeur's call

for a second naiveté achieved in and through the critical interpretation of symbols in order to bring us to a "postcritical
equivalent of the precritical hierophany"[32] is still a most promising wager for the contemporary recovery of the religious
meaning of apocalypticism. It is my hope that the texts presented here will give some small help in this task.

One final note concerns the use of scripture in these
treatises and letters. I have elected to translate directly from
the texts given by the authors, rather than from any standard
modern translations, because these writings show considerable
freedom in their citation of scripture, a freedom that is at times
important to their argument.

There is always an end beyond the end, so it remains for
me to thank those whose help has made this book possible. My
gratitude is due first of all to Richard Payne, the editor of this
series, for accepting the idea of such a volume for The Classics
of Western Spirituality and for his constant help and encour-
agement. Michael Hollerich, Dominic Monti, O. F. M., and
James Moran, C. S. C., all gave very valuable assistance in
checking the translations and making many useful suggestions.
Whatever errors remain are my own. Finally, Professor E.
Randolph Daniel of the University of Kentucky, one of the
world's foremost Joachim scholars, provided the translation
and notes from a key section of his not yet published edition of
the abbot of Fiore's *Book of Concordance* for this volume.

Part I
LACTANTIUS

Even the students and admirers of Lactantius have not bestowed undue praise on him. To René Pichon, "Lactantius is 'mediocre' in the Latin sense of the word—and also a bit in the French sense";[1] to Vincenzo Loi, "Lactantius is neither a philosophical or theological genius nor linguistic genius."[2] Despite these rather cool remarks, it would be a mistake to underestimate this fluent Christian rhetorician whom the Renaissance Humanist Giovanni Pico della Mirandola once referred to as "the Christian Cicero." Like his pagan mentor, Lactantius's originality is not as important as his typicality. He is an important witness to many of the major themes of Patristic thought, not only the encounter between Christian doctrine and Latin Classical culture, but also the continued vitality of Christian apocalypticism.

The facts of his life can be briefly told.[3] L. Caecilius Firmianus Lactantius was born in North Africa before the middle third century. Jerome tells us that he was a student of Arnobius, another African rhetorician who converted to Christianity late in life. We do not know whether Lactantius's conversion took place before he was summoned to teach rhetoric at Nicomedia in Asia Minor by the Emperor Diocletian. At the beginning of Diocletian's persecution in 303, Lactantius had to retire from his position at court. He appears to have stayed in Asia Minor until 305, when he left for the West. The Emperor Constantine summoned the aged scholar to Trier in Gaul about 317 to tutor his son Crispus. It is not known when he died.

Although some of his works are lost, we can gain a good idea of his eclectic thought through the five that survive. The most important of these is the *Divine Institutes* in seven books composed between 304 and 313. Lactantius announces that he will treat of "hope, life, salvation, immortality, and God" (I.1)—in other words, a comprehensive summary of Christian teaching that also involved a refutation of the errors of pagan cult and thought. Books I and II attack Roman religion; Book III is a refutation of the philosophers. Book IV discusses the true wisdom brought by Christ; Book V treats of justice; Book VI of true worship; and the final book of the blessed life. The outline is more organized than the work since Lactantius was fond of orator's digressions.

Although the African teacher criticized pagan philosophers and held that no single philosophical school had more than a partial glimpse of the truth fully revealed in the scriptures, his knowledge of Classical thought, especially as filtered through Lucretius and Cicero, was large, and his indebtedness to philosophical categories for the presentation of his ideas was extensive. Lactantius's use of philosophy is scarcely systematic—his mingling of Platonism and Stoicism resulted in some serious ambiguities and confusions; nor was his presentation of Christian teaching without its peculiarities. Vincenzo Loi has shown that some of his most distinctive ideas, especially the strong dualistic tendency dependent on a doctrine of two antagonistic primal spirits, as well as his chiliasm, or literal acceptance of the thousand-year reign of Christ and the saints on earth, brought him within the orbit of Jewish-Christian traditions strong in Asia Minor where he taught at the court of the emperor.[4]

The second half of the seventh Book of the *Divine Institutes* is one of the most detailed and interesting treatments of Christian apocalypticism known. Lactantius not only summarized the essential elements of the ancient tradition of Jewish-Christian chiliasm, but also attempted to weave these together with a variety of other traditions concerning world judgment and renewal. The reason for the creation of this eclectic account was by no means purely speculative. Right belief about the coming judgment and reward was meant to provide motivation for Christians to live according to *justitia*, defined as "the devout and religious worship of the one God" (5.7), a basic theme of Lactantius's apologetic.

Lactantius's emphasis on apocalypticism appears to go counter to the generalization frequently made about the death of the apocalyptic mentality in post-New Testament times. The issues involved in these claims are complex, involving not only an evaluation of how important apocalypticism was to the earliest Christian communities, but also a position on how much apocalypticism was or was not present in Christianity after the mid-second century. These questions have often been answered in a simple and rigid manner; a true appreciation of the complexity of the relation between Christianity and apocalypticism explodes most of these generalizations.

As Ernst Käsemann put it in a much-quoted phrase: "Apocalyptic was the mother of all Christian theology."[5] Belief that the Resurrection of Christ had inaugurated the apocalyptic aeon and that the Risen Lord would soon return at the Parousia to manifest openly and universally the Kingdom that was already present in hidden reality was basic to earliest Christianity. But as the New Testament documents and the layers of tradition on which they rest seem to indicate, the variation in the ways in which this fundamental tenet came to be understood and related to other elements in Christian teaching and practice was considerable from the start. There are many theologies in the New Testament, and there are different forms of apocalypticism as well.

Some students of early Christian history, beginning from the premise that millennial and apocalyptic movements must be temporary by definition, have explained the survival and success of Christianity by surmising that hopes for the imminent return of Christ had to be replaced by something else. Martin Werner in his study *The Formation of Christian Dogma* saw the consistent-eschatological foundation of early Christian belief give way in the second century to a theology based on the institution of the sacraments.[6] More recently, John Gager, borrowing categories from the social sciences, explained the Church's success by an appeal to the phenomenon of "cognitive dissonance." According to Gager, embarrassment over the delay of the Parousia led to greater effort at proselytizing, which resulted in the formation of a unique sense of community and a Church that became the enemy of any form of apocalypticism or eschatology.[7] But Christianity, at least as far back as our sources will take us with any security, already seems too complex to be characterized as a simple apocalyptic movement or millenarian cult, and hence such explanations are too rigid to deal with the full range of the transformations and developments in early Christian beliefs. We cannot disregard the continuation of apocalyptic hopes after the middle of the second century nor dismiss these as anachronistic and unimportant for Christianity's growth and success.[8] The role that Lactantius gives to such beliefs argues to the inadequacy of this approach, and a glance at some other evidence from second- and third-century Christian history confirms this.

Irenaeus, bishop of Lyons from about 178 to 200, was among the most influential ecclesiastical authors of the second century. A forceful opponent of Gnostic heresy, as his major work *Against the Heresies* shows, he was also a good example of the monarchical bishop as guardian and interpreter of tradition, a type whose triumph was crucial to the future success of the nascent Christian movement. Nevertheless, this conservative institutional leader devoted an important part of the fifth book of his *magnum opus* to a detailed survey of the apocalyptic scenario that made use not only of scriptural materials, but also of a rich variety of themes that he probably inherited from his native Asia Minor.[9] Irenaeus gives no indication of how proximate he thought the return of the Risen Christ was, but there is no doubt that the events presaging the Parousia and the hope of a material thousand-year Kingdom on earth were very important to him. His absorption in the mysteries of the end may not be as all-encompassing as that of the first Christians, but it would be ludicrous to say that apocalypticism meant nothing to him.

It is unsure whether or not Lactantius knew the works of Irenaeus. The two share many apocalyptic themes, but these could have reached the African teacher through various common traditions. A similar observation may be made regarding the relation between Lactantius and Hippolytus (died 235). This learned Roman presbyter did not think that the return of Christ was imminent, indeed, a part of the message of his *Commentary on Daniel* was to prove that Christ had been born at the middle and not at the end of the sixth millennium of history so that over two hundred years remained before the establishment of the chiliastic reign of Christ.[10] But his works, especially the *Treatise on Christ and the Antichrist*, provided a summary of the full range of early Christian speculation on the final events of history.

The survival of apocalypticism in second- and third-century Christianity is amply documented not only in the case of the theologians, but also by the continued production of apocalyptic visions in Christian circles and by Christian involvement with the Sibylline tradition. Greek and Roman belief in female seers called Sibyls was ancient, but the oldest books of Sibylline verses that survive to us are the products of Hellenistic Jewish circles in Egypt written in the second century B.C. Though these verse prophecies differ in form from the intertestamental apocalypses, they share enough similarities in content, especially the emphasis on coming judgment for sin, to allow one authority to call them "the Apocalyptic of Hellenistic Diaspora Judaism."[11] Jewish production of the Sibyllines continued for many centuries; from about A.D. 150 Christian authors began to add to this literature as well, either reworking older poems in a Christian sense or producing new ones. Theologians like Justin Martyr, Theophilus of Antioch, Clement of Alexandria, Tertullian, and Hippolytus cited the Sibyls, especially for their monotheistic, ethical, and apocalyptic message. Christian fascination with the female seers reached its culmination in

Lactantius, who cites them at least fifty-one times in his surviving works—one and one-half times more than he cited the Old Testament![12]

The lengthy time of troubles that the Roman Empire entered upon in the third century may have been partly responsible for the periodic outbreaks of expectations of the imminent advent of the Antichrist that we find during the following century.[13] Even when there is no explicit reference to the proximity of the end there is evidence of considerable interest in a variety of apocalyptic themes. Efforts to work out the periods of history of the world, found in Christian authors since the first half of the second century, were expanded in the writings of the third-century chronographers.[14] Commodian and Hippolytus are monuments to the rich growth of legends concerning the Antichrist,[15] and at the end of the century Bishop Victorinus of Pettau's *Commentary on the Apocalypse*[16] taught a materialistic chiliasm close to that of Lactantius.

The Seventh Book of the *Institutes* was the heir and summation of these tendencies. Surprisingly little has been written about this fundamental source for the apocalypticism of the early Church.[17] A full analysis of the text would demand considerable attention to sources and to later influence; in the brief compass available here only the major themes can be summarized. The title itself, "The Blessed Life," sets the stage for the detailed treatment of the teleology of the divine *dispositio*, or plan for the whole of history, that gives structure to the book. Beginning from a consideration of the creation of the world and of man (chapters 3-7), Lactantius moves through a discussion of the immortality of the soul and the necessity of virtue (chapters 8-13) to conclude with a treatment of the goal of history in chapters 14 through 27.

Lactantius's doctrine on the ages of the world presented in chapters fourteen and fifteen is built on the theme of the cosmic week, that is, the parallel between the seven days of creation and the seven millennia of history popular among Christian authors for many generations. Like Hippolytus and his followers, he saw Christ's birth as coming in the middle of the final millennium and thus expected as much as two hundred years before the establishment of the millennial kingdom (7.25).[18] This breathing space was not to be taken as an argument for laxity or the abandonment of an attitude toward life deeply influenced by a sense of the approaching end; the signs of the times analyzed in chapters fourteen and fifteen show that Lactantius thought of his era as one of increasing gloom and troubles presaging the collapse of Rome and the coming of the two Antichrists whose careers are detailed in chapters sixteen through nineteen. This splitting of the Antichrist into two figures, the first a king who was to destroy the Roman Empire (usually from the West, but in the case of Lactantius from the more biblical North), the second a false teacher (usually Jewish in origin, but in Lactantius from Syria) who was to defeat the former, proclaim himself God, and persecute the Church, is found in a number of Patristic Authors.[19] In its detail and distinctive elements, Lactantius's description is the richest we possess.

After several chapters discussing the judgment and punishment of souls and the resurrection of the just at the end of the sixth millennium, Lactantius sums up traditions of early Christian chiliasm in his noted twenty-fourth chapter.[20] Basing himself on the literal materialistic reading of Apocalypse 20:1-6 that he probably learned in Asia Minor, he gives a full description of the joys of the just who will reign with Christ for a thousand years. Many traditions are utilized here, not only Sibylline and biblical, but also Classical notions of the Golden Age, seen as the poets' erroneous rendition of the prophetic revelation of the coming Kingdom. Chapter twenty-five returns to the question of the time of the Kingdom and the final two chapters take up the events at the end of the seventh millennium when Satan will be loosed for his final defeat, the general resurrection and judgment will take place, and the just will be turned into angels to enjoy forever their heavenly reward. The work ends on a typical moralizing note.

Perhaps the most striking thing about Lactantius's account of the events of the end-time is the range of sources he appeals to as *divina testimonia*, divine witnesses of the truth of what he predicts. A reference at the beginning of chapter twenty-five indicates that this was at least in part an apologetic strategy designed to confute the pagans from their own sacred authors, but the range of Lactantius's knowledge of exotic texts is still remarkable. The extensive use of Vergil and the Sibylline oracles may not surprise us, but the appeals to the Oracle of Apollo, the Hermetic Asclepius,[21] and the Oracle of Hystaspes are unusual. This last text, also known to Justin Martyr and Clement of Alexandria, has been shown to be a Greek version, probably of the first century B.C., of an authentic Iranian apocalypse incorporating themes still available to us through later Persian sources.[22] Explicitly cited in chapters fifteen and eighteen, it may also be used implicitly in a number of passages in chapters sixteen, seventeen, and nineteen.

In the long run, Lactantius is more the compiler than the creator, more the facile rhetorician than the visionary. Nevertheless, the importance that he gives to the apocalyptic message of Christianity and his desire to show that the same message had been foretold by the seers of all religions affords us a remarkable insight into the continued power of apocalyptic in the spirituality of the early Church.[23]

LACTANTIUS
"The Blessed Life", Book VII of *Divine Institutes*

1. "Good; the foundations are laid," as the famous orator says.[1] We have not only laid foundations that are strong and fit to support the work, but we have also almost finished the whole building with large and solid construction. The much easier part is left, the roof or ornament without which the earlier work is useless and thankless. What use is it to be freed from false religions or to understand the true religion? What use is it to see the vanity of false wisdom or to recognize the truth? What use is it to defend heavenly justice or to hold fast to the worship of God in the midst of great difficulties (the height of virtue), unless you gain the divine prize of eternal happiness?[2] We must speak of that prize in this book so that all the former material is not vain and fruitless. If we were to leave hanging what we have done all the rest for, one might think that all these labors were undertaken in vain and despair of the heavenly reward that God established for the man who scorns the earth's sweet goods in comparison with virtue alone.

We will construct this part of our work with scriptural testimonies and proven arguments to show that things to come are to be preferred to present things, divine things are to be preferred to earthly ones, and eternal things to passing ones. The rewards of vice are temporary, those of virtue eternal.

I will explain the world's makeup so that you can easily grasp when and why God made it. Plato, who spoke about the structure of the world, could not understand or explain this. He was ignorant of the heavenly mystery learned only by the prophets under God's instruction. Therefore, he says that the world was made from eternity.[3] It is far different, for whatever exists in material form necessarily has both a beginning at a certain time and an end. Aristotle, because he did not see how such a great mass could perish, wished to avoid this by saying that the world always was and always will be.[4] He understood absolutely nothing. Whatever exists necessarily has a beginning at some time and nothing at all can exist unless it has begun. When we see earth, water, fire—the parts of this world—undone, consumed, and extinguished, we understand that a whole whose parts are mortal is itself mortal. Whatever is born can die. Everything that is visible, as Plato says, is both corporeal and able to be dissolved.[5] Epicurus alone, following Democritus, was truthful here. He said that the world originated at some time and would perish at some time.[6] Nevertheless, he was unable to give any explanation, either by assigning the causes or by giving the time when so great a work is to end.

Since God has revealed it to us, we know it by heavenly gift and not by guessing. We will present it so zealously that those anxious for truth will see that the philosophers have not seen nor understood the truth, but were so lightly touched that they in no way perceived the source of the sweet and pleasant wisdom that breathed upon them. Meanwhile, it is necessary to warn the reader that evil and vicious minds whose higher powers are dulled by earthly desires that weigh down the senses and weaken them will not understand these teachings we pass on at all. Even if they do understand them, they will falsify them and not admit them to be true. Drawn by vices, they consciously favor their sweet captivating evil habits and they abandon the way of virtue whose bitterness offends them. On fire with avarice and an insatiable thirst for possessions, and unable to lead a modest life when the goods they love are sold or scattered, they surely would rather have what forces them to renounce their desires to be a fiction. In the same way, those who are led on by the stirrings of lust "dash into madness and fire," as the poet says.[7] They claim that we bring impossible teachings because we wound their ears with the commandment of continence that would forbid them the pleasures to which they have dedicated their bodies and souls. Those who put all their effort into gaining honors are blown up with ambition and enflamed with love of power. They would not adjust their belief to a teaching that if accepted would want them to hold all power and honor in contempt and to live so humbly that they could accept injury and not return it. No, not if we bore the sun itself in our hands![8] These are the men who with closed eyes rage against the truth in any way. But those who are healthy, that is, not so immersed in vices that they are incurable, will both believe and readily draw near. Whatever we say will seem open, plain, and simple to them, and, what is more, true and irrefutable.

No one favors virtue who does not pursue it, and to pursue it is not easy for everyone. Those whom poverty and want have trained and made capable can do it. If virtue is the ability to endure hard things, those who are always well-off do not understand it because they have neither experienced difficulties nor are they even able to because they have become accustomed to and desire only what they know. So the poor and humble who are free of things believe in God more easily than the rich, who are bound down by many burdens. They are bound and shackled, slaves to the whim of Lady Cupidity, who has ensnared them in unbreakable chains. They cannot look up to heaven because their minds are flat on the ground fixed to the dirt. The path of virtue does not accept those who carry much baggage; narrow is the way by which justice leads men to heaven. Only he who is free and clear of things can hold to it. Those who are rich and weighed down by vast burdens walk the way of death, a way that is so broad because destruction rules so widely. Whatever God commands for the sake of justice and whatever we say on the basis of God's teaching about virtue and truth is bitter and poisonous to them. If they dare to reject it, they must admit they are enemies of virtue and justice.

Now I come to what remains so that the work can be finished. What is left is our discussion of the judgment of God. The judgment is arranged so that when Our Lord returns to earth he will give each person either reward or punishment for his merit. Just as we spoke of the First Coming of the Lord in the Fourth Book, in this book we will speak of that Second Coming which the Jews also confess and hope for, though in vain, for he has to return to confound those[9] whom he first had come to call. For those who dishonored the Humble Man in an unholy fashion will experience the Victorious Man in his

27

power, and with God restoring the balance they will suffer all the things they read and did not understand. Those who were stained with every sin and above all covered with the holy blood are destined to eternal punishment by the very one on whom they laid unholy hands. But we will have a separate section against the Jews in which we will convict them of error and crime.

2. Now let us instruct the ignorant. The providence of Almighty God has ordained that this unjust age should reach an end after the course of the ages at a time when every evil shall be instantly destroyed and the souls of the faithful called back to a blessed life. Under the rule of God himself, there will then flourish that quiet, tranquil and peaceful age that the poets call "Golden."[10] For philosophers the principal cause of all error was they did not understand the order of the world that contains the whole of wisdom. That order cannot be grasped by one's own perception and interior understanding, but they wished to do it themselves without a teacher. So they fell into varying and frequently self-contradictory positions from which there was no exit. They stuck fast in the same mud, as the comic playwright says,[11] that is, their reasoning did not conform to their premises. Although they had assumed some truths, these could not be affirmed or proved without knowledge of the Truth and of heavenly things. As I have frequently said, these matters cannot be found in man unless they are received from God's teaching. If man were able to understand divine things, he would also be able to do them, for to understand is to do forthwith. Man cannot do the things that God can because he is endowed with a mortal body; therefore, he cannot even understand what God does. It is easy for each of us to judge whether this is possible from the greatness of these matters and of the works of God, for if you were to contemplate the world and everything in it, you would well understand how much God's work surpasses human works. Necessarily then there is as much distance between the wisdom of God and that of man as there is difference between divine and human works. Because God is incorruptible and immortal and perfect in his eternity, his wisdom is as perfect as himself.

Nothing is able to thwart it, because God himself is subject to nothing.

Since man is subject to passion, his wisdom is subject to error. Just as many things hinder human life and prevent it from being eternal, so too man's wisdom is necessarily hampered in many ways so that it cannot be completely perfect in perceiving truth. Thus human wisdom is useless if it strives to come to the idea of truth and knowledge through itself, because the mind of man is bound down to a weak body and imprisoned in a dark dwelling so that it cannot freely maneuver or clearly perceive the truth whose knowledge is divine. God alone knows his own works; man is able to attain his knowledge not by thinking or disputing, but by hearing and learning from him who alone is able to know and to teach. And so Cicero adopted from Plato Socrates' opinion. At the time when he was departing from life but those before whom he was arguing his case were still alive, Socrates said: "Which may be better, I think the immortal gods know, but no man."[12] For this reason all the philosophical sects are far from the truth because they were founded by men. They can have no foundation or firmness because they have no support from divine revelation.

3. Since we are speaking of the errors of the philosophers, the Stoics divide nature into two parts, the one that makes, the other that offers itself for formation. In the first there is power to understand, in the latter matter. The one can do nothing without the other. How can it be the same being that both forms and is formed? If someone said that the potter is the same as the clay or the clay the same as the potter, would he not seem clearly crazy? The Stoics include two completely different things, God and the world, the Maker and the work, under the single name of "nature." They say that the one can do nothing without the other, as though nature were God mixed in with the world. Sometimes they so confuse things that God himself is the mind of the world and the world the body of God, as if the world and God came into being at the same time and God did not make the world.[13] At other times they themselves admit creation when they announce that the world was made

29

for the sake of man, and that God, as a divine and eternal mind separated and free of a body, is able to exist without the world if he wished. Since they were not able to understand his power and majesty, they mixed him up with the world, that is, with his work. Hence the passage in Vergil:

Mind spread through all the limbs
impels the entire mass and mingles
itself in the vast body.[14]

Where then is what they say was both made by divine providence and is ruled by it? If he made the world, he existed without it. If he rules it, he does so not as mind rules the body, but as a master rules a house, a driver a chariot, that is, as not mixed up with the things they rule. If all the things we see are parts of God, because they lack perception he lacks perception also. He is mortal because the parts are mortal.

I can count how often lands shaken by sudden earthquakes have split open or sunk abruptly, how often cities and islands, submerged by waves, have gone to the bottom, how often swamps have swallowed up fruitful plains, rivers and lakes have dried out, and mountains have either cracked and fallen or been leveled with the plains. Hidden unknown fire has consumed many regions and the foundations of many mountains. It is not enough that God does not spare his own members; man is also allowed to act against God's body! Large bodies of water are formed, mountains are cut down and the inner bowels of the earth are dug out to find wealth.[15] Is plowing possible without tearing the divine body? We who violate the members of God are criminals and evildoers. Does God allow his body to be abused and himself weaken it or permit man to do so? Or perhaps that divine understanding that is mingled with the world and all its parts has abandoned the earth's outer surface and buried itself in the depths lest it feel some pain from continuous wounding. If this is vain and absurd, the Stoics are just as lacking in sense as the things of this world. They have not understood that the divine spirit is diffused everywhere and holds all things together, but not in such a way that the incorrupt God himself is mingled with the solid corruptible elements.

What they took from Plato was more correct: that the world was made by God and is governed by his providence. Plato and those who think the same must teach and explain what the cause and reason for making so great a work was, why and for whose sake he made it. The Stoics say, "The World was made for the sake of men." I hear it. But Epicurus did not know why men were made or who made them.[16] Lucretius, when he says that the world was not made by the gods, writes:

> To say that they wished to prepare the magnificent
>   nature
> Of the world for men's sake . . .
> Is foolish. With what reward can our thanks seek
> To enrich the immortal and blessed ones,
> So that they would undertake to produce something for
>   us?[17]

Very rightly so. For the Stoics bring forward no reason why the human race was either created or established by God. It is our task to explain the mystery of the world and of man whose inner truth they, as strangers, were not able to attain or see.

Therefore, as I was saying above, although they assumed what was really true, that is, that the world was made by God and made for man, they were not able to defend what they assumed because reason did not accompany their conclusions. Plato said that the world would last forever lest he make God's work frail and tumbling to ruin.[18] If it was made for men's sake and so made that it be eternal, why are they for whose sake it was made not eternal? If they for whom it was made are mortal, it too is mortal and able to be dissolved, for it is not greater than those for which it was made. If his reasoning were to square with that point, he would understand that it will perish because it was made. Nothing can be eternal except what cannot be handled.

He who denies that it was made for man's sake has no

explanation, for if he says that the Creator formed such great works for himself, why then were we born? Why do we delight in the world? What does the creation of the human race and the other species mean? Why do we interfere with other species? Why do we grow, decrease, and die? Why are we born? Why do we have succession? God certainly desired to see and to construct what pleased him with his various images like seals. If such be the case, he would have concern for all living things and especially for man, who rules all things.

Those who say that the world always existed have one response from me: If the world always was, it can have no plan. (I omit the argument that nothing can exist without a beginning, a point they are unable to escape.) What plan can there be in something that never began? Before anything comes to be or is fabricated there is need for advice so that it can be arranged as it should be; and nothing can begin without a plan. Thus, planning precedes every work; what is not made has no plan. Nevertheless, the world has a plan because it continues to exist and to be. Therefore, it was made; and if it was made, it will be dissolved.

Let the Stoics give a reason, if they can, either why it was made in the beginning or why it will be dissolved later on. Because Epicurus and Democritus were not able to give a reason, they said that it happened of its own accord in the manner of seeds joined together here and there.[19] When they are again dissolved, discord and destruction will follow. Each perverts what he rightly saw and by his ignorance of the plan completely overturns the whole line of reasoning. Each renders the world and all that is in it like the image of the emptiest dream, as if there were no plan in human concerns. A marvelous plan, as we see, rules the world and all its parts—the symmetry of heaven and the circle of stars and of heavenly bodies, regular for all its variety, the steady and wondrous arrangement of seasons, the variation in the fruitfulness of lands, the broad spread of plains, the masses and ranges of mountains, the blossoming and fruitfulness of groves, the healthy bubbling of springs, the timely overflowing of rivers, the rich and full tides, the varied and useful winds, and all the other things are ordered by a very deep plan. Who is so blind as to think that these things so wonderfully arranged by perfect planning were created without a cause? If nothing can exist without a cause, and if the providence of Almighty God is evident from the arrangement of things, his strength from their greatness and his power from their governance, then those who deny providence are stupid and insane. I should not attack them if they were to deny the gods in order to say that the one God exists; but when they do it to say there is no God, he who does not think they are insane is crazy himself.

4. We have spoken enough about providence in the first book. If providence exists, as is clear from the marvelous character of its works, then it is necessary that the same providence created man and all living things. Since it is correct to say with the Stoics that the world was created for men, let us see what the reason was for creating the human race. The Stoics erred not a little because they said for "the sake of men," rather than "of man," for the use of the singular embraces the whole human race. They spoke this way because they did not know that God had created a single man and because they thought that men had been produced like mushrooms in every land and field. Hermes knew that man came from God and was made to the image of God.[20] But now to return to the subject.

I think that there is nothing that is made for itself, but anything that exists must be made for some use.[21] Who is there so helpless and lazy that he would vainly try to do something from which he could hope to have nothing useful or advantageous? Anyone who builds a house builds it not just to have a house, but to live in it; anyone who makes a boat takes up the work not just to have a boat, but to sail in it. In the same way, anyone who constructs and molds some vessel does it not just for appearances, but so that the finished vessel can hold something he needs. And so anything else that is labored over is done for some useful purpose and not in vain.

God did not make the world for its own sake. Since it lacked sensation, it had no need for the sun's heat, the moon's light, the winds' breath, the moisture of showers, the nourishment of fruits. Nor can it be said that God made the world for himself, since he was able to exist without the world, as he had previously. And he does not use the things that exist in it or that are brought into being. Therefore, it is clear that the world was made for the sake of living things, because living things enjoy what it is made of. Everything necessary for them is supplied at fixed times so that they may live and persevere. Further, it is evident that other living things were made for man because they serve man and have been given into his charge and for his use. Whether they are of land or sea, they do not understand the order of the world as man does.

This is the place to respond to the philosophers, and especially to Cicero who asks: "When God made all things for our sake, why did he make such a vast supply of snakes and vipers? Why did he spread so many deadly things through land and sea?"[22] This is a large area for discussion, but it must be touched upon, if only briefly and in passing.

Because man was composed of different and contrary things, soul and body, that is, heaven and earth, the spiritual and the material, the eternal and the temporal, that capable of understanding and that without understanding, that which gives light and that which is dark, reason itself and blind necessity demand that both good and bad things should be presented to man—good things to use, bad things to avoid and guard against. He was given wisdom to know the nature of good and evil, and thus to exercise his reason in following good and avoiding evil. Wisdom was not given to the other animals; they were defended and armed by natural gifts. God gave man reason alone, the most significant thing, in place of all the rest. Naked and defenseless he created him, so that wisdom might defend and protect him. He set up his defense and his adornment within and not without, not in the body, but in the heart.[23] There would be no need for wisdom were there no evils to avoid or to distinguish from what is good and useful. Cicero ought to know that reason was given to man so that he could catch fish for his own use and avoid snakes and vipers for his safety. Because he had received wisdom, good and evil were put before him, for the whole force of wisdom is in discriminating between good and evil.

Great and fitting and worthy of admiration is the power, the reason, the might of man for whom God made the world and all things. He held him in such honor that he placed him above everything, since man alone was able to appreciate God's works. Our Asclepiades, discussing the providence of Almighty God in the book he wrote me, well says:

> Everyone ought to know that divine providence rightly gave the place nearest itself to one able to understand its regulation. There is the sun. Who can regard it in such a way that he understands that it is the sun and that it bears so much favor to the rest of creation? This is heaven: who can regard it? This is the earth: who will cultivate it? This is the sea: who will sail it? This is fire: who will use it?[24]

Therefore, Almighty God made all things not for his own sake, because he needed nothing, but for the sake of man to use them in fitting fashion.

5. Now let us explain why he made man himself, something that had the philosophers known, they would either have defended the truths they discovered or not have fallen into great errors. This is the high point, the hinge of everything: If someone does not hold on to it, all truth will escape him. This made the philosophers disagree with reason. The Academy would never have strangled discussion and the whole of philosophy if this truth had shone on them, if they had recognized the total mystery of man. Just as God did not make the world for himself because he did not need its goods, but made it for the sake of man who uses it, so too he made man for himself. "What use has God for man," says Epicurus, "that He should create him for his own sake?"[25] So that there should be someone to understand his works, someone able to be astonished in mind and declare in speech the foresight of his arrangement, the order of his creation, and his power to perfect. The height of all this is that there should be someone to worship God.

The man who understands this is giving worship. He who measures the power of God's majesty in the planning, the beginning, and the perfecting of his works is giving the Maker of all things, his true Father, due veneration. What clearer argument can be made that God created the world for man and man for himself than that man alone of all living things is formed so that his eyes are directed to heaven, his face looks up toward God, his countenance has something in common with his Maker, so that with outstretched arm God seems to have raised man from the dust and lifted him up to his own contemplation? Epicurus says: "What does man's worship give to God who is blessed and needs nothing? Why did God make man mortal and weak if he held him in such honor that he made the world for him, instructed him with wisdom, made him lord of the living, and loved him like a son? Why did he hinder him whom he loved with every kind of evil, especially since man, who was closely linked to God and an immortal being, ought to be blessed like the God he was created to worship and contemplate?"[26]

Although here and there in the previous books we talked about this, it must be explained more carefully and more fully now because we are going to discuss the blessed life. We do so in order that God's providence, work, and will may be recognized. Though he could always produce countless souls by means of his immortal spirits (just as he had created the angels whose immortality endures without any danger or fear of evil),[27] he nevertheless devised something indescribable. According to this he created an infinite multitude of souls, which he first set up midway between good and evil and bound to fragile and weak bodies. He then set virtue before these beings of double nature so that they would not be able to attain immortality easily and gently, but could arrive at that inexpressible prize with the greatest difficulty and labor. In order to clothe them with heavy and tiresome limbs, he first of all decreed a seat and dwelling place for them since they could not have remained in the midst of the void with the weight and heaviness of the body pressing them down. And so the making of the world was begun with ineffable power and splendid might. With the light elements hung in the heights and the heavy elements sunk in the depths, he fixed the heavens firm and made fast the earth. It is not necessary now to pursue the details, since we described them all in Book Two.[28]

He placed lights in the heavens whose regularity, brightness, and motion were most fittingly ordered to the use of living creatures. To the earth, which he wished to be their seat, he gave fruitfulness in bearing and bringing forth different things, so that it could provide nourishment for the nature and use of each kind of being by the richness of fruits, herbs, and growing things. Then, when everything that belonged to the establishment of the world had been completed, he formed man from the very earth that he had prepared as a dwelling place for him from the beginning. He clothed and wrapped his spirit up in an earthly body, so that, composed of different and warring elements, he might be capable of good and evil. Just as the earth itself is rich in fruits, so man's body, which was taken from the earth, has abundant power to generate and bring forth offspring. Hence a man, since he was made of frail matter, cannot endure. When the period of his earthly life is finished, he departs and renews in a perpetual succession the frail weak body he bore.

Why did God make the one for whom He built the world mortal and frail? First, so that an infinite number of souls might be brought forth and fill the earth with their number. Second, that he might set virtue, that is, the enduring of evils and labors, before man so that he could gain the prize of immortality through it. Because man consists of two things, body and soul, one of which is earthly, the other heavenly, two kinds of life are attributed to him—one temporal, assigned to the body; the other eternal, belonging to the soul. We receive the former when we are born; we attain the latter by effort so that immortality is not granted to man without difficulty. The former life is earthly like the body, and therefore comes to an end; the latter is heavenly like the soul and has no end. The first we receive unconsciously; the second consciously because it is granted not to nature but to virtue.

God wanted us to gain life for ourselves in the midst of life. Therefore, he gave this present life so that we might either lose that true and eternal one by vice or merit it by virtue. The highest good is not in this bodily life, because as it was given us by divine necessity so too will it be taken away. What ends in this way cannot be the highest good. The highest good is contained in that spiritual life which we acquire through ourselves. It can have no evil or end. The nature and arrangement of the body provides an argument for this. Other animals bend toward the ground because they are earthly; they do not receive the immortality that is from heaven. Upright man gazes into the heavens because immortality is offered to him,[29] but it does not come unless it is granted to him by God. There would be no difference between the just and the unjust if every man who was born were to become immortal. Therefore, immortality is not a result of nature, but the prize and reward of virtue. Finally, man does not walk upright as soon as he is born, but he first goes on all fours because we share the condition of the body and of this life with the dumb animals. After he has arrived at his strength he stands up, his tongue is ready to speak, and he ceases to be a dumb animal. This teaches that man is born mortal, but afterwards becomes immortal at the time when God raises him up to see the heavens and divinity, when he begins to live from God, that is, to follow the justice that is found in the worship of God. This happens when he is purified by the heavenly water of baptism, and puts aside infancy with every stain of his former life, becoming a full and perfect man by receiving the aid of divine strength.[30]

Because God has set virtue before man, the body and soul are opposed and make war against each other, even though they are associated. The goods of the soul are the evils of the body—think of flight from wealth, forbidding of pleasures, contempt of pain and death. In the same way, the goods of the body are the evils of the soul, such as avarice and lust. Through them we desire wealth and the sweetness of different pleasures, things that weaken and kill the soul. The just and wise man has to live in the midst of every evil, because fortitude conquers evil. The unjust man must live amidst wealth, honor, and power. These are corporeal and earthly goods. The unjust man leads an earthly life and is not able to gain immortality because he has given himself up to the pleasures that oppose virtue.

This temporal life ought to be subject to that eternal one just as the body is to the soul. Whoever prefers the life of the soul must necessarily despise the life of the body; there is no way to strive for the summit without condemning the depths. Whoever has embraced the life of the body and its desires has been cast down to earth and is not able to attain that higher life. Those who prefer to live well forever will live in discomfort for a time and will be afflicted with every difficulty and hardship while they are on earth so that they may have divine and heavenly consolation. He who prefers to live well for a time will live in discomfort forever. God's judgment will condemn him to eternal punishment because he preferred earthly things to the good things of heaven. For this reason God wishes to be worshipped and honored by man as a Father, so that man may cling to the virtue and wisdom that alone bring immortality. He alone possesses it, and he alone is able to give it. He will grace the faithfulness by means of which man has given honor to him with this reward—blessedness for eternity, ever in and with God.[31]

6. Now I will round off the whole argument with a brief summary.[32] The world was made so that we should be born. We are born so that we should acknowledge God, our Maker and the Maker of the world. We acknowledge him in order to worship him; we worship him in order to receive immortality for the reward of our labors, since the worship of God consists of many labors. We are graced with the prize of immortality so that made like the angels we may serve our Highest Father and Lord forever and be an eternal kingdom to our God. This is the summation of everything, God's hidden secret, the world's mystery. Those are far from it who by following present pleasure have devoted themselves to weak and worldly goods and have plunged souls that were made for heaven in the mud and mire by means of these deadly delights.

Let us now in turn ask if there is any sense in the worship of the gods. Are there many gods? Do men worship them only so that the gods may give them wealth, victory, honors, and things useful in the present alone? Are we born without purpose? Is there no providence involved in the procreation of men? Are we born by chance only for ourselves and for our pleasures? Are we nothing after death? If this all were true, what could be as empty, useless, and vain as the human situation and the world itself, which though it be of vast size and made with marvelous planning is dedicated to useless things? Why do the winds push the clouds along? Why do flashes of lightning blaze forth, thunders rumble, rains fall? Why does the earth produce fruits and nourish its progeny? Why finally does the whole natural order labor so that nothing that sustains man's life may be lacking, if it is vain, if we are reduced to nothing, if there is no gain for God in mankind? If it is unspeakable and unthinkable that what you now see so rationally ordered was created without any rational order, what rationality can there be in the errors of wretched religions and in the opinion of those philosophers who think that souls die? None at all. What explanation do they have why the gods give men everything in due season? Is it that we may give them grain and wine and the odor of incense and the blood of beasts? But these things are perishable and cannot be welcome to the immortals. Since they are made for the use of corporeal beings, they cannot be used by those lacking bodies. If the gods were to desire them, they could give them to themselves whenever they wished. Therefore, whether souls perish or remain forever, what sense was the worship of the gods? By whom was the world created? Why or when or for how long or to what extent or for what reason were men produced? Why are they born and die, why succeed one another or be renewed? What do the gods gain from the worship of those who will be nothing after death? What can they give or promise or threaten that is worthy of either men or gods? If souls remain after death, what are they doing or will they do about them? What do they need in a treasure house of souls? From what source do they themselves come? How and why and whence are they a multitude? So if you stray from that summary of all things which we gave above, all rationality perishes and everything is reduced to nothing.

7. The philosophers did not understand that summary nor were they able to grasp the truth, even though they had seen and explained almost everything that made up the whole. Different ones brought forth all the issues in differing ways without joining the causes, conclusions, and relations of things in order to put together and complete the totality that contains everything. It is easy to show that almost the entire truth has been divided up among the various philosophers and their Schools. For we do not overthrow philosophy as do those Academic thinkers who propose to answer all questions — something that is rather a joke or a mockery. We teach that no School was so wayward, no philosopher so empty, as to be without a share of the truth. But as long as they were insane with the desire for contradiction, as long as they defended their own falsehoods and undermined the truths of others, not only did the truth they pretended to seek escape them, but they also lost it by their own sin.

But if there had been anyone to bring the truth scattered through individuals and Schools together into one and reduce it to a body, he surely would not have disagreed with us. No one can do this unless he is steeped in truth, and no one can know what is true who has not been taught by God. There is no way to reject what is false, to choose and approve of what is true. If someone were to do this by chance, he would most certainly be a philosopher, even though he would not be able to defend these matters by divine witnesses. Still, the truth itself would shine out with its own light. Those who approve of some group and join themselves to it are guilty of an unbelievable error when they condemn other groups as false and empty and arm themselves for battle although they do not know what they ought to defend or what to refute. They hatefully attack at random everything those with whom they disagree bring forward.

Because of their totally obstinant quarrels there is no philosophy that comes near to what is true. The truth that is whole they grasp in a partial fashion. Plato said that the world was made by God;[33] the prophets said the same and it is clear from the poems of the Sibyl.[34] They are therefore in error who said that all things were born spontaneously or from tiny atoms that had come together. A thing so great, so beautiful, so vast, could not come to be nor be arranged and set in order without a Maker of the highest wisdom. The very order that they understand establishes and rules all things gives witness to a Maker of sagacious mind. The Stoics say that the world and everything in it was made for the sake of men: the Scriptures teach us the same. Democritus, who thought that men were produced from the earth without rhyme or reason in the manner of worms, was therefore in error. Because he was not able to grasp the sacred mystery why man was created, he reduced human life to nothing. Ariston taught that men were born to pursue virtue;[35] the prophets teach and warn us of the same. Aristippus, who subjected man to pleasure, that is, to evil, like a beast, is wrong.[36] Pherecydes and Plato contended that souls are immortal;[37] this teaching is at home in our religion. Therefore Dicaearchus and Democritus, who argued that they perished with the body and were dissolved, are in error.[38] Zeno the Stoic taught that there is an underworld and abodes for the holy that are separated from the wicked. He also taught that the good dwell in peaceful and pleasant regions and the evil undergo punishment in dark places and in fearful chasms of filth.[39] The prophets make the same clear to us. Therefore Epicurus erred when he thought that it was all an invention of the poets and interpreted the punishments of the underworld that are spoken of as taking place in this life.[40] Philosophers reached the whole truth and every secret of divine religion, but when others refuted them they were not able to defend what they had found because no system joined each of the points together, nor were they able to reduce all the things they knew to be true to a summary as we have done above.[41]

8. Immortality is the unique highest good. From the beginning we were created to attain it. We were born for it. We are striving toward immortality: Human nature inclines us to it;

virtue draws us to it. Because we discern it as a good, we must now discuss it.

Although Plato's arguments add much to the subject, they have little weight for proving and rounding out the truth. He did not complete the explanation of the whole mystery nor did he unify it. He did not understand the highest good. Even though he knew the truth about the immortality of the soul, he did not speak about it as the highest good. We are able to choose the truth through more secure signs. We do not acquire it by doubtful guessing, but know it by divine tradition. Plato argued thus: That which both knows through itself and is always moved by itself is immortal. What has no beginning of motion will not have an end because it cannot depart from itself.[42] This argument would grant eternity to dumb animals unless he had modified it by a wise addition. To avoid this joining of men and animals he added:

> The human soul, whose wonderful dexterity in discovery, quickness of thought, ease of perceiving and learning, memory of the past, foresight of the future and knowledge of unnumbered skills and matters lacking in other living things appears divine and celestial, cannot be other than immortal. The origin of the soul that can grasp and contain so many things is not to be found on earth; indeed, it has no trace of earthly matter. What in man is weighty and able to be dissolved must be dispersed into the earth; what is fine and subtle is indivisible. When it has been freed from the habitation of the body as from a prison it will fly to heaven and to its nature.[43]

This is a brief summary of Plato's doctrine, which is explained in detail in his works.

Earlier Pythagoras and his teacher Pherecydes, whom Cicero believed was the first to discuss the immortality of the soul, held the same view.[44] They all were very convincing, but in this quarrel those who held the opposing viewpoint, first Dicaearchus, next Democritus, and finally Epicurus, had no less authority, so that what they were fighting about was undecided. When Cicero had set forth all their views on immortality and death, he finally proclaimed that he did not know what was true. He says: "Let some god see which of these opinions is true."[45] And again in another place: "Because each of these opinions has very learned authorities, what is sure cannot be divined."[46] We have no need of divination; divinity itself has revealed the truth to us.

9. The eternity of the soul can be proven by arguments that neither Plato nor anyone else discovered. We will briefly collect them, because our presentation wants to proclaim God's great judgment destined to take place on earth as the end of the world draws near.

The first argument. Because God cannot be seen by man, among his other wonderful ordinances he made many things, such as noise, odor, and wind, whose power is evident but whose substance cannot be seen, so that no one might think that there is no God just because mortal eyes cannot see him. Following their example and proof, we behold God by his power, purpose, and works even though he is invisible. What is louder than noise, stronger than the wind, more penetrating than odor? When they are borne through the air, come to our senses, and incite them with their force, they are not beheld by light's power, but are felt by the rest of the body. Likewise, we do not comprehend God by sight or any other feeble sense, but we are to see him with the mind's eye when we behold his wonderful and splendid works. I would say that those who claim there is no God at all are not only not philosophers but not even men. They are most like the dumb beasts, made up of body alone, discerning nothing through the intellectual soul, referring everything to the body's sensation, and thinking nothing exists that cannot be seen. Because they saw adversities overtake good men and prosperity attend the evil, they believed that everything took place by chance and that the world was made by nature and not by providence.

They have already fallen into the nonsense that necessarily follows such an opinion. But if God is incorporeal, invisible, and eternal, it is not likely that the soul perishes just because it is not visible after it departs from the body. It is clear that alive and intelligent things exist that cannot be seen. But it is diffi-cult for the mind to grasp how the soul can understand without the bodily parts adapted for understanding. What about God? Is it easy to grasp how he lives without a body? If the philos-ophers believe that there are gods (who, if they exist, must surely be without bodies), they must believe that human souls exist in the same way, because good sense and reason under-stand that there is a likeness between god and man. Cicero's argument is also quite solid: The soul can be known to be eternal because "there is no other animal that has any knowl-edge of God," and religion is almost the only thing that dis-criminates man from the beasts.[47] Since this happens only in man's case, it surely testifies that we strive after, desire, and cultivate that which is familiar to us, what lies right ahead.

Can anyone have considered the nature of other living beings, which Almighty God's providence created humbled with bent bodies and prostrate upon the earth, and not have understood that they have no relation with heaven? Can he not understand that man is the only divine and heavenly animal, he whose body is raised up from the ground and whose counte-nance is held high? In his upright state he seeks his origin. Contemptuous of the lowliness of earth, he stretches out to the heights because he understands he is to seek his supreme good on high. Mindful of the creation by which God made him special, does he not look toward his Maker? Trismegistus very rightly called this looking "contemplation."[48] It does not exist in animals. Because the wisdom given to man alone is nothing else than knowledge of God, it is clear that the soul does not perish or dissolve. It lasts forever because it seeks and loves the eternal God. By the prompting of its nature it understands where it has come from and where it is going.

That man alone makes use of the heavenly element is no small argument for immortality. The universe consists of these two elements, fire and water, mutually opposed and at odds with each other. The one belongs to heaven, the other to earth. The other living things, because they are earthly and mortal, use the earthly and heavy element; man alone has the use of fire, the light, lofty, and heavenly element. Heavy things press down to death, light things rise up to life, because life is above, death below. Just as light cannot exist without fire, so life cannot be without light. Fire is the element of life and light; hence it appears that man who uses it is immortal in his condition, because he is at home with that which causes life.[49]

Virtue, which is also given to man alone, is a potent argument that the soul is immortal. If the soul dies, virtue would not be natural, because it is harmful in the present life. This earthly life that we have in common with dumb animals both desires pleasure, whose various fruits and sweets it delights in, and flees pain, whose harshness injures living beings with bitterness and pushes them toward devouring death. Therefore, if virtue denies man the goods naturally desired and compels him to undergo evils naturally avoided, it is an evil, an enemy of nature. He who follows it must be judged a fool who injures himself by fleeing the good things in front of him and seeking evil things without hope of a better reward. For when we could enjoy ourselves with the most delightful pleasures does it not seem senseless to prefer to live in humility, need, contempt, and dishonor—or, rather, not even to live, but to be tortured by pain and be on the point of death? And does it not seem foolish that we should gain nothing from these evils to pay back for the pleasure lost? But if virtue is not an evil, and acts rightly in its strong condemnation of vicious and shameful pleasures, and does not fear pain or death in the discharge of its duty, it must then gain a good greater than those it spurns. But once death has come, what other good than eternity can be hoped for?

10. Now we ought to move on to the things that are contrary to virtue. They too demonstrate the immortality of the soul. All vices are temporary; they are aroused for the present moment. The force of anger is quieted when vengeance has been taken; the pleasure of the body is the goal of lust. Either enough of what we want or the arousal of other feelings does away with avarice; ambition grows old after the honors it desired have been gained. So also the other vices cannot remain firm or permanent, but reach their end in the very fruit they await. They come and go, but virtue is constant without inter-

ruption. The man who has taken it up once and for all cannot abandon it. If it were to have an interruption, if at some time we were able to do without virtues, the opposing vices would immediately return. If virtue departs, if at some time it withdraws, it was not really embraced. When it has made itself a stable home, it is necessarily part of every action. It cannot faithfully drive out vices and put them to flight unless it fortifies the breast in which it dwells with a permanent watchpost. The permanent character of virtue shows that the human soul, if it has grasped virtue, will also last, because virtue is eternal and only the human soul contains it.

Because vices are opposed to virtue, their whole explanation must of necessity be different and opposite. Vices are stirrings and disturbances of the soul; virtue on the contrary is a calmness and tranquility of soul. Vices are temporary and brief in duration; virtue is lasting, constant, and always consistent. Pleasures, the fruits of vices, are as temporary and brief in duration as they are; the fruit and reward of virtue must be eternal. Vices' profit is in the present, virtue's in the future. There is no reward for virtue in this life because virtue must be itself. Just as vices reach their fulfillment in the act and their pleasure and reward attend them, so when virtue has been perfected its reward will follow it. Virtue is perfected only in death in that its highest task is undergoing death. So the reward of virtue is after death. In his *Tusculan Disputations* Cicero understood, even though hesitantly, that man's highest good happened only after death. "If so it is to be," he says, "with steadfast soul one will march to the death in which we have recognized there is either no evil or the highest good."[50] Death does not snuff out a man, but admits him to virtue's reward. Cicero also says that anyone who has befouled himself with vices and crimes and has been a slave to pleasure is condemned to pay an eternal penalty (what the scriptures call the second death).[51] This is eternal and full of the most severe tortures. Just as two lives are proposed to men, the one of the soul, the other of the body, so also are two deaths proposed, the one pertaining to the body, which all must discharge according to nature, the other belonging to the soul, which crime gains and virtue avoids. Just as this life is temporary and has definite limits because it belongs to the body, so also death is temporary and has a fixed end because it affects the body.

11. Death itself will end when the time that God set for it will have been fulfilled. Because temporary death follows temporary life, souls will rise to eternal life when temporary death has ended. On the other hand, just as the life in which the soul receives the divine and inexpressible fruits of its immortality is itself eternal, so too the death in which it pays unfailing penalties and infinite torments for its sins must be of equal duration. It has been arranged that those who are happy in this bodily and earthly life are soon to be unhappy forever because they have already gained the good they preferred. This happens to those who worship the gods and neglect God. Those who sought justice in this life were unhappy, despised, and in need. They frequently suffered insults and injuries for the sake of justice, because virtue can be possessed in no other way. They are soon to be happy forever, so that since they have already suffered evil they may also enjoy good. This surely is the case for those who reject the earthly gods and passing pleasures to follow the heavenly religion of the God whose pleasures are as eternal as he is. What? Do not the works of the body and soul show that the soul is free of death? Because the body is weak and mortal, whatever it does is equally passing. Cicero says that there is nothing done by human hands that is not eventually destroyed either by men's violence or by devouring old age.[52]

We see that the soul's works are eternal. Those who strove for contempt of present things left behind the evidence of their character and great deeds and certainly gained an imperishable name for their genius and virtue. If the works of the body are mortal because the body is, it follows that the soul is immortal from the fact that we see that its works do not die. In the same way, the desires of the body and the soul prove that the one is mortal and the other not. The body desires only what is temporal, that is, food, drink, clothing, rest, pleasure (although these things cannot be sought after or acquired without the will and aid of the soul). By itself the soul desires things that do not serve the body's enjoyment, things not passing, but eternal, such as the reputation for virtue and a good memory. Contrary to the body, the soul desires a worship of God that consists in abstinence from desires and passions, endurance of pain, and contempt of death. So it is credible that the soul does not die, but is separated from the body, because the body can do nothing without the soul, whereas the soul is able to do many great things without the body. Is it not true that visible and tangible things cannot be eternal because they can undergo external violence, but that the things that cannot be seen or touched are everlasting because they suffer no such force? Only their power, their order, and their influence are evident. If the body is mortal because it is subject to sight and touch, then the soul is immortal because it can neither be touched nor seen.

12. Now let us refute the arguments of those who hold the opposite view. Lucretius has set them out in his third book. He says that the soul is born with the body and it must perish with the body.[53] But their manner of existence is not the same, for the body is solid and perceptible to the eyes and hand; the soul is immaterial and evades touch and sight. The body is made of earth and has density; the soul has nothing compound in it, no earthly weight, as Plato says.[54] If it were not from heaven, it could not have such great dexterity, power, and quickness. Because the body is formed of a heavy and corruptible element and is tangible and visible, it is corruptible and perishes; it cannot resist violence because it can be seen and touched. But the soul, because in its fineness it evades all touch, cannot be destroyed by any attack. Although they are born joined together and connected, and the one that is formed from earthly matter is like a vessel for the other that is drawn from a heavenly intangibility, when some power separates them (the separation called death), each returns to its own nature. What was taken from the earth is released to the earth; what was from the heavenly spirit always lasts and lives, since the divine spirit is eternal. Lucretius, forgetting what he had put forward and what teaching he defended, wrote these verses:

> That which previously came from the earth returns again
> To earth, but what was sent from the world of the ether
> The shining temples of heaven take back again.[55]

He who taught that souls perished with bodies had no right to say this, but he was overcome by truth and right reason stole upon him unaware. Furthermore, the position he summarizes here, namely that the soul is dissolved, that it perishes together with the body because they are born together, is false and capable of being reversed. They do not both perish together, but when the soul departs the body remains whole for many days and frequently lasts a very long time when it is embalmed. If they both perished together as they are born together, the soul would not suddenly depart and leave the body, but at one instant both alike would disperse. The body with the breath still in it would dissolve and perish as quickly as the soul withdrew, and with the dissolution of the body the soul would vanish like water poured from a broken vase.

If the weak earthly body does not immediately melt away and decay into the earth that was its source after the departure of the soul, then the soul, which is not feeble, will last forever because its origin is eternal. Lucretius says that because the mind increases in children, is vigorous in the young, and weakened in the old, it is proven to be mortal.[56] First of all, the soul is not the same as the mind, for that by which we live is different from that by which we think. The mind and not the soul of those asleep is unconscious. In the insane the mind is extinguished but the soul remains, and therefore they are termed "demented" and not "lifeless." The mind, that is the intelligence, is increased or diminished according to age; the soul is always in its own state of being, and it stays the same from the time when it receives the power of breath until the end when, sent forth from the prison of the body, it flies back to its own home. Second, although the soul is breathed in by God, nonetheless, because it is imprisoned in the dark home of earthly flesh,[57] it does not have the knowledge that belongs to divinity. It hears and learns all things, and gains wisdom by hearing and learning. Old age increases rather than diminishes wisdom, if youth has been passed in virtue.[58] If excessive old age weaken the limbs, if sight vanishes, the tongue grows mute, and the hearing deaf, it is the body's fault and not the soul's. But the memory does fail.[59] What wonder if the mind is weighed down by the ruin of its collapsing dwelling place and forgets the past? How else can it be divine in the future if it does not flee the prison that hampered it?

Lucretius says the same soul is subject to pain and grief and raves in drunkenness, and so it appears fragile and mortal.[60] Therefore, virtue and wisdom are necessary so that fortitude may repulse the sorrow incurred by seeing and suffering unworthy things, and abstinence in drink and in other matters may overcome pleasure. If the soul lacks virtue and is given over to pleasures and effeminacy, it will become subject to death, because virtue produces immortality and pleasure death, as we taught.[61] As I have shown,[62] death does not completely destroy and obliterate the soul, but inflicts eternal punishments on it. The soul cannot die completely since it has its origin in the eternal Spirit of God.

The soul, Lucretius says, also feels the body's illness and is forgetful of itself. It frequently grows sick and is healed.[63] This is especially why virtue is to be employed, so that the mind, not the soul, may not be broken by any pain of the body or undergo self-forgetfulness. Because mind lives in a definite part of the body, when an attack of disease has injured that part it moves its place and leaves its home in shaken fashion, ready to return when medicine and health shall have restored its dwelling place. Because the soul is joined to the body, the body's contact will weaken it if it lacks virtue, and the helplessness coming from association with weakness will reach the mind. When freed from the body, it will flourish of itself and not be tempted any longer by any kind of weakness because it has cast off its frail clothing. Just as the eye torn out and separated from the body can see nothing, he says, so the separated soul can sense nothing because it is a part of the body.[64] This is false and unlikely. The soul is not a part of the body, but is rather in the body. Just as what is in a container is not a part of the container, nor are the things that are in a house said to be parts of the house, so too the soul is not a part of the body because the body is either the vessel or container of the soul.

A much sillier argument says that the soul seems to be mortal because it does not leave the body quickly but gradually departs from all the members beginning from the bottom of the feet.[65] If it were eternal, it would burst forth in an instant as happens in the case of those who perish by the sword. Those whom sickness kills breathe their last over a duration so that the soul is gradually exhaled as the limbs grow cold. Since it is contained in the blood like light in oil,[66] when the blood is consumed by hot fevers some extremities of the limbs must grow cold. The smaller veins extend to the extremities of the body and the last weaker streams dry up when the inner source of the fountain fails. It must not be supposed that because bodily perception fails, the soul's perception is dead and gone. The body becomes like a brute beast when the soul departs and not vice versa because the soul takes all perception with it. Since the soul when present gives the power of perception to the body and makes it live, it is not possible that the soul, being itself the power of perception and life, does not live and perceive through itself.

As for his statment:

> If our mind were immortal,
> It would not so much complain that it is dissolved in
>   dying,
> But rather of going forth and changing its garment like a
>   snake,[67]

I have never seen anybody who complained that he was "dissolved in death." Perhaps Lucretius saw some Epicurean being a philosopher as he was dying and discoursing on his own dissolution in his last breath. How can we know whether he felt that he was being dissolved or liberated from the body when there is no speech at the moment of departure? As long as he had sensation and could talk, he was not yet dissolved; when he had been dissolved, he could no longer sense or speak. He either could not yet or could no longer lament dissolution. "But before he is dissolved he understands that it will happen." What about the fact that we see many of the dying do not complain about dissolution, as he says, but testify by gesture or if they still can by voice that they are going forth, setting out, walking away? So it is clear that there is no dissolution but a separation. This says that the soul remains.

Other arguments of the Epicurean teaching oppose Pythagoras, who said that souls leave bodies that are worn out by age and death and enter those that are new and just born. The same souls are always being reborn, now in men, now in cattle, now in wild beasts, now in birds. Thus they are immortal because they frequently change dwelling places made up of various and different bodies. This view of a crazy man ought not even have been seriously refuted, ridiculous as it was and more suited to a farcical actor than to a School of philosophy. Anyone who acts this way seems to be afraid that someone will believe him. Let us then omit the arguments in behalf of error put forth against error; it is enough to have refuted those put forth against the truth.

13. I have set forth, I think, that the soul is incapable of dissolution. What remains is to cite texts whose authority strengthens the arguments. I will not call on the prophets whose teaching and predictions were established to teach that man was created to worship God and to receive immortality from him, but will rather call on those whom the opponents of truth must believe. In describing the nature of man in order to teach how he was made by God, Hermes says the following:

> And the same made a single human nature from each of two natures, the immortal and the mortal, and thus made it partly immortal and party mortal; and he took it and set it up between the divine and immortal nature and the mortal and mutable nature, so that it might look upon all and wonder at all.[68]

Someone might number him among the philosophers and grant him no more authority than Plato or Pythagoras, although he has been placed among the gods and honored by the Egyptians under the name Mercury. A greater testimony is needed. A man named Polites asked Apollo of Miletus whether the soul remained after death or was dissolved, and he responded in these verses:

> The soul, as long as it is held fast to the body by bonds,
> Knowing corruptible sensations, is subject to mortal pains.
> But when it has gained a very quick release from
>   mortality,
> The body being wasted, it is carried completely into the
>   air;
> Ageless always, it remains imperishable forever,
> For the first-born divine foreknowledge has arranged
>   this.[69]

Don't the Sibylline verses prove it to be so when they announce that the time will come when God will judge the living and the dead? We will give examples a little later.

Therefore the opinion of Democritus, Epicurus, and Dicaearchus about the dissolution of the soul is false. They did not dare to talk about the destruction of souls when any magician was present who knew that souls are raised up from the underworld by special verses, that they draw near and present themselves to be seen by human eyes and speak and predict the future. If they did dare, they would have been overcome by the fact itself and the proofs presented. They said that the soul dies because they did not consider its character, which is so subtle that it escapes the eyes of the mind. What about Aristoxenus, who denied that there was any soul at all, even when it was in the body?[70] He thought that just as the unified sound and song that musicians call harmony is made in the lyre from the stretching of the strings, so the power of perception is found in bodies from the structure of the internal organs and the strength of the external members. Nothing could be more foolish than that! He truly has good eyes but a blind heart who has not seen that by which he is alive, and has not seen the mind by means of which he had the thought! Many philosophers have thought that nothing existed that was not visible, even though the power of the mind ought to be clearer than that of the body when we perceive things whose power and nature are felt rather than seen.

14. Because we have spoken of the immortality of the soul, it follows that we ought to teach how and when this will be given to man.[71] In this readers may also see the errors that come from the malice and folly of those who think that some mortals have been made gods by men's decrees and orders, supposedly either because they invented arts, or taught the use of the fruits of the earth, or discovered things useful for human life, or killed fierce beasts. How far these services are from deserving immortality we have taught in the former books and now teach again, so that it may be clear that justice alone brings eternal life to man and God alone bestows it. Those who are said to have been made immortal by reason of their merits gained not immortality but death by their sins and lusts. They had neither justice nor true virtue. They merited no heavenly reward, but the infernal punishments that hang over them and all who worship them. I will show that the time of this judgment is near. In it the just will receive fit reward and the unjust well- merited punishment.

Plato and many other philosophers, because they were ignorant of the source of things and of the exalted time when the world was made, said that many thousands of years had passed since this most beautiful world order had appeared. Perhaps they followed the Chaldeans, whom Cicero in the first book of his *On Divination* noted wildly claimed to have four hundred and seventy thousand years worth of records.[72] They thought that because they could not be refuted they could freely lie. We, on the other hand, are taught the knowledge of truth by the holy scriptures and know the beginning and the end of the world. We will now speak of the latter at the conclusion of our work, having already explained the beginning in the second book.

Let the philosophers who count thousands of years from the beginning of the world know that the six thousandth year has not yet been completed. When this number has been reached, a consummation must come and the condition of humanity must be transformed for the better. The evidence for this will be first set forth so that the calculations may be clear.[73]

God created the world and this wonderful work of nature in the space of six days and hallowed the seventh day on which he rested from his works, as we find in the mysteries of holy scripture. This is the sabbath day, which in Hebrew is named from the number seven, and hence seven is the prescribed and perfect number. There are seven days by whose orderly revolutions the circles of the years are made up, seven stars that never set, and seven planets whose different and unequal paths and movements are thought to cause changes of times and events. Therefore, since all of God's works were completed in six days, the world must remain in this stage for six ages, that is, for six thousand years.[74] God's "great day" is bounded by a thousand years, as the prophet points out in saying: "Before your eyes, O Lord, a thousand years are like one day" (Ps. 89:4). Just as God worked those six days in making such great things, so his piety and truth must work during these six thousand years that are under the domination and power of evil. Because when his works were completed he rested on the seventh day and blessed it, at the end of six thousand years all evil must be taken away from the earth and justice reign for a thousand years. There will be tranquillity and rest from the labors that the world has already long endured. I will give an orderly explanation of how it will happen.

We have frequently said that smaller and lesser matters are figures and foreshadowings of greater ones. Our day, bounded by the rising and the setting of the sun, has a likeness to the "great day" that is fixed by the circuit of a thousand years. In the same way, the creation of the earthly man foreshadowed the making of the heavenly people. As God made man himself last on the sixth day when everything fashioned for his use had been finished and brought him into this world as if into a house carefully prepared for him, so now on the sixth "great day" the true man, that is, the holy people shaped to justice by God's teaching and command, is being formed by the Word of God. Again, as at that time a mortal and imperfect man was fashioned from the earth to live a thousand years in the world, so now the perfect man is being formed from the earthly age so that given life by God he might rule in this same world for a thousand years.

If anyone searches the sacred scriptures he will find how the consummation will take place and what sort of fate hangs over human affairs. The voices of the prophets of this world agree with those of the other and announce the proximate end and destruction of all things. They describe the final old age of a world that is tired and collapsing. I will present now a summary and collection of the things the prophets and seers have said are coming before that final end arrives.[75]

15. Among the mysteries of holy scripture is the story of how a prince of the Hebrews compelled by the lack of grain crossed over into Egypt with all his house and kin.[76] When his descendants had lived in Egypt for a long time and grown into a great people they were afflicted with the heavy and unbearable yoke of slavery. God struck Egypt with an incurable plague, freed his people, and led them through the midst of the sea so that they walked over dry land when the waves had been split and moved to each side. When the Egyptian king tried to follow them in their flight he was cut off with all his forces as the sea returned to its place. Though so famous and wonderful a deed shows God's power to men in the present, it was also the presignification and figure of something greater that God is to do in the final consummation of the ages—he will free his people from the slavery of the world. Then, because there was one people of God who dwelt in the midst of one nation, Egypt alone was struck; now, because the people of God are gathered from all languages and dwell among all nations and are oppressed by their rule, all nations, that is, the whole world, must be struck by divine blows, so that God's just and devout people may be freed. Just as then signs were given that showed the coming slaughter to the Egyptians, so at the end there will be fearful prodigies in all the world's elements by which all nations will grasp the imminent destruction.

As the end of this world draws near the human situation must change and decline while evil grows strong. Our own times, in which evil and malice have increased precipitously, can be judged fortunate and almost golden in comparison to the incurable evil of that era. Justice will grow so rare, impiety, avarice, covetousness, and lust increase so greatly, that even if good men exist they will be the sport of the wicked and will be attacked on all sides by the unjust. Evil men alone will be rich; the good will be cast down in calumnies and in want. All justice will be disturbed, the laws will perish. There will be no possessions except what will be gained and defended by one's own hand. Insolence and violence will take hold of everything. There will be no faith, peace, humanity, shame, or truth among men, and hence neither safety, nor government, nor respite from evils. The whole earth will be in chaos, wars will rage everywhere, all nations will be in arms and will attack each other. Neighboring cities will battle each other. Egypt, the first home of all foolish superstitions, will pay the penalty and be covered with blood like a river.[77] Then a sword will travel through the world cutting down everything and laying all things low like a harvested crop.[78] The cause of this devastation and confusion will be the fact that the Roman name, which now rules the world, will be taken from the earth. Empire will return to Asia and once again the East will rule and the West will serve.[79] My minds shrinks from saying it, but say it I will because it is to come! It should not seem astonishing that a kingdom founded with such might, built up for so long by many great men, and finally made solid with such wealth will nevertheless collapse at some time. There is nothing built by human effort that cannot be destroyed by human means: Mortal are the works of mortals. Other earlier kingdoms, though they had flourished for a long time, were finally destroyed. It is recorded that the Egyptians, the Persians, the Greeks, and the Assyrians all ruled over lands. After they were all destroyed the supreme position came to the Romans.[80] Just as they surpassed all the rest in the greatness of their realm, so will their fall be the greater, because a building that is higher than the rest has more to destroy.

Seneca skillfully divided the periods of the city of Rome into ages. He said that the first age was infancy under King

Romulus, the time when Rome was born and educated. Then came childhood under the other kings who expanded the city and formed it by many teachings and laws. During Tarquin's reign, when it already began to be adult, it did not brook slavery, but threw off the yoke of proud domination and preferred to be ruled by laws rather than by kings. When its adolescence was finished at the end of the Punic War, it then began to flourish in its resolute strength.[81] With the removal of Carthage (for so long a rival in empire) Rome stretched out her hands by land and sea to the whole world. Finally, when all kings and nations had been subdued to her rule so that the very cause of wars had disappeared, she abused the might by which she had been built. This was her first old age, when, torn by civil wars and beset by internal evils, she returned once more to one-man rule as if going back to a second childhood. She lost the liberty she had defended under the leadership of Brutus and grew so old that she was not able to support herself without depending on the assistance of her rulers. If this be the case, what remains except for destruction to follow on old age? Under other words of terse obscurity (lest anyone easily understand),the discourses of the prophets announce that it will happen. The Sibyls openly say that Rome will perish by God's judgment because she hated the divine name and as an enemy of justice killed the people who were the disciples of truth.[82] Hystaspes also, a very ancient king of the Medes from whom that stream that is now called Hydaspes took its name, handed on to posterity a wonderful dream concerning the meaning of a boy who uttered prophecies. Long before the Trojan race was founded he announced that the Roman Empire and name would be taken from the world.[83]

16. I will describe how it will take place so that you do not think that it is incredible. First of all, the empire will grow but the supreme directing power will weaken and will be scattered and divided among many. Then civic quarrels will continually spread abroad and there will be no end of deadly wars until ten kings will emerge simultaneously. They will divide the world to destroy and not to govern it.[84] They will greatly expand

their armies and devastate the farmlands—the beginning of destruction and death. They will lay waste, crush, and devour everything.

Then a mighty enemy from the far North will suddenly rise up against them. When he has destroyed the three who control Asia he will be taken into alliance with the others and will be made their chief.[85] He will afflict the world with unbearable tyranny, will mix up human and divine matters, and will work for things abominable and accursed. He will ponder novel notions in his heart: to set up his own empire, change the old laws and ratify his own, contaminate, ravage, despoil, and kill. Lastly, when the name of the empire has been changed and its seat moved, the confusion and disorder of the whole human race will follow. Then will come a hateful and detestable time when no one will enjoy life.

Cities will be destroyed from their foundations. They will perish, not only from fire and sword but also from frequent earthquakes, floods, plagues, and famines. The air will be poisoned and will be corrupt and pestilential, at one time from unseasonable rains or unusual dryness, at another from excessive cold or hot spells. The earth will not give her fruit to men. Neither grain, nor tree, nor vine will bear; but rather, after they have given the greatest hope in the blossom, they will cheat at harvest. Springs and rivers will dry up so that they will not provide a drink; waters will be changed to blood and bitterness. Because of this the animals will desert the earth, as will the birds the air and the fishes the sea. Wondrous portents in heaven, as well as comets' tails, eclipses of the sun, the moon's color, and falling stars will confuse the minds of men with the greatest fear. These things will not happen in the usual way, but unknown and unseen stars will suddenly shine forth. The sun will be perpetually darkened so that one can scarcely distinguish between night and day. The moon will fail, and not just for three hours; constantly covered with blood, it will complete unusual orbits so that men will not be able to know either the courses of the stars or the calculation of time. Summer will come in winter, or vice versa. Then the year will be shortened, the month diminished, the day compressed to a brief moment. The stars will fall en masse so that the entire sky will appear blind, without any lights. The highest mountains will also be brought low, level with the plains; the sea will be made unnavigable.[86]

So that nothing may be lacking to the misfortunes of mankind and of the world, a trumpet will be heard from heaven. The Sibyl describes it this way: "The trumpet from heaven shall send forth its wailing voice."[87] All will tremble and be afraid at that mournful sound. Then through the wrath of God against those who did not acknowledge justice, sword, fire, famine, and disease will rage. Fear will hover continually over everything. Men will call upon God and he will not listen; they will hope for death and it will not come. Not even night will allay the fear nor will sleep be possible, but anxiety and sleeplessness will torment men's hearts. They will weep and groan and grind their teeth; they will congratulate the dead and mourn for the living. These and many other evils will cause desolation on the earth; the globe will be corrupted and deserted. In the Sibylline verses it is thus described: "With the destruction of men the world will no longer be the world."[88] The human race will be so diminished that scarcely a tenth will be left; a hundred will go forth from where a thousand once went out. Two-thirds of the worshipers of God will perish; the third that will remain will have been tested.[89]

17. I will explain more clearly how it will take place. When the end of time is already close God will send a great prophet who will convert men to him and who will receive power to perform miracles.[90] Wherever men will not listen to him, he will close up heaven and hold back the rain, change water into blood, and torture them with hunger and thirst. Whoever attempts to injure him will be burned by fire coming out of his mouth. By these miracles and works of power he will convert many to God's worship.

When his works are finished, another king, born of an evil spirit, will arise from Syria.[91] He will be the subverter and destroyer of the human race. At the same time he will destroy that first evil king and anything that he has left. He will fight against God's prophet, overcome and kill him, and see to it that he lies unburied. But after the third day the prophet will arise and in the wondering sight of all he will be snatched up to heaven.[92] That king will be completely loathsome himself, a prophet of lies. He will set himself up and call himself God,[93] and will command that he be worshipped as the son of God. He will be given the power to do signs and wonders in order thus to ensnare men to worship him. He will command fire to come down from heaven, the sun to stand still outside its orbit, and a statue to speak.[94] These will all happen at his word. By these miracles he will even attract many of the wise to himself. Then he will try to destroy the temple of God and will persecute the just people; there will be affliction and sorrow such as has never been from the beginning of the world.[95]

Those who believe him and join him he will mark like cattle; those who refuse his mark will either flee to the mountains or be captured and killed with the most exquisite tortures. (He will wrap up just men in the scrolls of the prophets and burn them.) He will be allowed to desolate the earth for forty-two months.[96] That will be the time when justice will be cast out and innocence will be hated, when the evil will prey on the good in hostile fashion. Neither law nor order nor military discipline will be preserved; no one will reverence white hairs; the duty of piety will not be acknowledged; neither sex nor infancy will be spared. All things will be confused and mixed together contrary to the divine law and to the laws of nature. The whole earth will be laid waste as though by a single universal act of robbery.

When these things have taken place, then the just and those who follow truth will leave the wicked and flee to the desert. The Unholy One will hear of this and enflamed with rage will come up with a great army. He will bring up all his forces and in order to capture the just he will surround the mountain where they are waiting. When they see that they are shut in and besieged on all sides, they will call out to God with a great voice and beg divine aid. God will hear them and from heaven will send the Great King, who will rescue them and free them. He will destroy all the wicked with fire and sword.[97]

18. These things will take place in this way as all the prophets who speak by God's inspiration and the seers who speak from the prompting of demons have announced. Hystaspes, whom I mentioned above, after describing the wickedness of this last age, said that the pious and faithful who fled their persecutors would stretch out their hands to heaven with tears and groans and would implore Jove's protection. Jove would look down on the earth, hear the voices of man, and destroy the wicked.[98] All of this is true with the exception of the fact that he said Jove would do what God will do. Misled by demons, he also left out that the Son of God would be sent by the Father to free the faithful after all the wicked have been destroyed. Hermes did not hide that. In the book entitled *The Perfect Treatise*, after he mentioned the evils we spoke of, he adds:

> But when these things thus come to pass, O Asclepius, then he who is Lord, Father, God, and Creator of the first and one God, looking upon the deeds of men and opposing his own will (that is, Goodness) to disorder, abolished error and purged wickedness by washing it in much water and by burning it with raging fire and sometimes by subduing it with wars and pestilences. He brought back and restored his world to its ancient state.[99]

The Sibyls also show it that the Highest Father will send the Son of God to free the just from the hands of the wicked and destroy the unjust and their cruel tyrants. One of them put it this way:

> He will come and wish to destroy completely the city of
>   the blest,
> And a mighty king will be sent from God against him
> Who will destroy all the powerful kings and important
>   men.[100]

Another wrote:

> Then God will send the king from the rising of the sun
> Who will free the whole earth from the evil of war.[101]

PLATE I:

THE RETURN OF THE RISEN LORD
Detail of the apse mosaic of the Church of Saints Cosmas and Damian in Rome, c. 530
A.D. Reproduced from W. Oakeshott, *The Mosaics of Rome* (London: Thames and
Hudson, 1967), Plate XI.

And another:

> Behold the mild King comes to take our yoke,
> The intolerable slavery that now lies on our necks;
> He will free us from godless sentences and oppressive
>   changes.[102]

19. The world will be oppressed because human might will have failed to destroy this powerful tyranny. It will fasten on the captive world with great armies of thieves. Divine aid will be needed in such a calamity. Moved by the threatening danger and the pitiable complaint of the just, God will immediately send the Deliverer. On a dark and stormy night heaven's vault will be opened so that the light of the descending God may be seen through the whole world like lightning. The Sibyl has spoken of it in these verses:

> When he comes there will be fire in the darkness
> Of the black night.[103]

This is the night we celebrate with a vigil because of the coming of our King and God.[104] It has a double meaning: because in it he once received life after he had suffered, and in it he will later receive the kingdom of the world. He whom we call Christ, Defender, Judge, Avenger, King, and God will give this sign before he descends. A sword will suddenly fall from heaven so that the just may know that the Leader and the holy army is about to come down. Accompanied by angels he will descend in the midst of the earth. An inextinguishable flame will precede him. The power of the angels will deliver the army who besieged the mountain into the hands of the just; they shall fall in battle from the third hour until the evening, and blood will flow like a torrent. With all his forces destroyed, the Unholy One will flee all alone. His power will desert him.

This is the one called Antichrist. He will lyingly say he is Christ; he will fight against the truth. When conquered he will flee. He will frequently renew the war and frequently be overcome, until in the fourth battle, when all the wicked have been slain, he will be completely conquered. He will be cap-

65

tured and finally pay the penalty for his crimes. The other rulers and tyrants who wasted the world will be brought bound to the King together with him. He will rebuke them, refute them, charge them with their crimes, and will condemn them and hand them over to deserved tortures. When evil has been thus snuffed out and impiety suppressed, the world, which through so many centuries had been subject to error and crime and had borne heinous slavery, will be finally at peace. Gods made with hands will no longer be worshiped. The idols will be cast from their temples and couches and burned. They will burn along with their wondrous gifts—something the Sibyl in agreement with the prophets predicted would happen: "The idols and all their riches will be cast away."[105] The Erythraean Sibyl promised the same thing: "The idols made by hands shall be devoured by fire."[106]

20. After this hell will be open and the dead will rise. The same King and God to whom the Supreme Father will give the ultimate power of judging and ruling will make the Last Judgment on them. The Erythraean Sibyl speaks thus about this Judgment and Kingdom:

> When this day of fate has found its accomplishment,
> The Judgment of the Immortal God will come to mortals,
> The Great Judgment and rule shall come upon men.[107]

Another Sibyl says:

> Then the earth will gape apart and show the abyss of
>   Tartarus,
> All will come to the royal judgment seat of God.[108]

In another place in the same Sibyl:

> I will roll up the heavens and open up the abysses of the
>   earth,
> And then I will raise the dead, loosing Fate

And the sting of Death; immediately I will come to
    Judgment,
Judging the life of men both pious and wicked.[109]

Not all will then be judged by God, but only those who
gave God reverence. Those who did not recognize God, because no judgment can absolve them, are already judged and
condemned as the holy scripture testifies, ". . .the wicked shall
not rise to judgment."[110] Therefore, those who knew God shall
be judged and their crimes, that is, their evil deeds compared
and weighed with their good ones. If the good and just deeds
are more numerous and important, they will be granted blessedness; if evil deeds win out, they will be condemned to punishment.

Here perhaps someone will say: "If the soul is immortal,
how is it able to suffer and feel pain? If it is to be punished for
what it has merited, it will indeed feel pain, and death as well;
if it is not subject to death, neither is it to pain. Therefore it is
not able to suffer." The Stoics meet this demand or argument
in the following manner. The souls of men are eternal and are
not annihilated by death, but those that were just return home
to the heavenly seat of their origin, pure, impassible, and
blessed. Otherwie, they are taken to those fortunate fields
where they enjoy wondrous delights. The souls of the wicked,
however, because they stained themselves with evil desires,
hold a middle place between mortal and immortal nature and
possess weakness from the flesh's contagion. Addicted to the
flesh's desires and lusts, they bear a certain indelible stain and
earthly blot that with length of time completely penetrates
them. It renders them of such a nature that while they cannot
be totally destroyed because they are from God, they can be
punished through the stain that sins have burned into the body
and that produces the sensation of pain. The poet explains this
opinion thus:

When at the last day life has departed,
Nonetheless, not every evil and bodily curse completely
Departs from the wretched; many hardened stains have

Long grown within in wondrous ways.
Therefore they must be disciplined by punishments and
Pay the penalty of old sins.[111]

This is quite near the truth. As the same poet says, when the soul is separated from the body, "it is like light wind and very similar to fleeting sleep."[112] It is a spirit and in its subtlety cannot be grasped by us who are bodily, but it can be grasped by God, to whom all things are possible.

21. We say that God's power is such that he perceives even incorporeal things and influences them as he wishes. The angels fear God because he can discipline them in an indescribable way, and the demons dread him because he torments and punishes them. Why wonder that even though souls be immortal they are still able to suffer at the hands of God? Since they have nothing hard and tangible, they cannot suffer violence from solid and corporeal things. Because they live on the level of spirits, they yield only to God whose power and substance is spiritual.

Holy scripture teaches us how the wicked are to be punished. Because they contracted sin while in the body, they will again be endowed with flesh so that they can absolve their crime in the body. It will not be a flesh like the earthly one that God clothed man with, but it will be indestructible and eternal so that it can bear torments and perpetual fire. This fire will be different from the one we use for the necessities of life, which is extinguished if it is not nourished by some fuel. That divine fire always lives by itself and thrives without any nourishment. There is no smoke mixed with it, but it is pure and flowing, as liquid as water. It is not driven upward by some force as is our fire, which by reason of its material defect and the smoke with which it is mixed must blaze out and fly up toward heaven in confused fashion. The divine fire will both burn and renew the wicked by one and the same force and power. It will restore whatever it takes away from bodies and will provide its own eternal nourishment: something the poets transferred to the vulture of Tityus.[113] It will burn and cause pain with no loss to the bodies that are being restored.

When God has judged the just he will also prove them with fire. Those whose sins have greater weight or number shall be scorched with fire and burnt; those who have been dyed in the fullness of justice and the maturity of virtue will not feel the flame,[114] because they will have something divine in them that will repel and reject it. Such is the power of innocence that the fire will leave it unharmed because God has given this fire the ability to burn the wicked but to spare the just. Do not think that souls are judged immediately after death. All are held in common custody until the time comes when the greatest Judge will examine their merits. Then those whose righteousness is proven will receive the prize of immortality; those whose sins and crimes are found out will not rise but will be buried with the wicked in the darkness and destined to sure punishments.

22. Some say these are poets' fictions because they do not know where the poets learned them. They deny that they can happen. This is no wonder because the matter is different from what the poets said. Although the poets are more ancient than historians and orators and other kinds of writers, because they did not know the mystery of the divine secret and because news of the future resurrection had reached them only as an obscure rumor, they reported what they had heard as casually and lightly as if it were a fiction. They also claimed that they did not follow secure authority, but mere opinion, as Vergil said: "If I can speak what I have heard." [115] Though they partly corrupted truth's hidden secrets, the message is guaranteed to be true because it partly agrees with the prophets. For us that is proof enough.

There is an explanation for their error. In frequent discourses the prophets preached that the Son of God would judge the dead. This prediction was not concealed. Since the poets thought that Jove was the god who ruled heaven, they entrusted judgment in the underworld to a son of Jove, not Apollo, or Liber, or Mercury, the celestial sons, but one who was mortal and righteous, such as Minos, or Aeacus, or Radamanthus. Therefore, with poetic license they corrupted what they had received, or else imagination altered a truth that had been spread through various mouths and repetitions. They sung that souls would again be restored to life after a thousand years in the underworld, as Vergil says:

> All these, when the wheel has turned through a thousand
> years,
> God will call to the river Lethe in a great band;
> Unremembering, they visit once more the vault of heaven
> and begin
> Again to yearn to return to bodies.[116]

This explanation was wrong, because the dead will not rise a thousand years after their deaths, but restored again to life they will reign a thousand years with God.[117] God will come so that he can raise the revived souls whose bodies have been renewed to eternal happiness when this world has been purged of every stain. Except for the water of forgetfulness the rest is true. They made that up lest an opponent say: "Why do the souls not remember that they were once alive and who they were and what they did?" But this is not plausible, so the whole matter is rejected by some as a fanciful and fabulous creation.

When we affirm and teach concerning the resurrection that souls return to another life remembering who they are and in the same disposition and form, an opponent says: "So many centuries have passed and what single person has ever risen from the dead to prove that it is possible?" But the resurrection cannot take place while injustice still rules. In this world men are violently slaughtered by the sword, by ambushes and poisons; they are harassed by injuries, want, prison, torture and proscription. On top of this, justice is hated, and all who wish to follow God are not only despised, but are also vexed with every kind of punishment. They are made to worship idols not through reason and truth but by heinous mangling of their bodies.

Should men be resurrected to the same conditions? Should they return to a life in which they cannot be safe? Because the just are held in such low esteem and because they are so freely killed, what would it have been like if someone had come back from the dead and received life by a return to his former state? He would have been immediately snatched from the eyes of men, lest seeing and hearing him everybody abandon the gods and convert to the worship and religion of the one God. Therefore, the resurrection must take place once and for all when evil has been taken away, because those who have risen can no longer die nor be harmed in any way. Their death has been canceled so that they can lead a blessed life. Because the poets knew that this world was filled with every evil they made up the river of forgetfulness lest souls refuse to return to the upper world because of their memory of evils and labors. As Vergil puts it:

> O father, are we to think that any souls go up from here
> To heaven, and again return to their sluggish bodies?
> What is this so fearful longing for the miserable light of
>   day?[118]

They did not know how and when this was to happen and hence they thought that souls were reborn and once more sent into the womb and restored to infancy. Plato also says that souls can be known to be immortal and divine because native genius is quicker and more perceptive in boys. What they learn they grasp so quickly that they do not seem to be learning it for the first time but to be recalling and remembering it.[119] The philosopher foolishly believed the poets on this score.

23. They are not reborn—that is impossible—but they will arise and be endowed with bodies by God. They will remember all the deeds of their former life. Placed amidst heavenly goods and enjoying the delights of countless riches, they will give thanks to God present among them because he has destroyed all evil and has raised them up to the kingdom and to life everlasting.

The philosophers have also tried to say something about the resurrection, just as corruptly as the poets. Pythagoras discussed the passage of souls into new bodies, but he mistakenly held them to pass from men into cattle and from cattle into men. He thought his own soul came from Euphorbus.

71

Chrysippus, whom Cicero says was a Stoic,[120] does better when he speaks of the renewal of the world in the book he wrote *On Providence*:

> Because this is so, nothing is impossible. After our death, when certain periods of time have come round again, we are returned to the state in which we now exist.[121]

But let us return from human to divine testimonies. The Sibyl says:

> The whole race of men is faithless; but when
> The Judgment shall come over the world and men that
>   God himself
> Will make upon both the wicked and the just in the same
>   way,
> Then he will send the wicked into the fire of the darkness
>   below.
> All who are holy will live again on the earth,
> God giving them spirit, honor and especially life.[122]

If not only the prophets but also the seers, poets, and philosophers agree that there will be a future resurrection of the dead, let no one ask us how it will happen. No explanation can be given for God's works. If he created man in the beginning in an indescribable way, let us believe that the old man can be restored by the same God who made him when he was new.

24. Now I will add what remains. The Sibyl testifies that the Son of the Most High and Great God will come to judge the living and the dead:

> There will then be confusion of all mortals on earth,
> When the Almighty himself appears on the throne to
>   judge
> The souls of living and dead and the whole world.[123]

When he has destroyed injustice, completed the Great Judgment, and restored to life all the just who have existed from the beginning of the world, he will dwell for a thousand years among men, governing them with totally righteous rule.[124] Another Sibyl proclaimed in raving prophecy: "Listen to me, O mortals, an everlasting king will reign!"[125] Those who will live then will not die, but will propagate an infinite multitude through those thousand years. Their offspring will be holy and beloved by God.[126] Those who will be raised from the dead will rule over the living like judges.

The nations are not to be totally destroyed, but some will be left for God's victory so that the just can triumph over them and subject them to eternal servitude. At the same time the Prince of Demons, the author of all evil, will be bound with chains and imprisoned for the thousand years of the heavenly kingdom when justice will rule the world, lest he rouse any ill against God's people. After God's coming the just shall be gathered together from the whole world. The holy city will be built in the middle of world after the Judgment is finished. God will dwell in it as founder along with the just who rule the earth. The Sibyl points to this city when she says:

The city which God chose for himself He made
More gleaming than the stars, the sun and the moon.[127]

Then the darkness that covered and obscured the heavens will be taken away, and the moon will receive the sun's brightness and will not be lessened anymore. The sun will be seven times brighter than it is now. The earth's fertility will be opened and it will spontaneously bear the richest fruits. The mountain rocks will drip with honey, the brooks will run with wine, and the rivers overflow with milk. In that time the world itself will rejoice. The whole of nature, freed and delivered from the rule of evil, impiety, crime, and error, will be glad. During this time beasts will not feed on blood and birds on prey, but they will be peaceful and serene. Lions and calves will stand together at the manger, the wolf will not snatch the sheep, the dog not hunt, hawks and eagles not kill. The infant will play with serpents.[128] All the things that the poets said happened in the Golden Age when Saturn reigned will then take place.

The poets' mistake comes from the fact that the prophets

announced and revealed many future events as if they were already past. They saw the visions they were given by the Holy Spirit as if they had already happened. When rumor had gradually spread their prophecies abroad, those who were ignorant of the mysteries did not know the way in which they were put forth. They thought that the events were already all completed in former ages, things that could not have been done and fulfilled under any human rule. But when all evil religions have been abolished and crime has been subdued, the earth will be subject to God,

> The sailor himself shall give up the sea and the sea-going
> Ship not exchange merchandise; the whole earth will bear
>   everything.
> The ground shall not suffer the hoe, nor the vine the
>   pruning hook;
> The hardy plowman shall loose the yoke from the oxen.

And then:

> The plain shall grow slowly golden with the waving
>   grain,
> The purple grape shall hang from the uncut brambles,
> And the solid oaks shall sweat honey wet with dew.
> Wool will not learn to adopt falsely various colors,
> But the ram himself in the meadows will change his
>   fleece,
> Now to sweet purple, now to saffron yellow;
> Scarlet will cover the grazing sheep of its own accord.
> The goats will bring home udders swollen with milk
> And the herds will not fear the great lions.[129]

Vergil foretold this following the Sibyl's song, for the Erythraean Sibyl speaks thus:

> Wolves and lambs, devoutly joined, shall feast on the
>   mountains,
> And leopards shall feed with kids.
> Bears shall lie with calves and other small cattle,

74

LACTANTIUS

And the carnivorous lion shall eat like a cow at the
   manger;
Serpents and vipers shall sleep with infants.[130]

In another place she speaks of the fruitfulness of things:

Then God will give great joy to man,
For the earth and the trees and the innumerable herds of
   cattle
Shall give to mankind their true fruit
Of wine and sweet honey and white milk
And grain which is the most wonderful of all for men.[131]

Another Sibyl in the same way says:

The holy land of the pious alone will bear these things,
For all the just there will flow a stream from a rock
   dripping honey,
And from a fountain ambrosial milk.[132]

So men will live a very peaceful and abundant life and will
reign together with God. Kings of nations will come from the
ends of the earth with gifts and offerings to adore and honor
the great King whose name will be splendid and venerable to
all nations under heaven and to all kings who rule over the
earth.

25. These are the things that the prophets say are coming. I
have not thought it necessary to put down proof-texts and
exact words because it would be an endless task. The span of
one book could not contain such a multitude of things from so
many who speak the same truths in the one Spirit. It would
also have been an annoyance to the reader if I had compiled
what I collected and translated from all sources. I could have
confirmed what I said not from my own words but rather from
those of others, and thus taught that not only we but also those
who reproach us hold to the established truth they are hesitant
to recognize. If anyone wants more accurate information on
these matters, he should draw from that source and he will find
more wonders than we have included in these books.

75

Perhaps someone will now ask when these things we have spoken of will take place. I showed before that the transformation has to happen after six thousand years and that the final day of the last end is already drawing near. We can know this much concerning the signs predicted by the prophets; they foretold signs by means of which we could day-by-day await and fear the end of time. Those who have written about the ages deduce the number of years from the beginning of the world out of holy scripture and different histories and teach when the whole sum will be completed. Although they vary and disagree a bit about the number, no expectation seems to be more than two hundred years.[133] The current situation indicates that the collapse and ruin of everything will soon take place, unless nothing is to be feared because the city of Rome is still unharmed. But when the capital of the world will have fallen and begun to be a street,[134] as the Sibyls say will happen, who can doubt that the end of human affairs and the world has already come? This is the city that still upholds all things.[135] Let us entreat and implore heaven's God to put off his decisions and decrees, if possible, lest that terrible tyrant come more quickly than we think, he who will work so great an evil and dig out that eye at whose destruction the world itself will verge on collapse. Now let us go back to describe the other things that will then follow.

26. A little earlier, we said that at the beginning of the holy Kingdom God would overcome the Prince of Demons. But when the millennium of the Kingdom, that is, the seventh millennium has begun to reach an end, he will again be freed. He will come forth from prison and will march out and stir up all the nations at that time under the rule of the saints in order to make war on the holy city. A countless host of nations will be gathered from the whole world to besiege and surround the city. Then the final wrath of God will come upon the nations. He will vanquish them to the last man. First he will shake the earth with supreme power, a blow that will split the mountains of Syria, sink the valleys abruptly and knock down the walls of all the cities.[136] God will decree that the sun not set for three days. He will set it on fire. Severe heat and intense burning

will descend upon these enemies and unholy peoples, as well as showers of brimstone, a hail of rocks, and drops of fire. Their spirits will melt with the heat, their bodies will be destroyed by the hail, and they will strike each other with the sword. The mountains will be filled with corpses, the fields covered with bones. For three days God's people will hide in the caverns of the earth until his wrath against the nations and the Last Judgment will end.[137]

Then the just will go forth from their hiding places and will find everything covered with corpses and bones. Every wicked nation will be rooted out and God's people will be the only nation in the world. For seven uninterrupted years the forests will remain untouched and no wood will be cut from the mountain, but rather the arms of the nations will be burnt.[138] There will be no more war, but peace and eternal rest.[139] When the thousand years shall have been completed, God will renew the world, heaven will be folded up, and the earth will be changed. God will change men into the likeness of angels. They will be white as snow and always live in the sight of the Most High. They will sacrifice to their Lord and will serve him forever. At the same time the second and public resurrection of all will take place. In this one the wicked will rise to eternal punishment. These are the ones who worshiped idols, who either did not know or denied the Lord and Parent of the world. Their Master and his ministers will be taken and condemned to punishment in the sight of the angels and the just. Because of their sins the whole host of the wicked will be burned by eternal fire along with him forever.[140]

This is the teaching of the holy prophets, which we Christians follow. This is our wisdom, which those who worship feeble idols or defend empty philosophy deride as foolishness and vanity. We do not usually defend or maintain this publicly since God has commanded that we peacefully and silently keep his secret hid within our conscience. He also commanded that we do not engage in obstinate battle against those who are ignorant of the truth, those who for the sake of accusation and mockery and not for learning harshly attack God and his religion. How faithfully ought the mystery to be hidden and concealed, especially by us who bear the name of the faith! They condemn this silence of ours as if it were bad conscience, and so they make up detestable rumors about chaste and innocent people and freely believe what they have made up.

27. We have reached the goal after completing the seven books of our proposed work. What remains is to exhort everyone to take up wisdom and true religion. Religion's power and office is to direct us to the eternal rewards of heavenly treasure after we have condemned earthly cares and cast off the errors that once held us slaves to the desire of passing things. In order to gain these rewards we must discard the seductive pleasures of the present life as soon as possible. They charm souls with destructive delight. How greatly should we value the happiness that removes us from the stains of earth and sets us on the path for the Most Just Judge and Kindest Parent who bestows rest instead of labor, life instead of death, light instead of darkness, and eternal and celestial goods instead of brief earthly ones. The bitterness and distress we suffer in this world when we perform justice's works can in no way be compared or put on the same footing with this reward.[141] If we would be wise and happy, we should consider and meditate upon that saying of Terence, ". . . ground as in a mill, flogged and put in bonds."[142] Much worse things than these must be borne—prison, chains, and torture. We must suffer pains, and finally accept and bear death itself, because it is evident to our conscience that no fleeting pleasure will be without punishment and no virtue without divine reward.

All ought to make an effort either to put themselves on the right path as quickly as possible or else to deserve divine consolation by taking up virtue, working at it, and patiently completing life's labors. Our Father and Lord, who founded heaven and made it firm, who established the sun and other stars, who by his greatness fortified the earth he had weighed out with mountains, who surrounded it with the sea and divided it with rivers, and who created whatever exists in this world from nothing, saw the errors of men and sent a leader to open up for us the path of justice. Let us all follow him and pay heed to him. Let us obey him with great devotion, for he alone, as Lucretius says:

> Purified the hearts of men with true sayings
> And fixed a limit to desire and fear;
> He set forth what the Highest Good to which we all
> strive
> Might be, and he showed the way by which on a narrow
> path
> We can march directly towards it.[143]

He not only showed the way, but he also walked it before us so that no one would shrink from the path of virtue because of its difficulty. Let us abandon, if possible, the path of destruction and fraud in which death lies hidden, concealed by the allurements of pleasure. The more that anyone in his declining years sees the day approaching when he must depart from this life, the more he should ponder on how pure he must set forth, how innocent he must come before the Judge. Do not act like those whose minds are blind. When warned of the presence of their destiny by the failure of the body's powers, they try to drink down lusts more eagerly and ardently. Get free of that abyss while you can, while the ability is still there. Be converted to God with your whole mind so that you can safely await that day when the Ruler and Lord of the world will judge the deeds and thoughts of each man. Neglect and flee the things that are coveted here, and judge your souls more important than the fleeting goods whose possession is insecure and transitory. Such things vanish every day, leaving much quicker than they came. Even if we could enjoy them to the very end, we would surely have to leave them behind to others. We can take nothing with us except a good and innocent life. He who has continence, mercy, patience, charity, and love for companions will come to God both rich and splendid. This is the inheritance that can neither be taken away from anyone nor given to another. Who is the man who desires to acquire and obtain these good things?

Let those who are famished come that they may lay aside perpetual hunger and be filled with heavenly food. Let those who thirst come that they may draw saving water with full throats from the everlasting source. By this divine food and drink the blind will see, the deaf hear, the dumb speak, the lame walk, the foolish become wise, the sick well, and the dead live again.[144] That Supreme and True Judge will lift up to life and perpetual light anyone who has trodden down the seductions of the earth. No one should trust in riches, high office, or even royal power—these things do not make one immortal. Whoever ceases to be human and prostrates himself on the dirt by pursuing the pleasures of the moment will be punished as a deserter of his Lord, Emperor, and Father. Seek after justice, which like an inseparable companion will lead us to God. While the spirit rules these limbs,[145] fight for God with unwearied courage, practice stations and watches, contend in strength with the enemy, so that as victors who have triumphed over the conquered foe we may attain the reward of virtue promised by the Lord.

Part II

ADSO OF

MONTIER-EN-DER

Despite the pessimism of Lactantius, he wrote at a time when the Roman Empire, far from sinking under the weight of its problems, was reorganizing itself to deal successfully with these difficulties. The full story of this reorganization (that is, the history of the Christian Roman Empire) cannot be told here. In order to understand the world in which the monk Adso was writing some six centuries after Lactantius, however, it is important to recognize that although this reorganization was only temporarily successful in the West, it was crucial to the history of the Middle Ages and to the apocalyptic beliefs held throughout that period.

Constantine's shift of the capital to his new city on the border between Europe and Asia was an early but decisive moment in the orientalization of the later Roman Empire. By A.D. 950 this process, coupled with the massive displacement of peoples that accompanied the period of the invasions, had resulted in a world that, however much it lived under the shadow of Rome, was no longer Roman in the classical sense of the term. Three successor empires laid claims to the lands once united under Roman sway—the Eastern Empire of Byzantium, the most direct descendant of the Christian Roman Empire inaugurated by Constantine; the Abbasid Caliphate, the successor to the state founded on the religious fervor of the Moslem religion that in the seventh century had decisively broken the unity of the ancient Mediterranean world; and the shattered fragments of the revival of the Roman Empire in the West that had been the work of Charlemagne, the last and greatest of the barbarian warlords.

Two apocalyptic figures are central to this brief treatise in letter form that Adso addressed to Queen Gerberga about 950—first, the Antichrist himself, mankind's final dread enemy; and second, a coming Frankish ruler who would restore the Roman Empire and whose voluntary abdication and death would be the sign for the Antichrist's rise to power. A brief glance at the history of these figures in the later Roman Empire is necessary to understand the place of Adso's text in apocalyptic traditions.

The Antichrist had been born in intertestamental Judaism, received his name and job description in the New Testament, and come to take on a more inflated stature in the patristic period as developing Christology and popular belief collaborated in producing a more detailed and heroic "Antichristology."[1] We have seen how rich these accretions to New Testament understanding had become by the time of Lactantius.

In scriptural texts, the Antichrist appears not only as the final individual opponent of Christ and the Church, but also as a multitude, that is, the succession of all evil forces and persons in the course of history.[2] Thus while individuals, such as the wicked rulers Nero and Domitian, were frequently identified with the Antichrist or with one of his predecessors, from the fourth century collective interpretations also became common, such as those that saw various heretical groups like the Arians as the Antichrist, or that of the Donatist exegete Tyconius, whose influential *Commentary on the Apocalypse* identified the Antichrist with the cumulative body of evildoers within the Church. But the strength of the individual interpretations continued. In the late fourth century Martin of Tours told his followers that the Antichrist had already been born,[3] and a century and a half later Procopius of Caesarea painted Justinian in unmistakable Antichrist language.[4] The dual interpretation carried over into the barbarian West in later centuries. In the late eighth century the Spanish monk Beatus of Liébana wrote a *Commentary on the Apocalypse* that relied heavily on Tyconius and thus encouraged the collective approach,[5] while in 826 Agobard of Lyons wrote to the Emperor Louis the Pious advising that someone undertake a systematic survey of traditional teaching on the coming individual final enemy.[6] This task was not to be fulfilled until Adso took pen in hand over a century later.

We may be puzzled over this fascination with the Antichrist. Why did the pious Queen Gerberga request such a treatise from Adso? Carolingian intellectuals, of course, delighted in producing handy and simple compendia of the complex heritage of the patristic past, but there is good reason why a compendium on the Antichrist fitted the world of the mid-tenth century even better than that of the early ninth. Adso and Gerberga lived in the midst of what was by any standards a society of the most extreme violence. On any level, life in the tenth century involved constant struggle against a variety of foes. External invasion by Vikings, Moslems, and Magyars was still a real threat (the victory over the Magyars at the Lechfeld in 955 has been seen as a crucial moment in Western Europe's independence). The collapse of the Carolingian Empire had produced a state of social disorder in which a class of violent armed warriors, or *potentiores*, was left free to pursue their own ends through the oppression of the lower classes, or *humiliores*, without the interference of the legal and coercive institutions of any real form of state. What spiritual life existed at the time could not abstract from this grim situation. It is scarcely surprising that in the spiritual writings of the time the present world and everything that smacked of it were viewed with intense pessimism. Life was seen as a constant struggle between good and evil, and the forces of evil always seemed to have the upper hand here below. The lot of the good man was to endure evil and persecution with patience in hope of a future glorious reward.[7] The conflict between good and evil was to culminate in the last and worst persecution by the most powerful opponent of goodness, the Antichrist. Antichrist's evil campaign was to be more insidious than that of rampaging Vikings or even of the oppressive local nobility, for he would advance his cause under the banner of seeming goodness, even to the point of performing signs and wonders. To be forewarned was to be forearmed. In order to survive in the coming ultimate struggle with the Antichrist, one needed to be instructed about his origin, career, and the signs of his coming. In its attention to these goals, Adso's treatise fulfilled a very practical purpose for the spirituality of the tenth century.

Adso's apocalyptic outlook, however, tempered pessimism with a splash of optimism through his teaching regarding the role of the Roman Empire and its final ruler in the drama of history. The problem of the apocalyptic significance of the Roman Empire went back deep into the patristic past. Rome had first appeared in a negative role, as the persecuting Whore of Babylon of John's Apocalypse; but from about A.D. 200 the teaching of the Second Epistle to the Thessalonians regarding a mysterious restraining force or person whose presence held back the advent of the Antichrist (2 Thess. 2:6–7) was taken by many of the Fathers to refer to the Roman Empire. Within the same perspective, the equally puzzling "defection" (*apostasia*) of 2 Thessalonians 2:3 could be interpreted as the final breakup of Roman unity. Since Rome had come to be identified with the last of the four world empires symbolized by the statue of the second chapter of Daniel, her empire was meant to endure down to the end of the world. Even such a harsh opponent of pagan Rome as Tertullian could pray for the preservation of the empire in order to allow time for more conversions to the true religion.[8] This more positive evaluation of the historical role of Rome received immense support from Constantine's conversion and the Christianization of the empire in the fourth century. Henceforth the fortunes of *Romanitas* and *Christianitas* seemed indissolubly linked to most Christian authors (Augustine was an exception), and the enemies of the new Christian Rome might easily come to be seen as the Antichrist, or his predecessors.

Loyalty in the Roman Empire, especially in the army and among the common people, centered on the person of the emperor, God's vicar on earth and the divinely appointed head of both the ecclesiastical and civil hierarchies. This traditional picture was not changed, but rather underlined by the conversion of Constantine. But the imperial office itself had heretofore no corresponding positive function in the Christian understanding of history. This new situation called for an apocalyptic validation of the transhistorical significance of the empire and its leader in the light of the Christian teleological view of history where events achieved their meaning in direct relation to their connection with the end of history. The result was the creation of a potent new apocalyptic myth in the time of the later Roman Empire, the legend of the Last World Emperor.[9]

The earliest surviving witness to the Last Emperor occurs in the *Revelations* ascribed to the third-century martyr bishop Methodius, a text actually written in Syriac by a pro-Byzantine monk in the latter seventh century. This popular work was soon translated into Greek and Latin, as well as into a number of eastern languages, and was widely read for over a millennium.[10] The Syrian author is not likely to have invented all the details of the legend, however much he may have been responsible for its final shaping. It is possible that the figure of a final Christian emperor may have been present in the lost fourth-century Latin translation of a Greek Sibylline text,[11] and a mass of traditional legendary traditions was certainly gathering about the person of the *basileus*, or Christian emperor, during the fifth and sixth centuries. The Pseudo-Methodius text does emphasize that the rise of the new religious force of Islam, the second great shock to traditional understandings of sacred history in the late antique world, had much to do with the explicit emergence of the myth of the Last Emperor.

The sudden appearance of the new opposition force at a time when the Romans had finally won a decisive victory against the age-old Persian challenge, coupled with the rapid loss of large portions of the heritage of the empire to Islam, was a crisis of no mean proportions, not least of all to Christian optimistic understandings of history. Belief did not waver, however, in Rome's destiny to last until the final age of the persecution of the Antichrist; and, in optimistic fashion, the Moslem attack was generally not identified with that of the final enemy.[12] According to the Pseudo-Methodius, the terrible persecution of the Ishmaelites, that is, the Moslems, was to be brought to a dramatic end.

> The king of the Greeks, that is, the Romans, will come out against them in great anger, roused as from a drunken stupor like one whom men had thought dead and worthless. He will go forth against them from the Ethiopian sea and will send the sword and desolation into Ethribus their homeland, capturing their women and children living in the Land of Promise. [13]

This final ruler who was to conquer the Moslems would restore the fullness of the Roman Empire and establish a messianic reign of peace and plenty. In his time the unclean northern races of Gog and Magog, which legend had it were shut out by Alexander the Great with his famous gates, would break out to ravage the earth,[14] but God would send an angel to destroy them. Finally, when the Antichrist had arisen, the Last Emperor would give up his crown, kingdom, and life to God in the Holy City of Jerusalem, thus marking the end of the Roman Empire.

The legend of the Last World Emperor, as it appears in the Pseudo-Methodius and in many later transformations, was both a message of consolation to an empire on the defense (frequently against Islamic forces) and a call to arms for the defense of *Romanitas*. In times of trouble men were not to despair of empire and emperor, but to be prepared to take up arms in support of the coming messianic ruler.

Adso's Letter is the earliest surviving Western version of the myth of the Last World Emperor, though the Merovingian translation of the Pseudo-Methodius and probably other traditions no longer textually extant had made knowledge of the new messianic figure known in the West since the eighth century. The political and religious context within which the abbot of Montier-en-Der wrote helps explain the character of his adaptation of the traditions regarding the coming ruler. Adso lived in an era that despite its disorganization and decay had already begun to see glimmers of the hope of *renovatio*, or renewal. *Renovatio* had become a fact in the monastic world with the foundation and spread of the reform movements connected with the monasteries of Cluny and Gorze. Adso himself, who was born about 910, was a member of reforming monastic circles and a noted hagiographer. *Renovatio* of the empire was also an object of hope in tenth-century Europe among the claimants to the Carolingian heritage in both East and West Frankish lands. It was Gerberga's powerful brother, Otto the Saxon, who was crowned emperor at Rome in 963, and not Louis IV (ruled 936–954), her weak husband who was overshadowed throughout his life by the powerful nobles of his realm. Adso's treatise reflects this political situation and is in part a manifesto for the hopes of the West Frankish realm against both the French barons and the rising Saxon power.[15] The reforming abbot emphasizes the shift in power from East to West; and though he admits that the Roman Empire is now in ruins, he claims that its dignity belongs by right to the line of the West Franks from whom will come the Last World Emperor.

Considerable scholarship has recently been devoted to the question of the sources used by the abbot. The work of M. Rangheri and D. Verhelst has shown how closely Adso follows a few early medieval authorities, especially Bede (d. 735) and Haymo of Auxerre (d. c. 865), themselves compilers of traditional patristic material.[16] But Adso's dependence on earlier authors should not be allowed to mask his originality, especially with regard to the form he adopted for his treatise. R. Konrad has pointed out that the Letter is modelled on the most popular form of spiritual literature of the time, the saint's life.[17] As a practiced hagiographer, Adso could scarcely help but be marked by the influence of this widespread genre. The clarity it gave to his presentation of the origin, career, and fate of the Man of Perdition will be evident to anyone who compares his work with the rich but diffuse *Treatise on Christ and the Antichrist* written by Hippolytus about the year 200.

The influence of Adso's Letter was immense. Its popularity led to no less than seven subsequent revisions of the text in the eleventh and twelfth centuries that circulated under the names of such prestigious authors as Augustine, Alcuin, and Anselm of Canterbury—a typical example of apocalyptic pseudonymity. D. Verhelst, whose critical edition of the versions of the Letter has provided a solid critical basis for all subsequent study, has identified some 170 manuscripts of the various renditions of the text.[18] The diffusion of the work and its impact on later medieval presentations of the career of the Last Emperor and of the Antichrist, as in the case of the Latin *Play of Antichrist* composed in Germany about 1160, show that even in comparatively less violent times correct and accessible information about the Final Enemy was considered important to Christian piety.

ADSO OF MONTIER-EN-DER
Letter on the Origin and Time of the Antichrist

PROLOGUE TO GERBERGA

Brother Adso, the last of all her servants, sends best wishes and eternal peace to her highness Gerberga, most excellent Queen, mighty in royal dignity, beloved of God and cherished by all the saints, mother of monks and leader of holy virgins.

Because I have won the favor of your kindness, Royal Mother, I have been always faithful to you in everything like a dutiful servant. Even though my prayers do not deserve anything from God, I beseech the mercy of our God for you and for your husband, the Lord King, as well as for the safety of your sons. May he deign to preserve the imperial dignity for you in this life and after it cause you to reign happy with him in heaven. If the Lord gives you good fortune and bestows longer life on your sons, we know without doubt and do believe that God's Church must be exalted and the monastic order must be multiplied more and more. As your faithful one, I wish for this and strongly desire it. If I were able to gain the whole kingdom for you, I would do it most gladly;[1] but since I cannot do that, I will beseech the Lord for the salvation of you and your sons that his grace may always precede you in your works and his glory may follow you in loving kindness. Because grace is directed to the divine commandments, you can fulfill the good that you desire so that the crown of the heavenly kingdom will be given to you.[2]

You have a pious desire to listen to the scriptures and often to speak about our Redeemer. You even want to learn about the wickedness and persecution of the Antichrist, as well as of his power and origin. Since you have deigned to ask your servant, I wish to write to you to tell you something about the Antichrist, although you do not need to hear it from me because you have Don Rorico at your side, that most prudent pastor and brilliant mirror of all wisdom and eloquence, a man indispensable to our age.[3]

When you wish to be informed about the Antichrist the first thing you want to know is why he is so called. This is because he will be contrary to Christ in all things and will do things that are against Christ.[4] Christ came as a humble man; he will come as a proud one. Christ came to raise the lowly, to justify sinners; he, on the other hand, will cast out the lowly, magnify sinners, exalt the wicked. He will always exalt vices opposed to virtues, will drive out the evangelical law, will revive the worship of demons in the world, will seek his own glory (John 7:18), and will call himself Almighty God. The Antichrist has many ministers of his malice. Many of them have already existed, like Antiochus, Nero, and Domitian.[5] Even now in our own time we know there are many Antichrists, for anyone, layman, cleric, or monk, who lives contrary to justice and attacks the rule of his way of life and blasphemes what is good (Rom. 14:16) is an Antichrist, the minister of Satan.[6]

Now let us see about the Antichrist's origin. What I say is not thought out or made up on my own, but in my attentive reading I find it all written down in books. As our authors say, the Antichrist will be born from the Jewish people, that is, from the tribe of Dan, as the Prophet says: "Let Dan be a snake in the wayside, an adder on the path."[7] He will sit in the wayside like a serpent and will be on the path in order to wound those who walk in the paths of justice (Ps. 22:3) and kill them with the poison of his wickedness. He will be born from the union of a mother and father, like other men, not, as some say, from a virgin alone.[8] Still, he will be conceived wholly in sin (Ps. 50:7), will be generated in sin, and will be born in sin (John 9:34). At the very beginning of his conception the devil will enter his mother's womb at the same moment. The devil's power will foster and protect him in his mother's womb and it will always be with him. Just as the Holy Spirit came into the mother of Our Lord Jesus Christ and overshadowed her with his power and filled her with divinity so that she conceived of the Holy Spirit and what was born of her was divine and holy (Luke 1:35), so too the devil will descend into the Antichrist's mother, will completely fill her, completely encompass her, completely master her, completely possess her within and without, so that with the devil's cooperation she will conceive through a man and what will be born from her will be totally wicked, totally evil, totally lost. For this reason that man is called the "Son of Perdition" (2 Thess. 2:3), because he will destroy the human race as far as he can and will himself be destroyed at the last day.[9]

You have heard how he is to be born; now hear the place where he will be born. Just as Our Lord and Redeemer foresaw Bethlehem for himself as the place to assume humanity and to be born for us, so too the devil knew a place fit for that lost man who is called Antichrist, a place from which the root of all evil (1 Tim. 6:10) ought to come, namely, the city of Babylon.[10] Antichrist will be born in that city, which once was a celebrated and glorious pagan center and the capital of the Persian Empire. It says that he will be brought up and protected in the cities of Bethsaida and Corozain, the cities that the Lord reproaches in the Gospel when he says, "Woe to you, Bethsaida, woe to you Corozain!" (Matt. 11.21). The Antichrist will have magicians, enchanters, diviners, and wizards who at the devil's bidding will rear him and instruct him in every evil, error, and wicked art.[11] Evil spirits will be his leaders, his constant associates, and inseparable companions. Then he will come to Jerusalem and with various tortures will slay all the Christians he cannot convert to his cause. He will erect his throne in the Holy Temple, for the Temple that Solomon built to God that had been destroyed he will raise up to its former state.[12] He will circumcise himself and will pretend that he is the son of Almighty God.

He will first convert kings and princes to his cause, and then through them the rest of the peoples. He will attack the places where the Lord Christ walked and will destroy what the Lord made famous. Then he will send messengers and his preachers through the whole world. His preaching and power will extend "from sea to sea, from East to West" (Ps. 71:8), from North to South. He will also work many signs, great and unheard-of prodigies (Apoc. 13:13). He will make fire come down from heaven in a terrifying way, trees suddenly blossom and wither, the sea become stormy and unexpectedly calm. He will make the elements change into differing forms, divert the order and flow of bodies of water, disturb the air with winds and all sorts of commotions, and perform countless other wondrous acts. He will raise the dead "in the sight of men in order to lead into error, if possible, even the elect" (Matt. 24:24). For when they shall have seen great signs of such a nature even those who are perfect and God's chosen ones will doubt whether or not he is the Christ who according to the scriptures will come at the end of the world.[13]

He will arouse universal persecution against the Christians and all the elect. He will lift himself up against the faithful in three ways, that is, by terror, by gifts, and by prodigies.[14] To those who believe in him he will give much gold and silver. Those he is not able to corrupt with gifts, he will overcome with terror; those he cannot overcome with terror, he will try to seduce with signs and prodigies. Those he cannot seduce with prodigies, he will cruelly torture and miserably put to death in the sight of all.[15] "Then there will be tribulation such as has not been on earth from when the nations began to exist up to that time. Then those who are in the field will flee to the mountains, and he who is on the roof will not go down into his house to take anything from it" (Matt. 24:21, 16; Dan. 12:1). Then every faithful Christian who will be discovered will either deny God, or, if he will remain faithful, will perish, whether through sword, or fiery furnace, or serpents, or beasts, or through some other kind of torture. This terrible and fearful tribulation will last for three and a half years in the whole world. "Then the days will be shortened for the sake of the elect, for unless the Lord had shortened those days, mankind would not have been saved" (Matt. 24:22).

The Apostle Paul reveals the time when the Antichrist will come and when Judgment Day will begin in the Epistle to the Thessalonians, chapter two ("We beseech you through the coming of Our Lord Jesus Christ"), in the place where he says: "Unless the defection shall have come first and the man of sin and the Son of Perdition shall have been revealed" (2 Thess. 2:3). For we know that after the Greek Empire, or even after the Persian Empire, each of which in its time had great glory and flourished with the highest power, at last after all the other empires there came into existence the Roman Empire, which was the strongest of all and had all the kingdoms of the earth under its control. All nations were subject to the Romans and paid tribute to them. This is why the Apostle Paul says that the Antichrist will not come into the world "unless the defection shall have come first," that is, unless first all the kingdoms that were formerly subject shall have defected from the Roman Empire.[16] This time has not yet come, because even though we may see the Roman Empire for the most part in ruins, nonetheless, as long as the Kings of the Franks who now possess the Roman Empire by right shall last, the dignity of the Roman Empire will not completely perish because it will endure in its kings. Some of our learned men say that one of the Kings of the Franks will possess anew the Roman Empire.[17] He will be in the last time and will be the greatest and the last of all kings. After he has successfully governed his empire, he will finally come to Jerusalem and will lay aside his scepter and crown on the Mount of Olives.[18] This will be the end and the consummation of the Roman and Christian Empire.[19]

Immediately, according to the saying of Paul the Apostle cited above, they say that the Antichrist will be at hand. And then will be revealed the man of sin, namely, the Antichrist. Even though he is a man, he will still be the source of all sins and the Son of Perdition, that is, the son of the devil, not through nature but through imitation because he will fulfill the devil's will in everything.[20] The fullness of diabolical power and of the whole character of evil will dwell in him in bodily fashion; for in him will be hidden all the treasures of malice and iniquity.[21]

"He is the Enemy," that is, he is contrary to Christ and all his members, "and he is lifted up, that is, raised up in pride above everything that is called God" (2 Thess. 2:4), that is, above all the heathen gods, Hercules, Apollo, Jupiter and Mercury, whom the pagans think are gods.[22] Antichrist will be lifted up above these gods because he will make himself greater and stronger than all of them. He will be lifted up not only above these gods, but also "above everything that is worshiped," that is, above the Holy Trinity, which alone is to be worshiped and adored by every creature. "He will exalt himself in such a way that he will be enthroned in God's Temple, displaying himself as if he were God."

As we said above, he will be born in the city of Babylon, will come to Jerusalem, and will circumcise himself and say to the Jews: "I am the Christ promised to you who has come to save you, so that I can gather together and defend you who are the Diaspora." At that time all the Jews will flock to him, in the belief that they are receiving God, but rather they will receive the devil. Antichrist also "will be enthroned in God's Temple," that is, in Holy Church, and he will make all Christians martyrs. He will be lifted up and made great, because in him will be the devil, the fountainhead of all evil "who is the king above all the sons of pride" (Job 41:25).

Lest the Antichrist come suddenly and without warning and deceive and destroy the whole human race by his error, before his arrival the two great prophets Enoch and Elijah will be sent into the world. They will defend God's faithful against the attack of the Antichrist with divine arms and will instruct, comfort, and prepare the elect for battle with three and a half years of teaching and preaching.[23] These two very great prophets and teachers will convert the sons of Israel who will live in that time to the faith, and they will make their belief unconquerable among the elect in the face of the affliction of so great a storm.[24] At that time what scripture says will be fulfilled: "If the number of sons of Israel be like the sand of the sea, their remnant will be saved" (Rom. 9:27). When, after three and a half years, they shall have finished their preaching, the Antichrist's persecution will soon begin to blaze out. He will first take up his arms against them and will slay them, as it says in the Apocalypse: "And when they have finished their witness the

PLATE II:

ANTICHRIST SLAUGHTERS THE TWO WITNESSES
In the lower register of this illumination the giant figure of the Antichrist is seen
(third from the right) in the act of killing the two witnesses Enoch and Elias
according to Apoc. 11:7-10. Folio 136v of the Beatus of Urgel, c. 970 A.D. Reproduced
from *Les jours de l'apocalypse* (La Pierre-Qui-Vire: Zodiaque, 1967), Plate 38.

beast which will ascend from the abyss will make war against them and will conquer and kill them" (Apoc. 11:7). After these two have been slain, he will then persecute the rest of the faithful, either by making them glorious martyrs or by rendering them apostates.[25] And whoever shall have believed in him will receive his brand on the forehead (Apoc. 20:4).

Since we have spoken about his beginning, let us say what end he will have. This Antichrist, the devil's son and the worst master of evil, as has been said, will plague the whole world with great persecution and torture the whole people of God with various torments for three and a half years. After he has killed Elijah and Enoch and crowned with martyrdom the others who persevere in the faith, at last God's judgment will come upon him, as Saint Paul writes when he says, "The Lord Jesus will kill him with the breath of his mouth" (2 Thess. 2:8). Whether the Lord Jesus will slay him by the power of his own might, or whether the Archangel Michael will slay him, he will be killed through the power of Our Lord Jesus Christ and not through the power of any angel or archangel.[26] The teachers say that Antichrist will be killed on the Mount of Olives in his tent and upon his throne, in the place opposite to where the Lord ascended to heaven.[27] You ought to know that after Antichrist has been killed the Judgment Day will not come immediately, nor will the Lord come to judge at once (Isa. 3:14); but as we understand from the Book of Daniel, the Lord will grant the elect forty days to do penance because they were led astray by the Antichrist.[28] No one knows how much time there may be after they shall have completed this penance until the Lord comes to judgment; but it remains in the providence of God who will judge the world in that hour in which for all eternity he predetermined it was to be judged.

EPILOGUE

So, Your Highness, I your loyal servant have faithfully fulfilled what you commanded. I am prepared to obey in other matters what you shall deem worthy to command.

Part III
JOACHIM OF FIORE

Reading Joachim of Fiore today, it may be initially difficult to discern the fascination that the Calabrian holy man had for his contemporaries and for so many subsequent readers. Joachim's three major works, the *Exposition on the Apocalypse*, the *Book of Concordance*, and the *Ten-Stringed Psaltery*, are lengthy, repetitious, and difficult for those not well acquainted with his intricate exegesis and symbolism. His occasional treatises, some of considerable length, do not always display the fundamental characteristics of his thought as clearly as does the trilogy on which he labored for almost twenty years.[1] One might be tempted to regard the Calabrian as an important figure for the history of apocalyptic theory but not as a cogent representative of apocalyptic spirituality. Such a judgment, however, does not stand up to a careful reading of Joachim's surviving works in full.

Joachim was born about 1135 in Calabria, the son of a notary of the resplendent Sicilian court.[2] Educated to follow in his father's footsteps, after a pilgrimage to the Holy Land he dedicated his life to the pursuit of God. For a time he lived as a hermit on Mt. Etna, then was a wandering preacher in his native Calabria before being ordained and entering the Benedictine monastery of Corazzo. Joachim soon became abbot, and during the 1180s was involved in a long campaign to have the house incorporated into the Cistercian order. It was during this time that he first came to the attention of Pope Lucius III, who encouraged him to put his apocalyptic theories in writing.[3]

In 1188 when Corazzo was finally accepted into the Cistercians, Joachim and a group of followers had already begun to separate themselves from the monastery. By 1192 he had founded a new house at San Giovanni da Fiore in the high Sila plateau—and had been denounced as a renegade by the Cistercian General Chapter. Despite the remoteness of his new establishment, during the final decade of his life Joachim had numerous contacts with the great and powerful of his day. Kings and queens, popes and princes sought his advice.[4] By the time of his death on March 30, 1202, he was one of the most noted religious figures of the day. The order that he founded experienced such an expansion in the following decade that it was hailed by the Fourth Lateran Council in 1215 as one of the four pillars of the Church. Although the Florensian order soon stagnated, the fame of its founder, whether positively or negatively viewed, continued to grow for centuries.

Joachim of Fiore shares much with the Jewish and Christian apocalyptic prophets and scribes of the biblical period. A sense of immediately impending crisis, more evident in him than in either Lactantius or Adso, provides the motive for the proclamation of his message. Two letters translated here, the "Letter to All the Faithful" and the "Letter to the Abbot of Valdona," make this abundantly clear.[5] Like the prophet Ezechiel whom the Lord had made the watchman over Israel, the Calabrian felt compelled to announce the message of coming doom to his generation. Even though his admonitions to do penance might be disregarded by most, they must still be preached in season and out.

Powerful as was the abbot's deep pessimism concerning the coming troubles, in the manner of many Old Testament prophets, or of the John of the Apocalypse, he holds out hope for the blessed remnant who will remain faithful during persecution. This optimistic vision of coming terrestrial reward appears in the letters translated here as well, though the distinctive characteristics of Joachim's millenarian hope could scarcely be spened out in detail in such brief texts.

A second note of Joachim's apocalyptic spirituality is the distinctive way in which he received his message. The abbot describes two revelations made to him at the beginning of his apocalyptic career while he was visiting the Cistercian house of Casamari in 1183 and 1184.[6] The first happened at midnight on Easter after he had been stymied for a year in his attempt to understand a passage in the Apocalypse. It was "a revelation of the fullness of the Apocalypse and of the complete agreement of the Old and New Testaments perceived with clear understanding by the mind's eye."[7] No image or figure accompanied this Christological illumination that was so central to Joachim's exegesis and theory of history. This is what the Augustinian doctrine of the kinds of visions would term an "intellectual vision," a truth infallibly revealed without the aid of images internal or external.[8] Here the illumination came first and then Joachim had to seek verbal and visual ways to portray it. But the abbot of Fiore also had "spiritual visions" in the Augustinian sense,[9] that is, showings in which something was revealed through a form or symbol seen within the mind. Joachim describes the one he had on Pentecost Sunday at Casamari in the following words:

> In the meantime, when I had entered the church to pray to Almighty God before the holy altar, there came upon me an uncertainty concerning belief in the Trinity as though it were hard to understand or hold that all the Persons were one God and one God all the Persons. When that happened, I prayed with all my might. I was very frightened and was moved to call on the Holy Spirit whose feast day it was to deign to show me the holy mystery of the Trinity. The Lord has promised us that the whole understanding of truth is to be found in the Trinity. I repeated this and began to pray the psalms to complete the number I had intended. Without delay at this moment the shape of a ten-stringed psaltery appeared in my mind. The mystery of the Holy Trinity shone so brightly and clearly in it that I was at once impelled to cry out, "What God is as great as our God?"[10]

The ten-stringed psaltery is one of the fundamental symbols, along with trees, eagles, circles, and the alpha and omega, that appear throughout Joachim's main works.[11] It is tempting to think that all these symbolic forms may have been revealed to the abbot, but he is silent about other visions.[12]

Despite these special revelations, Joachim did not consider himself a prophet in the sense that Ezechiel, Daniel, and John had been. In answer to Adam of Persigny's question about the source of his predictions, he said that he had received no gift of prophecy, nor omen, nor revelation, "but that God who once gave the spirit of prophecy to the prophets has given me the spirit of understanding to grasp with great clarity in His Spirit all the mysteries of sacred scripture, just as the prophets who once produced it in God's Spirit understood these mysteries."[13] This important key to Joachim's self-understanding highlights an essential characteristic of his apocalyptic mentality that is at once traditional yet also highly distinctive in the way Joachim developed it—its hermeneutical nature.

Joachim did not put himself forward as the prophet of a new revelation, but as the exegete to whom God had granted the gift of understanding the truth already revealed but hidden in the Bible. Apocalypticism had indeed been a literary phenomenon from the start—a message put down in books. The reinterpretation of received writings had formed an essential part of Christian apocalypticism from the earliest days. The key apocalyptic sections of the New Testament were consciously based on the classical Jewish apocalypses, such as the Book of Daniel. As the authoritative writings of the Christian religion were shaped into the primitive canon of the New Testament, the dissemination and amplification of apocalyptic views of history found an increasingly larger role for the genre of the commentary, the text upon a text. The obscurity of apocalyptic literature invited and encouraged such an approach. It is no accident that the earliest surviving complete Greek biblical commentary is that of Hippolytus on Daniel and the earliest surviving Latin one is that of Victorinus on the Apocalypse, the one from the beginning, the other from the end of the third century. While new "revelation" as a source of information about what was to come in history did not die out—witness the strength of the Sibylline tradition in the Middle Ages—medieval apocalyptic traditions never strayed far from their base in the exegesis of the canonical apocalypses.

In his claim to found his vision of history not on a new divine communication, but on understanding the scriptures, Joachim was a faithful witness to this tradition. But the abbot of Fiore's theology of history was a new creation in many respects, and therefore it should not surprise us that the hermeneutical theory underpinning it was also novel. The dominant tendency in the interpretation of the Apocalypse since the end of the fourth century had been an individualizing and moralizing approach that, following the authority of Tyconius and Saint Augustine, had used John's imagery to describe the soul's warfare against vice. Some twelfth-century authors began to move away from this type of exegesis toward one that made use of the Apocalypse as prophecy for identifiable historical events, some already fulfilled, others still to come. Joachim formulated this tendency into a coherent new theory of hermeneutics.[14] The abbot's theory of interpretation is notoriously complex, but the investigations of H. Grundmann, H. De Lubac, and most recently H. Mottu have done much to clarify its essential features.[15] With the help of the categories of Professor Mottu,[16] a brief presentation of the main lines of Joachim's hermeneutics is possible. In the twelfth century traditional exegesis was based on the distinction between the literal and the spiritual meanings of scripture and generally accepted a division of four senses: the literal, the allegorical or doctrinal, the moral or tropological, and the anagogical or heavenly.[17] Joachim's enumeration of senses, on the other hand, is based on a distinction between allegory and typology, or, as the text translated here from the *Book of Concordance* has it, between *allegoria* and *concordia*.[18] Under the *allegoricus* or *spiritualis intellectus* he counted five species or types, related to the traditional four senses. These historical, moral, tropological, contemplative, and anagogic types were designed to show the gradual transition from slavery to freedom in the course of the history of salvation. The historicizing tendency of his

101

hermeneutics is even more evident in the seven species of the *typicus intellectus*, which aim to show the historical concordance (*concordia*) between the unfolding of history in the Old Testament and that in the New. These letter-to-letter comparisons and parallels between the Testaments are not used merely to understand the past, but also, and far more daringly, to reveal the future. As Mottu has shown, the notion of *concordia* involves not just a synoptic attempt to harmonize texts, or to compare parallel series of events from the Old and the New Testaments, but also the working out of the structural conformity or correlation of the two Testaments necessary to understand the coming third stage of history.[19] The Old Testament, the New Testament, and especially the Book of the Apocalypse, when illuminated by the typological understanding, can show the meaning of what is to come in the light of the relation of history to the most basic mystery of the divine life, God's existence as a Trinity of Persons.

The relation of hermeneutical theory to the Trinity and to the meaning of history is discussed in detail in the passage from the *Book of Concordance* given here. Chapters four through twelve of this selection demonstrate how Joachim made use of both a pattern of twos and a pattern of threes in his attempts to structure history, as Marjorie Reeves has pointed out.[20] The proper exegesis of scripture reveals not only the grand plan of the two Testaments, but also a scheme of three periods of time (*tempora*), or what Joachim says are more properly called states (*status*). These three states are complex, organic, progressive, and interlocking in character. The first began with Adam and lasted to Christ. It was ascribed to God the Father and was the time of the order, or way of life, of the married. The second started with King Josiah, began to bear fruit in Christ, and lasts until the present. It is ascribed to the Son and is the time of the order of clerics. The third *status*, the time of the monastic order, is ascribed to the Holy Spirit. It began with Saint Benedict and will bear fruit in the last times down until the end of the world.

The pattern of twos is also trinitarian in nature. The Holy Spirit proceeds from both the Father and the Son, and hence the spiritual understanding of both Testaments has a double beginning that signifies this: once in the prophet Elisha in the Old Testament (showing the Spirit's relation to the Father), and once in Saint Benedict in the New Testament (showing the relation to the Son). Because both the pattern of twos designated by the Greek omega and the pattern of threes designated by alpha are trinitarian, Joachim always sees them as complementary. The double procession of the Holy Spirit is essential to each, as chapter ten of the selection indicates. This fundamental harmony is not always as clear to the modern reader as it was to the abbot of Fiore—an important reason for at least some of the disagreement about his thought. Joachim did claim that the time of the New Testament would last until the end of the world—and thus appears fully at one with traditional Christian theology of history. But many other passages on the third *status* can be read as expressing hope in a coming historical era that, whatever its deep roots in the abbot's organic view of the past, was to be a form of new creation.

The application of this apocalyptic theology of history to the abbot of Fiore's beliefs about the crisis confronting his own time can be seen throughout his writings, but nowhere more clearly than in the celebrated *Book of Figures*. Joachim has been described as a "picture thinker,"[21] one whose mind moved according to the rich combinations of symbolic thought rather than the clarity of the logical or discursive mentality.[22] In his later years, he apparently began to organize and correlate the primary symbols through which the mystery of the Trinity and of history had been manifested to him into increasingly richer combinations. As these figures (*figurae*), which were at times geometrical forms, at times luxuriant organic images, grew more complex, Joachim explained them by means of captions and comments that in some cases amounted to brief treatises. The figures were collected and edited after his death by his immediate disciples into the *Book of Figures*. Despite the doubts expressed about its authenticity after its rediscovery in 1937, the careful study of M. Reeves and B. Hirsch-Reich has demonstrated their claim that Joachim's "strange and intricate patterns of thought convey themselves more immediately today through these powerful *figurae* than through the endless repetitions of his somewhat turgid Latin."[23]

Five of the sixteen basic illustrations that make up the *Book of Figures* are given here, together with translations of two of the brief treatises that accompany them.[24] No figure more immediately conveys the abbot's pattern of threes than the so-called Trinitarian Tree Circles.[25] In this symbolic presentation the tree of history springs up from the head of Noah, the just man, who represents God the Father. Noah's three sons are figured in three offshoots—Ham is a barren stump, but Shem on the left (the Jewish people) and Japheth on the right (the Gentiles) are the two peoples whose destinies will unfold God's plan throughout history. The first circle, the *status* of the Father, saw the flourishing of the Jews and a lesser growth for the Gentiles. The second circle, the state of the Son, reverses the picture: Now the Gentiles are more fruitful than the Jews. But in the final uppermost circle, the coming state of the Holy Spirit, both Jews and Gentiles will give fruit in supreme abundance. The melioristic character of Joachim's theory of history is especially evident in this figure.

Another key figure illustrates the full complexities of Joachim's notion of the three *status* and its relation to his understanding of the Trinity. The figure of the "Three Trinitarian Circles" (Plate III) shows the relation of this basic symbol to that of the Alpha and Omega, as well as to the abbot's special sense of the meaning of the Tetragrammaton, the Hebrew name for God.[26] Three interlocking rings demonstrate how the mystery of the Trinity relates to the course of history. The first circle in green belongs to the Father and forms the time of the Old Testament. The middle blue circle, that of the Son, interlocks with both extremities—the median that joins the extremes. The final flaming red circle of the Holy Spirit indicates the double procession of the Third Person by its intersection with both the green and the blue circles. Its internal rubric of *novum testamentum* shows that the New Testament is not to be superceded; but the noninterlocking area of this last circle does suggest a coming special era within history, not unrelated, but still superior to what has gone before. The other elements,

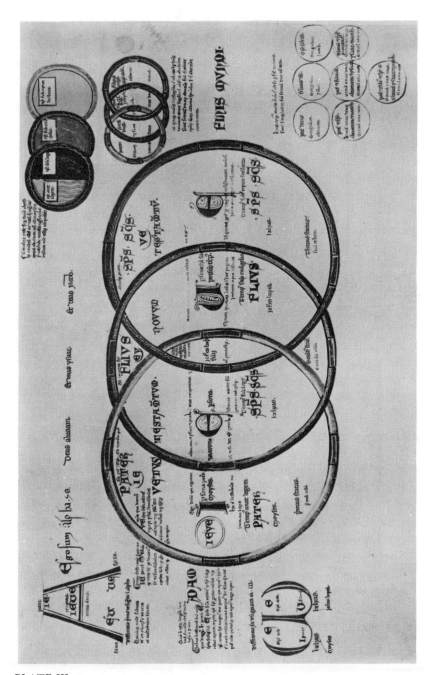

PLATE III:

THREE TRINITARIAN CIRCLES
Reproduced from *Il Libro delle Figure*, Plate XI b.

especially the Alpha and Omega on the left side (figuring the pattern of threes and the pattern of twos), reflect the same central message about the Trinitarian structure of history.[27] The fascination of this *figura* was not lost on later thinkers. An extensive literature exists about the relation between Joachim and Dante, and many of the suggested parallels between the two great authors are too general to be really convincing. But at the supreme moment of the *Paradiso*, when the poet attempts to express his vision of the three persons in one God, it is hard not to think that the image he is recalling is not that of this figure:

> That light supreme, within its fathomless
> Clear substance, showed to me three spheres, which
>   bare
> Three hues distinct, and occupied one space;
> The first mirrored the next, as though it were
>   Rainbow from rainbow, and the third seemed flame
>   Breathed equally from each of the first pair.[28]
>
> (Canto XXXIII, 115-20)

Like other apocalyptic authors, the abbot believed that future triumph would come only after present trials. Joachim's sensitivity to impending crisis is evident in his letters, but the *Book of Figures* shows how his distinctive hermeneutic enabled him to find a potent scriptural symbol to express his views. The great seven-headed dragon of the twelfth chapter of the Apocalypse is the image in which the abbot sees the whole history of the Church's persecutions, past, present, and future, revealed to the believer. In this figure and its accompanying text Joachim historicizes the symbolism of the final book of the New Testament by making it an explicit prophecy of the seven major persecutions of the Church of the second *status*.[29] The abbot thought that Saladin's triumph over the Christians of the East (Jerusalem had fallen in 1187) was a sign that the Church's tribulation was reaching its culmination. The imminent seventh head of the dragon, the Antichrist himself, would be a false teacher from the West who would ally himself with

Saladin or with one of his immediate successors. Joachim's initial reputation was as a prophet of the Antichrist. When we study the powerful figure of the seven-headed dragon we can well see why. But not even this drawing is totally pessimistic. The gap between the seven heads and the dragon's tail suggests a millennial period of peace after Christ's defeat of the last head and before the mysterious final Antichrist denoted in the tail.

It is the *Book of Figures* again that provides us with the most ample and accessible presentation of the abbot's view of the coming *status* of the Holy Spirit. In order to understand the special way in which Joachim spelled out his millenarian hopes, we must remember that the abbot's personal history suggests that his life is to be seen as a continuing search for the most perfect form of the monastic life. The progressive nature of his pursuit of this ideal must have had a deep effect on his theology of history. For Joachim history was the story of the gradual triumph of spirit over flesh, of contemplation over literal-mindedness. This triumph was inseparable from the history of monasticism.

One of his early works, the *Treatise on the Life of St. Benedict and the Divine Office according to His Teaching*, already made clear the connection, and it is also evident in another of the arboreal images of the *Book of Figures*, the "Tree with Side-Shoots."[30] The two trees of this illustration form a concordance of the lines of promise of the New and the Old Testaments. The tree on the left shows how of the sons of Abraham it was Isaac on the trunk and not Ishmael (the side-shoot) who was chosen as the heir of God's promise, just as Jacob was chosen over Esau, Joseph over Ruben, and Ephraim above Manasses. The right tree sketches a similar pattern of election in the time of the second *status*, beginning from its germination in the patriarchs through a succession of further divisions in which the trunk represents those who are chosen, the side-shoots the rejected— Gentiles over Jews, Latins over Greeks, monks over clerics, and Cistercians over Cluniacs. The Cistercians do not mark the final stage in contemplative evolution. Still to come (signified by the rich foliage at the top of the tree) is the monastic perfection of the third *status*.

It was the future, not the past, of monasticism that was Joachim's real concern. Though he himself was a monastic reformer, there is no evidence that he ever saw the Florensian order as any less of an interim stage than the Cistercians. Joachim never showed the depths of his understanding of the spiritual longings of his time to better effect than in the hopes he expressed for imminent more perfect forms of the religious life. The prodigious spiritual ferment of the twelfth century that had led to the creation of so many experimental forms of the perfect life, both orthodox and heterodox, had whetted the hopes of men rather than exhausted them. Such hopes usually centered on the image of the "apostolic life," the imitation of Christ and the apostles, and were, for the most part, backward-looking, given life by their attempt to revive a golden past. For Joachim, however, the renewal of monasticism was to be a new eruption of the power of the Holy Spirit within history—a *renovatio* from the future rather than from the past.[31]

According to Joachim, there would be two stages in the coming more perfect realizations of the monastic life. First of all, during the imminent crisis of history two new religious orders would arise to confront the Antichrist and his forces: an order of preachers in the spirit of Elijah and an order of hermits in the spirit of Moses.[32] Despite the vagueness of the abbot's descriptions of these orders, it would demand consider-able effort for the well disposed not to see in his descriptions a prophecy of the two mendicant orders that were born in the decade after his death. A generation later, various thinkers, especially within the Franciscans, were finding in both the authentic Joachim and the many works that came to be pseud-onymously ascribed to him even more precise confirmation for the apocalyptic significance of their groups.[33]

The two orders of the coming crisis were not the final word in history's drive toward the perfect terrestrial state of contemplation. Joachim's most original contribution to the theology of history, his belief in the three states, also included an essentially monastic component.

There are numerous hints at this in the course of the three major works, but the most detailed treatment of the abbot's

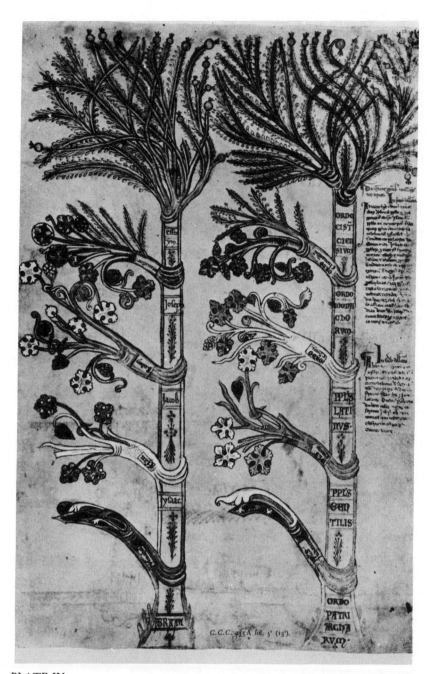

PLATE IV:

THE TREE WITH SIDE-SHOOTS
Reproduced from *Il Libro delle Figure*, Plate XXIII.

PLATE V:

THE TRINITARIAN TREE CIRCLES
Reproduced from L. Tondelli, M. Reeves, and B. Hirsch-Reich, *Il Libro delle Figure*
(Turin: SEI, 1953), Vol. II, Plate XXII.

vision of the future state of the Church is found in the figure known as "The New Order of the People of God."[34] Despite the detail of the accompanying text, and the helpful studies of Grundmann and Reeves,[35] there are still elements of obscurity in this fascinating diagram of the coming monastic utopia. The first involves its relation to an outside population, because details of the text indicate that Joachim expected that even after the Antichrist's persecution there would be some who would not belong to the ideal community. A second, more difficult question, concerns the relation of the monastic utopia to the institutions of the Church of the second state. Few areas of Joachim studies have involved more heated debate than his views concerning the future of the papacy. Proponents of Joachim's radicalism would have it that the third *status* represents a clear break with the framework of the medieval church, but the basic conservatism of the abbot and his close contact with many of the popes of his time make this position difficult to sustain, at least as a key to his intentions. The opposite position, for which Marjorie Reeves has been the most cogent proponent, tends toward a more spiritual and mystical reading of the figure and related texts, and thus would emphasize the inner evolution of the contemplative state, a reality not to be measured by chronological boundaries or institutional details. The debate cannot be settled in this context. The evidence of the *Dispositio* figure, however, does seem to provide some important principles. The details of the rule and physical arrangement of the monastic utopia indicate that Joachim had a material community in mind, and not merely some heavenly or internal reality. The coexistence of other Christians with the monastic utopia is not totally anomalous, because the text shows that the community is the religious center for all. Finally, the "Spiritual Father" who controls all facets of the coming contemplative society that embraces monks, clerics, and laity seems to be the equivalent of the spiritual pope of the coming *status* spoken of in other texts,[36] despite the lack of any explicit identification.

So brief a look at the enigmatic Joachim is bound to leave many questions unanswered. Even a detailed treatment of the complexities of his thought and a richer selection from his writings might not bring us nearer to final answers, but only heighten the difficulties. Joachim himself probably would not have worried much about the problems that later interpreters have had with his thought. He never considered himself anything more than a servant of sacred scripture—God's revelation about the meaning of history had already been made, and he alone would choose those to whom he would reveal it.

In the midst of the repetitions and obscurities of his thought, the abbot of Fiore is always able to reveal the sense of the divine presence on which his spirituality is based. The coincidence of opposites of optimism and pessimism in Joachim's theology of history found striking expression in a passage from his treatise *The Articles of Belief*.

> David the Psalmist says, "Taste and see how sweet the Lord is" (Ps. 33:8), but for Paul "It is a fearful thing to fall into the hands of the living God" (Heb. 11:31). Since almost every page of scripture proclaims both how lovable and how terrifying God is, it is perfectly right for people to ask how such great opposites can be put together, so that a person can rejoice for love's sake in his fear and tremble with dread in the midst of love. But according to scripture, the just and loving God is like fire, for it says: "Hear, O Israel, your God is a consuming fire" (Deut. 4:24). Why is the fire which so frequently burns homes and whole cities sought out with such eagerness by those trapped in darkness? Why is it so cherished by anyone who has endured real cold? If one and the same material reality can be so loved and feared, why is it that Almighty God in whom we live and move and have our being (Acts 17:28) is not both cherished for his indescribable loveliness and still feared for his transcendent greatness?[37]

SECTION A
Letter to All the Faithful[1]

The beginning of the letter of the Abbot Joachim. Brother Joachim called Abbot of Fiore advises all Christ's faithful whom this letter reaches to watch and pray so that they do not enter into temptation (Matt. 26:41). When the Lord spoke to the prophet Ezechiel whom he set up as a watchman over the house of Israel at the time of the removal to Babylon,[2] after he commanded him to write down many things he warned him: "If I say to a wicked man 'You will surely die,' and you do not make it known to him, he will indeed die in his iniquity, but I will require his blood from your hand" (Ezech. 3:18). Since what at that time was entrusted to one person in particular, in these days holds for all who seem to have received more information than others, by a common law everyone is bound to render an account of the function he has received.

The abbot writes. This is how it looked to me in the case of the divine plan I seem to understand in the true scriptures, especially since some monks have most urgently advised me that I have an obligation not to keep silent about the wrath of the Judge so soon to be revealed from heaven upon all the wickedness and injustice of men who are unwilling to do penance for their sins. If I am permitted to speak out to urge and excite hearts to be on guard I do not hesitate to say with the Apostle Paul, "I am innocent of the blood of all of you" (Acts 20:26). For some time I wished to cast anchor in the harbor of silence in deference to my priors, so as not to seem to stir up scandal or bickering in Christ's Church, especially because of those who run about more than others shouting, "Thus saith the Lord," when He has not commissioned them. But now: "Hear, O young men, and pay heed, you old men" (Joel 1:2). I will not speak in riddles so that you cannot understand because of the depth of the obscure speech, but I will both openly declare what happened from our fathers' days and

113

will also incorporate what is to follow in our times so that even the little children can understand it plain and simple. You have read in the Apostle Paul what you see has been fulfilled for him and what you know has been truly foretold. He says, "In the last days dangerous times will come, and men will be lovers of themselves, covetous, puffed up, proud, blasphemers, disobedient to parents, ungrateful, wicked, without either affection or peace, calumniators, incontinent, unmerciful, without kindness, traitors, shameless, arrogant, lovers of pleasure more than God, making a pretence of piety, but rejecting its power. Stay clear of them" (2 Tim. 3:1–5).

All these statements, I say, and ones similar to what Paul said have been fulfilled. According to what is written in the Psalms: "You see that the land has been desecrated with blood and defiled by their crimes" (Ps. 105:38–39). "All flesh corrupted its way" (Gen. 6:12), and every generation of men has committed evil. According to that statement of Genesis ("The end of all flesh is known to God, and all men who dwell on earth will be destroyed with the earth" Genesis 6:13), what occurred there was a prior figure for what is happening now.[3] "The just man is also perishing, and there is no one who reflects in his heart. Merciful men are taken away because there is no one who understands" (Isa. 57:1). "They have all gone astray and become useless at the same time; there is no one who does good—no, not one" (Ps. 13:3). "They all seek gifts and expect a like return. They do not defend the orphan, and the widow's plea does not reach them" (Isa. 1:23). "The priests have not said, 'Where is God?' The magistrates ignored both the law and God" (Jer. 2:8). "The harp and the lyre, the timbrel and the flute are present at their feasts, but they do not regard the Lord's work" (Isa. 5:2). "There is no truth, nor mercy, nor knowledge of God on earth. Cursing and lying and murder, theft and adultery have overflowed and bloodshed has followed bloodshed" (Osee 4:1–2). As a result, there is no place for those who seek the Lord, and the angel has been abandoned by those who fear him.

Death cries out from the East, destruction from the West. The multitude of the Greeks has become Sodom, the Latins have become Gomorrah, with the Greeks publicly proclaiming Egypt's crime, the Latins Babylon's disorder. All have plotted together at the same time against God, and all, as the prophet says, "have abandoned God, have blasphemed the Holy One of Israel, and have gone backward in retreat" (Isa. 1:4). "They have transgressed the laws, they have changed the order of justice, they have broken the everlasting covenant" (Isa. 24:5). "All peoples, now listen attentively; give ear, all who dwell on earth. He who has fled from fear will fall into the pit, and he who shall be freed from the pit will be taken by the snare, because the flood gates of heaven are open and the foundations of the earth will be shaken. The earth shall be completely shattered and totally crushed; like a drunken man it shall be violently shaken and shall be borne away like a tent of a single night. Its iniquity shall weigh it down, and it will fall and not be able to rise again" (Ps. 48:2; Jer. 48:43–44; Isa. 24:19–21).

Take this to heart, apostate children (Isa. 30:1); think on it and be afraid. Perhaps you may do penance for having rejected God's word and abandoned the bosom of the Chaste Mother who is now lowly and despised and preferred the Whore who rules over the kings of the earth. Hear the judgment that the Lord will perform in your days, a judgment He has not made from days of old, from the birth of time. Lo, the pagan nations will plot together and the kings of the earth gather and assemble against you, daughter of Babylon. They will fight against you like the fury of the sea and will root your offspring from the earth. All you citizens will be swept from the earth. All these things will come about as we have read; they will be fulfilled as has been written.

Lest anyone say that these times are not very clear and excuse himself from understanding and personal involvement, let him know that all people found in the present world fall into three groups. The first are those who have fallen away from the faith, strangers to the Church's sacraments and to every good deed. The second is those who "believe, but fall away in time of temptation" (Luke 8:13). "They profess that they know God, but they deny him by their deeds" (Titus 1:16). "They are glad when they have done evil and rejoice in the most wicked things" (Prov. 2:14). The third is those whose faith and works are good, that is, those whom Almighty God foreknew would be such in belief and in deed.[4] The first have been called the "scarlet multitude," the second "Babylon," the third "Jerusalem." If you consider the crowd of those men who to the full measure of their damnation are counted as members of the Christian religion, you have what is called the first Babylon, because by Almighty God's just judgment the pagans will rise against the bad Christians, will wreak vengeance on the apostate nations and the revenge of the living God on wicked sons. The multitude of the wicked have prevailed because the just were tepid. As the sons of Jerusalem have vanished, the sons of the unholy woman have filled the earth.

There is nothing more to be awaited for the execution of the judgment, because surely the sentence has been put off till now not for the sake of the wicked but for the meek. For when there were fifty just people in the city of Sodom the Lord spared the city for the sake of the fifty who lived there (Gen. 18:26 ff). And He spared it for the sake of the forty and thirty, and up till the time that ten were found He was eager to spare it. But when only Lot was found in the city of the vicious, Almighty God did not wish to bear such a vast mass of crime for the sake of one just man, but led him out of the city. As Peter says, "He snatched the just man Lot from unholy contact with the wicked" (2 Pet. 2:7). God knows how to snatch good men from temptation. He punished all who lived by the fearful chastisement of his condemnation; but Noah, that just man, was preserved in the ark when the remaining crowd of wicked were destroyed by the flood's waters. These things happened to them in a figure (1 Cor. 10:11). Through these two judgments, which happened in the earliest times, coming generations of men could recognize the judgment that the Lord was to perform in the last days and also know and perceive by real experience and not by threat how fearful it is to fall into God's hand (Heb. 10:31).

What are we doing? We were seeking fifty, and hardly one is to be found. Whoever that person is who is signified by Lot, or whoever is designated by Noah, he should know that Babylon's judgment threatens in every way possible. Let him hear the Lord's voice as it mercifully cries out from heaven and says: "Go out from her, my people, so as not to share in her sins and so as not to partake of her punishments. For her sins have reached up to heaven and the Lord has remembered her iniquities" (Apoc. 18:4–5). Depart from her through confession and penance. Either ascend the mountain of contemplation, if you can,[5] or if this seems difficult, keep yourself in the humility of the active life which is denoted by Segor, though it be small and lowly.[6] Thus, our soul may live in it (Gen. 19:20). Otherwise, former generations and those of your fathers' days will not be pleased.

Forget the saying that "now it will not be today as it was yesterday and the day before" (1 Macc. 9:44). Truly, it will not be as it has been thus far for some of the sterile branches, but "the ax is already laid to the root of the tree and every tree that does not bear fruit will be cut down and thrown into the fire" (Matt. 3:10). This will not take place in the days of your grandchildren or in the old age of your children, but in your own days, few and evil. "This generation will not pass away until all these things have been accomplished" (Matt. 24:34). After this the Lord will console the remnants of his people and will relieve the oppression of his inheritance. He will restore his leaders as they were in the beginning and his counselors as they were of old, and He will descend upon them like a river of peace (Isa. 48:18) and like a tower glorifying those who give praise.[7] Do penance now and be converted and live, "lest He at sometime seize upon your souls like a lion, while there is no one to redeem you or save you" (Ps. 7:3). The End.

SELECTION B
Letter to the Abbot of Valdona[1]

Brother Joachim wishes the venerable Abbot who by God's grace is Lord of Valdona[2] an abundance of the power of God's love.

The true knowledge approved in Christ's sermons is that which is experienced in a vision by the spirit of piety and not that which is seen in bodily form by the eyes of the flesh. The bearer of this letter is Brother Al. of your monastery who came here and told me how your friendship, based solely on God and your own goodness, cherishes my lowliness. With complete trust in my ability he urged me in the heart of Christ (Phil. 1:8) to write something to your friendship, as if I were in debt to the love that shines out in you. Instead of displaying gratitude, I should thus appear to be someone who pays back grudgingly and ungratefully. He forced this letter from me rather than received it. This is not because I disdain requests, or, heaven forbid, despise them in my pride, but because a little later on, through the agency of the same brother, I was not able to "sing a song of Sion" (Ps. 136:3) within the borders of Babylon.[3] I should prefer to write these things to a friend caught in the toils of the Great Whore in order that they might forestall rejoicing.[4] Rather than the "song of Sion," we ought to cry out, "By the waters of Babylon there we sat and wept" (Ps. 136:1).

It is almost evening. We have been brought to the sunset of this life. For an hour we must put up with weeping so that in the morning we may find joy (Ps. 29:5). Now is the time for the elect to weep over the imminent destruction of that youngest Babylon lest perchance we share in her sins and be forced to partake of her punishments, as if we did not have the letter Thau written on our foreheads (Ezech. 9:4–6; Apoc. 7:4) and were not able to avoid her threatening destruction.[5] "Behold, the day of the Lord is coming; it is a cruel day, one full of shame, a day of wrath and fury that will make the earth waste and wipe out sinners" (Isa. 13:9).

Someone says: "How do you know this?" I think that I have given a full account in the corrected and emended versions of the minor writings that have already reached you. If only those who were born according to the flesh would stop persecuting those who want to walk according to the spirit! As if I had not told the brethren day and night how Joseph was sold into slavery and brought into Egypt by his owners! Those who seek to snuff out the spirit and who despise prophecy must exist, even in the present. Perhaps it is God's will that we cannot bring the mystery to completion soon. This provides no consolation. How many things distract me in many different ways and form a hindrance, with the result that he who is holy is still sanctified by faith and he who is filthy is still made unclean (Apoc. 22:11) until the hour of temptation suddenly arrives that is to come to prove those who dwell on earth.[6]

I am writing this to your goodness so that if there be talk of it in your area some who without cause demand among themselves my response can have an answer to their requests. Where there is faith and the desire for an explanation, let the whole Church realize that dangerous times approach in which her children will come to a situation in which there will be no power to produce anything. After the present temptation they will cry out at some time. Not too late Christians will be seen to come to the Lord and He will free them from the hand of the persecutor. When they have been freed they will once again take advantage of the peace that God has given to them.

The Lord will hand them over to their enemies so that they learn not to blaspheme (1 Tim. 1:20). But when the time of wrath and the hour of temptation will have been completed, the Lord will gaze upon his people. His heart will rejoice, and no man shall take his joy from them (John 16:22). There will be a little while when the humble will not see their king because the wicked will rule over the earth. And there will be another little while (Jo. 16:19). When this little while is finished they will begin to see a time of peace like nothing that has been since men began to exist on earth.[7] No one will take their peace away from them. Farewell in the Lord, and pray for the writer. Amen.

119

SELECTION C

The Book of Concordance, Book 2, Part 1, Chapters 2-12 (Translation and notes by E. Randolph Daniel)[1]

CHAPTER 2

We define *concordia* correctly as a similarity, equality, and proportion of the New and Old Testaments.[2] I call it an equality of number but not of dignity, when, by means of some likeness, one person and another person, one order and another order, one war and another war, seem to gaze into each other's faces. Abraham and Zachary, Sara and Elisabeth, Isaac and John the Baptist, Jacob and the man Christ Jesus, the twelve patriarchs and the same number of apostles, as well as all other similar cases, wherever they occur, are to be understood as parallels between the two Testaments, not as allegorical interpretations. Certainly a single spiritual understanding proceeds from both of these Testaments. If we have wisdom we know there are two that signify and one that is signified, showing us, who believe in the living God, that there is one Father to whom the Old Testament especially pertains, one Son of God to whom the New pertains especially, one Holy Spirit who proceeds from them both and to whom pertains especially that mystical understanding which, as has been said, proceeds from the two Testaments.

What has just been said ought to be explained more precisely. How can there be any greater similarity than when two old men from two sterile mothers procreate two only sons? You ought not to consider the fact that Isaac, the patriarch, generated Jacob as different, even though John did not generate but baptized Christ. In Jacob the generation of the flesh has been confirmed since he was the carnal father of that people called Israel on account of their father's cognomen. In John the Baptist the generation of the spirit has been confirmed since he was the father in the spirit of that people called Christian. For

120

just as the former people has been procreated by twelve patriarchs, the latter has been procreated by twelve apostles; but in
the former that which has been born from flesh is flesh, while
in the latter that which has been born from spirit is spirit.

Even if it is argued that the baptism of John, by which
Christ was baptized, did not have that same virtue[3] that baptism has in Christ, still the similarity of the mystery[4] is not
dissolved by this argument, because even if God the Father was
unwilling to send his Spirit upon others who had been baptized by John, he nevertheless sent him upon Christ, accompanied by the testimony of his voice when he said to him: "Here
is my beloved son. In you I am well pleased."[5] Because John
himself was filled by the Holy Spirit without any baptism even
when he was in the womb of his mother, I do not see any
objection to saying that at least a hidden grace of the Holy
Spirit has been given also to those who have been baptized by
John's baptism, just as such grace has been given to other
righteous men who merited to be saved by grace under the law
and the prophets. If you think this argument is irrelevant
because John did not give the Holy Spirit but Almighty God
sent him, by the same token the baptism of Christ in which the
apostles baptized is not relevant, because even if they were the
men who baptized, nevertheless God alone infused the grace,
he alone performed the works and virtues.

Therefore, just as according to the flesh the generation of
Isaac is different from that of Jacob, so in some way the
baptism of John is different from the baptism of Christ. Indeed,
the seed of Isaac was elected only in Jacob. It was condemned
in Esau in whose case neither paternal vows nor merits were
able to warrant salvation. Jacob alone was foreshadowed by
maternal grace and gained a paternal benediction, both surely
in himself and in his seed. For the seed of Jacob was not
condemned in part and elected in part, but the whole Israel has
been reckoned his seed, even if we realize that some reprobates
were present in it, because it is one thing when scripture refers
to the mystery of temporal election, another thing when it
refers to eternal. Similarly, the baptism of John was, as it were,
useless to the others whom he baptized[6] because it was not able

121

to confer eternal salvation. Nevertheless, in another way it was useful because it was like a road sign[7] that pointed toward the true baptism, that of Christ. Christ alone, foreshadowed by the grace of the Holy Spirit, has been constituted the heir of all the fathers of the prior Testament, so that those who have been baptized in him have been made sons of Abraham, even if among them there may have been weeds that ought to be burned as there were also among the sons of Israel.

According to this pattern, therefore, the persons of the one Testament and those of the other gaze into each others' faces. City and city, people and people, order and order, war and war, act in the same way, as well as any other things that are similarly drawn to each other by some affinity. The difference is that those of the Old Testament refer more to the flesh, these of the New more to the spirit, albeit it must be recalled that there were indications of the spirit in the former, reminders of the flesh in the latter. Therefore, not only may a person be a type of another person, but also a multitude of a multitude, as Jerusalem of the Roman church, Samaria of Constantinople, Babylon of Rome, Egypt of the Byzantine Empire, et cetera.

CHAPTER 3

Allegoria is the similarity of any small thing to an extremely large one, for example of a day to a year, of a week to an age, of a person to an order, or a city, or a nation, or a people, and a thousand similar instances. By way of illustration, Abraham is a single man who stands for the order of patriarchs in which there are many men. Zachary is an individual man who stands for this same order.

Sara is an individual woman who stands for the synagogue, not, I say, the synagogue of the reprobate, which Agar signified, but that sterile church of the just which groaned and wept daily over the shame of its barrenness, when it saw its rival—if I may touch on another mystery—rejoicing in its sons and holding a feast day amidst its riches. Sara has been given a son (a son not of the flesh but of the promise) in her old age, that is when the fullness of time has arrived, just as God sent his Son, born from a woman and put under the law, in order that he might redeem those who were under the law. Elisabeth, therefore, has the same significance because she also conceived in her old age after she had been sterile.

Furthermore, Jacob and Christ Jesus were born to young mothers, but Jacob was born when Isaac was sixty years of age. Christ was conceived in the sixth month after Elisabeth conceived, because the church of the spiritual men was extraordinarily sterile until the sixth *tempus* of the second *status*. Now is the time when this church should be multiplied by its children and "should extend its palm fronds even to the sea and its posterity even to the river."[8]

According to the anagogical sense, Abraham signifies God the Father, Isaac the Son, and Jacob the Holy Spirit. In the same way Zachary, the father of John, stands for the Son, the man Christ Jesus for the Holy Spirit. This is enough concerning the spiritual understanding that is rightly called *allegoria*.

CHAPTER 4

That understanding which is called *concordia* is similar to a highway that extends from a wasteland to a city. On the way it crosses valleys in which a traveler may wonder if he is on the right road and just as often passes over mountain heights from which he can see backward as well as forward and determine the right direction to take for the remainder of his journey by contemplating the road he has come. Every traveler who goes forward until the route ahead is unclear finds the correct route to proceed by looking backward. Where the traveler is not able to illuminate either the journey he has completed or that which he ought still to finish—as customarily happens in the valleys—he drags himself more by faith and reason than by vision to the peaks, in order that from there he may either correct his errors or reassure himself that he has traveled the right road until now.

This journey, however, on which we have begun to proceed with God's guidance has a more secure route than our traveler's, because our route is not left to chance as it was when the trip started, but it is guided by the wisdom and teaching of God, which has its inns[9] spaced at regular intervals. These intervals ought to be considered according to diverse modes, broadly and narrowly, that is by distinguishing greater blocks of time, medium blocks, and short blocks, all of which are calculated on the basis of the number of generations and of the particular property of a *tempus*. For that *tempus* in which men lived according to the flesh was one block of time, the period that began with Adam and continued up to Christ. This is another *tempus* in which people live between two poles, that is between the flesh and the spirit. This *tempus* had its starting point with Elisha, the prophet, or with Josiah, king of Judah, and has continued to the present time. There is still another *tempus* in which people live according to the spirit, a *tempus* that began in the days of Saint Benedict and will continue until the end of the world. Thus the harvest or the particular property of the first *tempus*—or as we ought better say of the first *status*— lasted from Abraham to Zachary, the father of John the Baptist.[10] The beginning of this first *status* was from Adam. The harvest of the second *status* began with Zachary and will last to the forty-second generation.[11] The second *status* began with Josiah or in the days of Asa under whose reign Elisha was called by Elijah to be a prophet. The harvest of the third *status* will last from that generation which was twenty-second from Saint Benedict until the consummation of the age. This third *status* started with Saint Benedict. These *status* are proposed and shown to us by faith but I know that few will accept them unless manifest reason provides proof. Accordingly, it is necessary in this second book to dig up those weedlike questions as if preparing a field for the seed, so that in the other books that are to follow, this cultivated earth, the divine page, may bear fruit more abundantly in the hearts of the faithful.

CHAPTER 5

Just as these alterations of *tempora* and works demonstrate that there are three *status seculi*,[12] although this whole present may be called one age, so there are three orders of the elect, although the people of God are one as we clearly know both according to the holy fathers' authority and according to the things themselves. The first of these orders is composed of those who are married, the second is composed of the clergy, the third of monks. The married order started with Adam and began to bear fruit with Abraham. The clerical order started with Josiah, who, because he was from the tribe of Judah, offered incense to the Lord, though not without fear of punishment. It bore fruit with Christ who is both true king and priest. The monastic order, according to a certain proper form in which the Holy Spirit, who is the author of good things, has shown his full authority, started with Saint Benedict, a man quite famous for his miracles, his work, and his sanctity. This order will bear fruit in the last times. There were, however, monks and justly famous monks before him, but the reason why the monastic order preceded him in certain people will be discussed below.[13] One ought to know, however, that this same order, which according to its proper form started with Saint Benedict, began according to one signification from Elisha, the prophet. It is evident that the same venerable Benedict came in his spirit as their similar positions in time and perfection of life prove.

CHAPTER 6

I want it to be carefully noted that when we talk about the beginnings of these *status*, we may accept the *tempus* of Abraham, of Isaac, and of Jacob as one beginning. In the same way the *tempus* of Zachary, of John the Baptist, and of the man Christ Jesus may be accepted as one *tempus*, so that, because such statements require reasons, there is no difference whether we set the beginning of the first *status* in Abraham or in Isaac or in Jacob; whether we begin the second in Zachary or in John, his son, or even in Christ Jesus; whether we begin the third in the forty-second generation or in the two preceding generations. When we say "even up to the present, even up to

125

these days," or something like this, it is to be taken as if ninety years were one *tempus* because the end of any particular *tempus* in scripture customarily is taken either broadly or narrowly.

CHAPTER 7

Our statement that three generations ought to be taken as one beginning does not conflict with the sacred mystery of the holy and indivisible Trinity. For if the Father, the Son, and the Holy Spirit are not three beginnings but one beginning, this is by reason of a mystery, so that any three righteous men who stand typologically for the Trinity can be taken as one beginning. Thus, any one of this trio may be accepted as a beginning and all three as one beginning. Indeed, the fact that the three orders spoken of above became illustrious in their proper times pertains to the mystery of the Trinity, as will be shown below.[14]

Thus the *concordia* between the three *status* of the world ought to be assigned to these same orders so that the *concordia* may not be diverted either to the right or to the left. Even if events are numerous, God still revealed them one after another even up to the third *status* so that he might show himself to be triune in his persons.[15] If God were one person, we ought not seek three distinct works nor assign the *concordia* to one of them alone. Because, in fact, there are three persons, although the three are one God, the Son says about the Father and himself: "My Father is working still, and I am working."[16] When did the Father work without the Son, or the Son without the Father? But the Son, who made the statement "is working still," wanted the particular properties of the images to be understood. Therefore, just as the likeness of the Father ought to be venerated in those who are called Fathers up to Christ, so in those who have been redeemed by his blood and have been born by means of water and the Holy Spirit we should venerate the image of the Son himself who has wanted to have brothers on earth (although he is Lord of all and Creator of the universe), in order that he should be, as Paul says, "the first-born of many brothers."[17] When in fact the apostles had performed baptisms already, the same Lord and Redeemer said: "You will be baptized by the Holy Spirit before many days."[18] Hence the work of the Holy Spirit will be revealed after these things in the spiritual men. This revelation, although it will have been foreshadowed in some persons, ought to be expected chiefly near the end of the age, when that promise of the Lord which has begun in a few will be consummated in many. This is the promise he made by means of the prophet Joel who said: "It will happen in the last days that I will pour out my spirit on all flesh; your sons and your daughters will prophesy."[19] But enough has been said on these matters for now.

Nevertheless, I will not keep silent on this point so that no one can object to the promise because it is not yet possible to assign works to the third *status* except in part, due to the works being mostly incomplete. We will say what we can about these in their place. Expectation of future events may be made certain by the unfolding of the present. With this all said, our struggle is still not finished. For we have spoken about the three *status* of this world according to the pattern that the three great patriarchs and the three angels who appeared to one of them, that is to Abraham, represent. We have not spoken according to the pattern that Aaron, Moses, and the two cherubim (whom we have mentioned above) represent. It is necessary, therefore, to count the *status* of the world differently on account of another trinitarian mystery, so that we who have attentively counted the three *status* of the world because of the three persons of the deity may by this different pattern count not three *tempora* but only two. It ought to be done thus because this way too has its rationale and its revelation of the truth.

CHAPTER 8

According to the pattern we are about to discuss, the *tempus* of the first Testament began with Adam and continued even to Christ, bearing fruit from Jacob. The *tempus* of the New

Testament began with Josiah, King of Judah, and will last until the consummation of the world, bearing fruit from Christ.

For we know that the carnal Jewish people imitated the first parent in sinful corruption. Just as he is the first of all men, so too is he recorded first in the order of fathers. The Roman people, who are Gentile, began from a certain Moechus, as Augustine teaches in his book *The City of God*.[20] He generated Romulus and Remus through adultery in the days of Josiah. Afterward both peoples of the Lord were shown mercy, the former from the days of Jacob, the latter from the time when Christ came into the world. Fathers were elected from the former people by means of the law and circumcision; from the latter people sons were chosen by means of the sacrament of baptism. The likeness of the Father is found in the former, the likeness of the Son in the latter. For this reason the former have been called fathers in a special way, the latter not fathers but sons.

Lest the likeness of the gifts of the Holy Spirit be missing—the Spirit who proceeds from the Father and the Son—the kingdom that has been called Israel has proceeded from the kingdom of the Jewish people. In the kingdom of Israel are found the remnants of the elect, as well as the spiritual men, among whom were Elijah and Elisha and the sons of the prophets who lived in Jericho. Likewise the Church of the Greeks has proceeded from the universal church committed to Peter. In this Church are found the remnants in their days and the renowned fathers who lived in the desert, like Elijah, Elisha, and the sons of the prophets who dwelled in Jericho. This should not be thought irrelevant to the mystery that then ten tribes seceded from the house of David and now the Greek churches have seceded as it were from the Roman Church, because it is true what the apostle says: "There are different kinds of grace, but the same Spirit."[21]

You ought also to note that the letter of the Old Testament was committed to the Jewish people, the letter of the New to the Roman people. The spiritual understanding that proceeds from both Testaments has been committed to the spiritual men.

CHAPTER 9

We ought to review what we have just discussed about the three orders and the two peoples, so that by paying attention to the one the other may be more easily understood. When the two peoples were discussed, it was demonstrated that the Holy Spirit is sent by the Father and Son. When he is sent, he breathes where he wishes and gives his gifts to individuals as he wishes.

The principle that the Holy Spirit proceeds from the Father and the Son without either beginning or end prompts us to consider the three orders we spoke of above, because what we unswervingly hold about his nature appears there even more lucidly. For when we dealt with these orders, we said that the order of monks according to one proper form was started by Saint Benedict, but according to a likeness by Elisha, the prophet. For we said: "There were monks, even rather famous monks, before the time of Saint Benedict in whom the monastic order had already preceded."

Both because this is the place to treat it and also because we are bound by our promise, we ought now to fulfill what we said when we vowed that we would explain the likeness of the sacred mystery of the Trinity in these three orders. Note here that he who made man in his image and likeness also created Abraham, Isaac, and Jacob in order that they might bear the type of the divine Trinity, just as he created many other trios. God wanted to establish those three orders so that they themselves might be the image and likeness of the Trinity, according to that saying of the apostle: "Until we all attain to the unity of the faith, into a perfect man in the measure of the age of the fullness of Christ."[22]

For God considers the whole multitude of believers as if they were a single man, created out of flesh, blood, and the breath of life. For as blood is the medium between the flesh and the soul, thus the clerical order is the medium between the married and the monks. The married order bears the image of the Father, because as the Father is the Father because he has a Son, so the married order has been established by God solely in order to procreate sons. This is so even though Moses allowed them something contrary on account of the hardness of heart that made them wise in the things of the world and Paul the apostle permitted them one thing lest a worse occur.[23]

The clerical order bears the image of the Son, who is the Word of the Father, because it has been established to preach and teach the people the way of the Lord and the rules of their God. The monastic order bears the image of the Holy Spirit, who is the love of God, because this order could not despise the world and those things that are worldly unless it was invited by the love of God and drawn by the same Spirit who drove the Lord into the desert. It is also called spiritual because it walks not according to the flesh but according to the spirit.

The first order was started by Adam; the second by Josiah, king of Judah; the third in one way by Elisha, the prophet, in another by Saint Benedict. Why is it thus? Because the Holy Spirit proceeds from the Father and from the Son. For if the Holy Spirit proceeded from the Father alone—like the Son—it would seem to be more suitable for the clerical and monastic orders both to begin simultaneously and to attain their consummation simultaneously. If, on the contrary, the Holy Spirit proceeded from the Son alone—as the Son did from the Father alone—then it would seem more suitable for the *third status* to pertain only to the Holy Spirit, just as the second would pertain to the Son. Because, in fact, there is one Father from whom the Son and the Holy Spirit proceed, one Spirit who proceeds simultaneously from the Father and the Son, two who proceed from one Father, the first *status* is correctly ascribed to the Father alone, the third to the Holy Spirit,[24] the second to the Son and the Holy Spirit in common.

I do not say this in order that one should believe that the kingdom or the work of one person should be divided from the kingdom or work of the two other persons—that would be abhorrent to the hearts of believers. This statement ought to be accepted simply in respect to the mystery.[25] For just as there are three persons and one God, so frequently in those things that are common to all three distinct significations are found that show the respective likeness of the persons. For example,

Abraham signifies the Father because he has primarily been called father. Isaac signifies the Son and Jacob the Holy Spirit. The first *status*, therefore, ought to be assigned to the Father, the second to the Son and to the Holy Spirit (although the works assigned to the Son may be more noteworthy in it as is fitting), the third *status*, to the Holy Spirit. For this reason the Holy Spirit will reveal his glory in the third *status*, as the Son revealed his in the second, the Father his in the first.

Thus, at that time when Christ came into the world, the Holy Spirit came also, first to the Virgin, then to those who were baptized in Christ as if to ones still infants in him. The brightness of the Holy Spirit who cannot be seen could not be manifested as could the brightness of the Son who had risen from the dead in that visible flesh which he had assumed. The Son says in the Gospel: "I will ask the Father and he will give you the Paraclete, the spirit of truth whom this world cannot receive because it neither sees nor knows him."[26]

CHAPTER 10

On account of these venerable mysteries, the married order started with Adam; the other two orders with Elisha, the prophet, and Josiah, king of Judah, although the monastic order, which has been seen to begin in one way with Elisha, in another way began with Saint Benedict. The explanation of the mystery has been given. In the first case the monastic order began with Elisha in order to demonstrate the procession of the Holy Spirit from the Father. In the second case it began with Saint Benedict in order to show the procession of the Holy Spirit from the Son. Although the monastic order has been started twice, generically, nevertheless, it is one. Although the Holy Spirit has been twice given, he himself is still one. Nor has the Son been separated from the Father (an abhorrent notion) as if the Holy Spirit were sent separately by the Father, separately by the Son.

Because the minds of carnal people were not able to understand this mystery unless it were shown in a clear way, on one occasion the Holy Spirit was sent upon the Son in the likeness of a dove in order to make it evident that he proceeded from the Father who had said to John the Baptist: "He upon whom you will see my spirit descending and remaining is the one who baptizes in the Holy Spirit."[27] On another occasion the Holy Spirit was breathed out by the Son upon the apostles in order to show that the Spirit proceeded also from him.[28] Nevertheless, even when the Holy Spirit was sent in the likeness of a dove, he was sent by the Son as well as by the Father. And when the Son breathed on the apostles and said: "Receive the Holy Spirit,"[29] the Holy Spirit was given by the Father as well as by the Son.

Thus the sacred mysteries are rightly to be understood not wholly according to what they signify, but in accordance with the Catholic faith. For it is not because a man speaks that his image speaks as well, or because a man sees and hears that his image is able to see, hear, work, eat, or walk. Nevertheless, each act has a meaning that enables us to contemplate in some way a man's outward appearance.

I do not think I should neglect to mention that just as the letter of the Old Testament pertains especially to the married order and the teaching of the New to the clerical order, so in addition to that understanding which pertains to the Holy Spirit in mystical fashion, the life-giving Rule of our holy father Benedict, even when held according to the letter, also pertains to the Holy Spirit. That which it contains about the monastic institution is spirit and life.[30] That which properly pertains to the Spirit is one thing, that which concerns the bestowal of gifts is another. Thus there is one significance for the Spirit himself, another that pertains to the bestowal of gifts.

Perhaps we might seem to merit reproach here because in a book on *concordia* we are discussing the Trinity, a topic that both on account of its loftiness and especially of our limited space ought rather to be venerated than written about here.[31] If I am reproached about this, I also reproach myself. Nevertheless, when someone asks me about some point: "Why is this?" I am obliged to explain it, especially where the point appears absurd, lest a sterile and unsupported argument be held in contempt by nitpickers, skeptics, rivals, and detractors. They do not understand that the whole universe has been made wisely and do not realize the greatness of the Lord's work, done in accordance with his will.[32]

Therefore, because there are two divine persons of whom one is ungenerated, the other generated, two Testaments have been set up, the first of which, as we have said above, pertains especially to the Father, the second to the Son, because the latter is from the former. In addition, the spiritual understanding, proceeding from both Testaments, is one that pertains especially to the Holy Spirit. Again, the letter of the Old Testament pertains particularly to the married, the letter of the New to the clerics, the Rule, under which monks live, to the order of monks itself.

Because there are three coeternal and coequal trinitarian persons, when we take into account that which exemplifies the likeness of these persons the first *status* is reckoned from Adam to Christ, the second from King Josiah to the present time, the third from Saint Benedict to the consummation of the age. When, however, we omit the initial *tempora* and concentrate on that phase which is crucial to each *status*, then the first *status* is reckoned from Abraham, Isaac, and Jacob, up to Zachary, the father of John, or even to John himself and to Christ Jesus. The second is reckoned from this same time up to the present. The third is reckoned from the present time to the end.

Again, because of the two persons in the Trinity of whom one is ungenerated, the other generated, the deeds of the first Testament ought to be ascribed to the ungenerated person. The *tempus* of this first Testament is reckoned from Adam to Christ. The deeds of the second Testament ought to be ascribed to the generated person. The *tempus* of this second Testament is reckoned from Josiah to the consummation of the age. When the initial *tempora* are omitted and we concentrate on the crucial phase of each *tempus*, then the first *tempus* is reckoned from Abraham to Zachary, the second from Zachary to the consummation of the age. Because, in fact, there is one person who proceeds from the two, and he is called the Holy Spirit, certain special deeds that proceed from the others ought to be ascribed to this person. These special deeds will be treated in their proper place.

CHAPTER 11

The first pattern is designated by alpha (A) which is a triangular figure. The second is designated by omega (Ω) in which figure one rod proceeds from the juncture of two. Both patterns ought to be grasped, because both are highly relevant to the Catholic faith.[33]

CHAPTER 12

Now we have shown why the *tempora* of the world ought to be assigned to these two patterns, an arrangement that John implied when he mentioned the stone water jars, each of which held two or three measures.[34] Next we ought to discuss whether these *tempora* are to be reckoned according to their number of years or according to some other measurement. Saint Augustine, when he discussed the ages in *The City of God*, said that there was one age from Adam to Noah, another age from Noah to Abraham. When he said this, he added: "Not because the second age has the same number of years as the first, but because it has the same number of generations."[35] These *tempora*, therefore, ought to be reckoned not according to their number of years but according to their number of generations. For there were also sixty-three generations from Adam to Christ and sixty-three generations from Josiah to the end of the second *status*. Indeed, the New Testament, which was confirmed in Christ, was begun with Josiah, lest the Old should appear to wither before the New, having been sown and taken root, should germinate and produce fruit from the earth. It is, indeed, written in the law of Moses that "you shall eat the old until the new is born."[36]

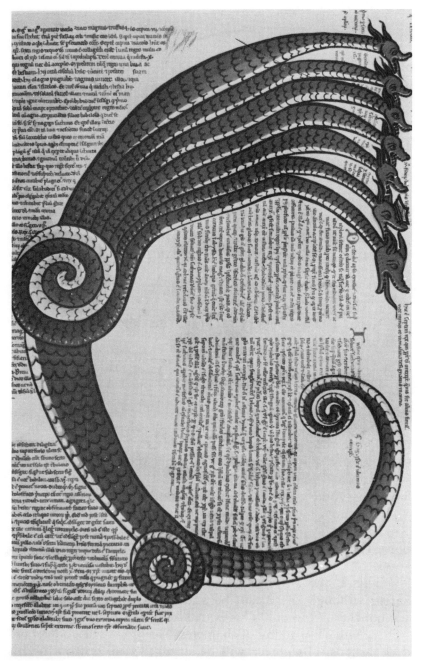

PLATE VI:

THE SEVEN-HEADED DRAGON
See the discussion of this figure in "Joachim of Fiore: Introduction" and the translation
of the accompanying text as Selection D under Joachim. Reproduced from *Il Libro delle
Figure*, Plate XIV.

SELECTION D
Book of Figures,
The Fourteenth Table,
The Seven-Headed Dragon[1]

I. THE CAPTIONS[2]

"There are seven kings. Five have fallen, one is present, and one has not yet come. When he comes, he must remain for a short time" (Apoc. 17:9–10).

Herod. The First Persecution, that of the Jews. The Time of the Apostles.[3]

Nero. The Second Persecution, that of the Pagans. The Time of the Martyrs.

Constantius.[4] The Third Persecution, that of the Heretics. The Time of the Doctors.

Mohammed. The Fourth Persecution, that of the Saracens. The Time of the Virgins.

Mesemoth.[5] The Fifth Persecution, that of the Sons of Babylon in the Spirit and not in the letter.[6] The Time of the Conventuals.[7] "These five have fallen" (Apoc. 17:10). The fifth persecution belongs to the King of Babylon. You will know later why you can write down Mesemoth for that king.

Saladin. The Sixth Persecution has Begun. The Seventh will Follow. "Another will arise after them and he will be more powerful than the previous ones" (Dan. 7:24). There are ten kings.

This is the Seventh King, who is properly called Antichrist, although there will be another like him, no less evil, symbolized by the tail. This is that king of whom Daniel says: "There will arise a king of shameless face who will understand dark designs. His power will be strengthened, but not by his own forces. He shall lay waste all things beyond belief" (Dan. 8:23–24).

Gog. He is the Final Antichrist.[8]

JOACHIM OF FIORE

II. The Commentary[9]

A. The Apocalypse: "A great sign appeared in heaven: a vast red dragon having seven heads and ten horns. His tail dragged down a third part of the stars of heaven and cast them to the earth" (Apoc. 12:3–4). The seven heads of the dragon signify seven tyrants by whom the persecutions of the Church were begun.[10] The dragon's sixth head has ten horns because in the time of the sixth king, he of whom it is said "He is one" (Apoc. 17:10), many kings by destiny will be brought together to do battle with Christ and his elect. As it says in the Apocalypse: "The ten horns which you saw are ten kings who have not yet received a kingdom, but will receive kingly power for an hour after the beast. They have one design, and their power and strength they will give to the beast. They will fight with the Lamb and the Lamb will conquer them. Those who are with him are called elect and faithful. And the ten horns which you saw on the beast will hate the Harlot and will make her desolate and naked. They will eat her flesh and burn her with fire" (Apoc. 17:12–16).

From all this it can be understood that first of all the sixth king must begin to rule alone, and then later gather many kings to fight with the Lamb and to smite the sons of Babylon who say they are Christians and are not, but are the synagogue of Satan (Apoc. 2:9, 3:9). Their intention will be wicked in all things and in every way. Even though they are unwilling and unknowing, they will do God's will in both cases: either by killing the just who are destined to be crowned with martyrdom, or by judging the wicked by whom the earth was corrupted with blood (Ps. 105:38).[11]

After this destruction, which has already in some part begun, the Christians will be victorious. Those who fear the name of the Lord will rejoice when that head of the beast over which the sixth king reigns has been brought almost to extermination and ruin. Then, after a few years, its wound will be healed, and the king who will be in charge of it (whether it be Saladin if he is still alive, or another in his place) will gather a much larger army than before and incite universal war against

God's elect. Many will be crowned with martyrdom in those days.[12]

In that time also the seventh head of the dragon will arise, namely, that king who is called Antichrist, and a multitude of false prophets with him. We think that he will arise from the West and will come to the aid of that king who will be the head of the pagans. He will perform great signs before him and his army, just as Simon Magus did in the sight of Nero.[13] "There will be great tribulation, such as has not been from the beginning, in order to deceive, if possible, even the elect. The Lord will shorten those days for the sake of his elect" (Matt. 24:21, 24, 22), so that they will not exceed forty-two months.[14]

I should like to consider more closely why the dragon's two heads are joined together at the same time, and why the Church's tribulations are doubled only in the sixth age so that a twin tribulation arises in this time alone.[15] Just as the old Babylon was struck under the sixth seal, so the new one will be pierced under the present sixth opening.[16] Also under the sixth seal next Holofernes, the leader of the army of the king of Assyria mentioned in the history of Judith, and then Aman from the land of Agag found in the history of Queen Esther hardened their faces to destroy the remnants of the Jewish people everywhere. In the same way, after the imminent tempest and the serenity of the peace that will follow, the eleventh king mentioned in Daniel (Dan. 7:24) will rise up from the Saracen race, though it might not be the one who is present now (because he could fall and rise again after his overthrow, or another could be raised up in his place). There will be another king from a group of heretics who will have an appearance of piety and who will lie hypocritically. I say that he is the king of whom it is said in Daniel: "There will arise a king with a shameless face who will hatch dark designs. His power will be strengthened, but not by his own forces. He shall lay waste all things beyond belief" (Dan. 8:23–24).

These two will make a conspiracy to wipe the name of Christ from the earth. But Christ will conquer them, he who is King of Kings and Lord of Lords (Apoc. 19:16). There are bound to be many who will fight them for the sake of the faith.

They will die for Christ's name and will at some time gain a triumph from the tyrants. Just as the sons of Israel used to walk through the desert for five days and on each morning of any week used to collect an omer of manna for the day, but only on the sixth day would gather a double ration so they could rest from labor on the sabbath (Exod. 16:16–23), so too he who says to his people "I will strike you seven times because of your sins" (Lev. 26:24) will permit the two final persecutions to happen in the one sixth time so that at the opening of the seventh seal peace may come and his faithful people can rest from their labors. Therefore, these two last heads are joined together, because both these tribulations of the final week are destined to be fulfilled under the one sixth time.

B. Paul writes about the Antichrist: "He is lifted up and opposed to all that is called God, or that is worshiped, so that he sits in God's Temple, showing himself as if he were God" (2 Thess. 2:4). We should not think, as the holy teachers say, that when he has been judged the end of the world will come soon, just because he is said to come at the end of the world. The end of the world and the last hour are not always to be taken for the final moment, but for the time of the end, as John who wrote over a thousand years ago openly teaches when he says: "Little children, this is the last hour, and as you have heard that Antichrist is coming, so now there are many Antichrists. Hence we know that it is the last hour" (1 John 2:18). But we must note that John and John's Master say many Antichrists will come. Paul, on the other hand, foretells that there will be one. Just as many holy kings, priests, and prophets went before the one Christ who was King, priest, and prophet, so likewise many unholy kings, false prophets, and antichrists will go before the one Antichrist who will pretend that he is a king, a priest, and a prophet.

After the destruction of this Antichrist there will be justice on earth and an abundance of peace, "and the Lord will rule from sea to sea and from the river to the ends of the earth" (Ps. 71:8). "Men will turn their swords into plowshares, and their spears into sickles. One nation will not lift up the sword against the other, and there will be no more war" (Isa. 2:4). The

Jews and many pagan races will be converted to the Lord,[17] and all people will rejoice in the beauty of peace because the great dragon's heads will be crushed and he will be imprisoned in the abyss (that is, in the remaining races who will live at the ends of the earth). God alone knows the number of the years, months, and days of that time.[18] When they have been finished and brought to end, once again Satan will be freed from prison to persecute God's elect, because there is still that other Antichrist who is symbolized in the dragon's tail.

At the end of the times and of the years "Satan will be freed from his prison, and will go forth and seduce the nations that are at the four corners of the earth. He will lead them in battle; their number will be like the sands of the sea. They will surround the camp of the saints and the beloved city" (Apoc. 20:7–8). That will be the final battle, in the last moment at the dragon's tail because the heads will have been already crushed.

Then the commander of the army will be Gog, the final Antichrist. God will judge him and his army by fire and brimstone poured down from heaven. The devil who led men astray to do all these evil deeds will be cast into the lake of fire and brimstone where the Beast and the False Prophet are (Apoc. 20:9–10). The Beast and the False Prophet (that is, the eleventh king mentioned in Daniel, along with his army) and the Seventh King written of above along with his group of false prophets are next thrown into the lake of fire. At the end Gog and his army will be judged; after them the devil and Gog himself will be cast into the lake of fire where the Beast and the False Prophet already are.

Among all the Antichrists who will appear in the world two are worse than the others: the one who is denoted by the seventh head and the one denoted by the tail. He who is denoted by the seventh head will come in hidden fashion like John the Baptist, who was not known to be Elias. He who is denoted by the tail will come in open fashion like Elias, who will come openly. The Lord promised one Elias and nonetheless two will come, one of whom will be called Elias. God's saints have specifically spoken of one Antichrist and nonetheless there will be two, one of whom will be the Greatest

Antichrist.[19] The devil strives for nothing more than to appear like the Most High in every way possible. Because Jesus Christ came in hidden fashion, Satan himself will do his works hiddenly, that is, signs and false wonders will be designed to seduce even the elect if possible. Because at the end of the world Jesus Christ will come to Judgment in open fashion, so too the devil himself will go forth at the end of the world and will appear openly in the days of Gog. He will incite the pagan nations and will lead them to war so that he can pretend that he is Christ come to judge with his saints, avenging all who have suffered wrong. Just as Jesus Christ came with true signs, but cloaked and hidden because of the likeness of sinful human nature so that he was hardly recognized as the Christ by even a few, so too the seventh king will come with false signs and will be hidden and cloaked because of his appearance of spiritual justice, so that only a few will be able to recognize that he is the Antichrist. For this reason even the elect may be led into error if possible. And because the same Christ Jesus will come openly in the glory of his majesty surrounded with a heavenly army of angels and men, so too Satan will appear openly with armies of wicked men, so that on the basis of dread of his forces he may pretend to be him who will come to judge the living and the dead and the world by fire.[20]

SELECTION E
The Book of Figures,
The Twelfth Table

The Arrangement of the New People of God[1] Pertaining to the Third State after the Model of the Heavenly Jerusalem

Paul the Apostle.[2] "Just as the body is one and has many members, all the members of the body, although they are many, are one body. It is the same with Christ. For a body is not one member but many. If the foot were to say: Since I am not a hand I do not belong to the body, it would not therefore not be a part of the body. And if the ear were to say: Because I am not an eye I do not belong to the body, it would not therefore not be a part of the body. If the whole body were an eye, where would the hearing be? If the whole body were hearing, where would the power of smell be? God put the members, each of them, into the body on purpose. If they all were one member, where would the body be? So there are indeed many members, but one body" (l Cor. 12:14–20).

John the Evangelist. "I, John, saw a door open in heaven and behold a throne was placed there. Around the throne and at its very center were four animals filled with eyes before and behind. The first animal was like a lion, the second animal like a calf, the third animal had a face like a man, and the fourth animal was like a flying eagle" (Apoc. 4:1–7). "Grace is given to each of us according to the measure of the gift of Christ. And hence he has said: 'Ascending on high he led captivity captive, and gave gifts to men' (Ps. 67:19). He gave to some the gift to be Apostles, some to be Prophets, some to be Evangelists, others to be pastors and doctors, for the fulfillment of the saints in their ministry in the building up of the Body of Christ, until we all come together into the unity of faith and the recognition of the Son of God, into the perfect man, into the measure of the maturity of Christ" (Eph. 4:7–13).

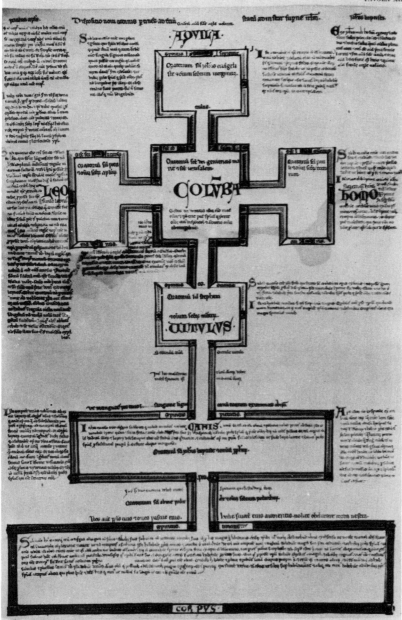

PLATE VII:

THE NEW ORDER OF THE PEOPLE OF GOD
Reproduced from *Il Libro delle Figure*, Plate XII.

I. The Oratory of the Holy Mother of God, Mary, and of Holy Jerusalem.[3] The Dove. The Seat of God. The Spirit of Counsel. The Nose.[4]

This house will be the mother of all. The Spiritual Father[5] who will be over all will be in it; all will obey his direction and authority.

The brethren of this house will live according to a rule in all things so that everyone else can be shaped by the example of their patience and sobriety. In fasts they will follow the model of the Cistercians. At the will of the Spiritual Father who will be in this house the brethren of the lower orders can move to the stricter life but in such a way that no one can do so without an examination, lest (God forbid!) someone who lacks the gift and calling of God desires the first place and must begin in shame to take the last (Luke 14:9).

II. The Oratory of Saint John the Evangelist and of all the Holy Men and Cloistered Nuns.[6] The Eagle. "The fourth animal was like a flying eagle" (Apoc. 4:7). The Spirit of Wisdom. The Eye.

In this oratory there will be approved and perfect men who are afire with spiritual desire and wish to lead a contemplative life. They will each have their own cells into which they can quickly enter when they wish to pray, but these will not be where each might have wanted, but next to the cloister according to the order and will of the Spiritual Father who will be over all. Their Prior will not rebuke them, but will entreat them like fathers and like those of the first rank who do not need compassion.

They will fast perpetually except in case of illness. They will drink no wine and will eat nothing seasoned with oil save for Sundays and major feasts. If anyone of them has such a stomach ailment that he cannot keep the established fast, he should be moved to the oratory of the aged and stay there until he be cured. These men will not have scapulars, but only cowls (except perhaps for some necessity), because they are not required to work but to pray and sing the psalms.[7]

III. The Oratory of Saint Paul and of All the Holy Doctors. The Man. "The third animal had a face like a man" (Apoc. 4:7). The Spirit of Understanding. The Ear.

In this oratory there will be learned men and also those to be instructed and taught by God (John 6:45). They desire and have more power than the others to devote themselves to reading and to apply themselves to spiritual teaching. Hence they have the means to bring forth new things and old (Matt. 13:52). They will fast every day in winter and three days in summer. Both in summer and winter they will always go without wine on Monday, without a meat dish on Wednesday, and on Friday will fast on bread and water, except in case of illness or if perhaps the Father of the monastery who rules all will wish to make a dispensation for the place or the time in someone's case.

IV. The Oratory of Saint Stephan and of All the Holy Martyrs. The Calf. "The second animal was like a calf" (Apoc. 4:7). The Spirit of Knowledge. The Mouth.

In this oratory will be those brethren who are strong in manual labor, but are not able to advance to a greater degree in spiritual discipline. They will fast three days in winter and one in summer, that is, on Friday. They will obey their Prior according to the order and will of the Spiritual Father who will be over all and who will render an account of all. They will not have cowls, but only scapulars and capes. They will work for themselves and also for those who lead the eremitical life so that what they fail to supply in prayer and abstinence may be made up for by those who live in a more spiritual manner.[8]

V. The Oratory of Saint Peter and of All the Holy Apostles. The Lion. "The first animal was like a lion" (Apoc. 4:7). The Spirit of Fortitude. The Hand.

In this oratory will be the old and the weak brethren who possibly because of stomach trouble are not able to bear the full austerity of the rule in fasting but who nevertheless strive to walk according to the purity of the rule insofar as they can and who for their simplicity and modesty invite a fitting respect. In wintertime they will fast daily insofar as they can, in summertime on Friday, but in such a way that there be a merciful regard for them so that if necessary they may anticipate the canonical hours. If possible let them have every day two cooked meat dishes and wine, but in such measure and temperance that the precept of the rule be not abandoned in their regard and a dispensation changed into wanton freedom. Let them be given as far as possible a house full of Christian love, and let them receive it with thanks and in all humility and fear of God. They are not to be compelled to go out in the fields to manual labor, but they will work inside on whatever is commanded them. Above all they will restrain themselves from idle words and they will keep the strictest silence whenever there is reading and especially on feast days. At other times when there is necessity let them speak with the Prior of the house in an orderly manner. Entry into this oratory will not be permitted to anyone of his own will and choice, but to whom the Abbot will have commanded upon consideration (as is found in the rule) of the real necessity of those in need and not the bad will of the envious. Anyone who has shown that he desires such a thing without the order of the Abbot is to be expelled from the monastery if he does not remain peacefully in his place.

Between this monastery and the clerics' place there ought to be a distance of about three miles.[9]

VI. The Oratory of Saint John the Baptist and of All the Holy Prophets. The Dog. The Spirit of Piety. The Foot. "So that your foot may be dipped in blood; your dogs' tongue have their share of your enemies" (Ps. 67:24).

In this oratory will be gathered priests and clerics who wish to live chastely and in common, but who do not wish to abstain completely from the eating of meat and warm clothing. In winter they will fast on Wednesday and Friday, and they will obey their Prior according to the direction and order of the Spiritual Father who will be over everyone. They will not use mantles, but only capes so that there may be a difference between their dress and that of the laity. They will study the art of grammar and teach the boys and young men to learn how to speak and write Latin and memorize the Old and New Testaments as far as they can. They will give a tithe of their labor and a tithe of the tithe they receive from the married into the hands of the Spiritual Father for the support of Christ's poor if they perhaps be in need of anything.[10]

They will receive tithes and offerings from the order of the laity, as much for their own use and that of the students who will be with them as for the support of the poor and strangers. They will not receive a sister in their oratory, but will enter the oratory of the laity on feast days and celebrate the liturgy with them. They should take care that no one ever dare spend the night within the confines of their enclosure. None of the priests or clerics should enter the house of any sister, sick or well, for a visit without approved and suitable witnesses. This should be done at the command of the Prior and according to the order of the Spiritual Father who will be in the Mother Church.

They will have a hospice outside the confines of their enclosure in which will be prepared beds and other things necessary for the use of guests both sick and well. It will have its own means of support according to its location and type of countryside, both with regard to livestock and to agriculture. It will have God-fearing servants who know how to show fitting honor to all so that God may be blessed in all things. If a rich person should wish to visit the oratories of the monks for the salvation of his soul, he should leave his horses there and proceed to them in a simple fashion. Strengthened by prayer, he may then return to his own.

Between these two oratories there ought to be a distance of about three *stadia*.[11]

VII. The Oratory of Saint Abraham the Patriarch and of All the Holy Patriarchs. The Sheep. The Spirit of Fear. The Body. "We are his people and the sheep of his pasture. Today if you would hear his voice, harden not your hearts" (Ps. 94:7–8).

Under the name of this oratory will be gathered the married with their sons and daughters living a common life. They will sleep with their wives for the sake of having children rather than for pleasure. At set times or days they will abstain from them by consent to be free to pray, taking into account the physical constitution and age of the young people lest they be tempted by Satan (1 Cor. 7:5). They will have their own dwelling places and will guard themselves from every accusation. They will have food and clothing in common, and will obey their Master according to the direction and order of the Spiritual Father to whom all these orders will be obedient like a new ark of Noah finished down to the cubit. They will fast in winter every Friday, except in the case of illness, and they will be clad with simple mantles only. No idle person will be found among these Christians, someone who will not earn his bread that he may have that from which to help those in need (Eph. 4:28). Let each one work at his own craft, and the individual trades and workers shall have their own foremen. Anyone who has not worked up to capacity should be called to account by the Master and censured by all. Food and clothing will be simple as befits Christians. Worldly garb will not be found among them nor dyed clothing. Honest and approved women will spin wool for the need of Christ's poor, and they will serve like mothers of the other women, instructing the young women and girls in the fear of God. They will give tithes to the clerics of all they possess for the support of the poor and strangers, and also for the boys who are studying doctrine. They do this so that in case they have more than they need and the rest have less, at the command of the Spiritual Father the surplus will be taken from those who have more and given to those who have less so that there may be no one in need among them but all things held in common.[12]

Part IV

THE FRANCISCAN SPIRITUALS

In the summer of 1317, while under house arrest and ban of excommunication at Avignon, a much-tried hermit who protested that the greatest trial of all was life at the Roman Curia sat down to pen a defense of himself and his followers to the implacable Pope John XXII. Angelo of Clareno's *Letter of Defense* brings us closer to the experience of the Franciscan zealots, or Spirituals as they are usually known, than any other contemporary document.[1] In at times gripping fashion, it recounts the story of the trials and tribulations of a group of Spirituals from the Province of the March of Ancona in east central Italy over the span of more than forty years. While it only touches on apocalyptic ideas in a few places (John XXII would scarcely have been placated by an apocalyptic manifesto!), the context within which the work is to be understood is based on Angelo's hopes for vindication of his form of life at the imminent end of the present evil age. A glance at his life and times will make this evident.

Angelo was born Peter of Fossombrone probably around 1250.[2] As a young man he entered the Franciscans at the convent of Cingoli, and first appeared in history in the late 1270s when, along with a number of the more influential

Franciscan radicals, he was cruelly imprisoned for his adherence to the standard of absolute poverty he found in the Rule and Testament of Saint Francis. The remainder of Angelo's long life spans the history of the encounter between the Spirituals and the established Conventual party.

It would be easy to simplify the struggle between the two parties within the Franciscan Order into an issue of black versus white, to see Angelo and his associates as either refractious fanatics or as spiritual idealists protesting against the corruption of their order and of the medieval Church. There is a bit of both sides in the Spiritual camp, and perhaps even in Angelo. In order to understand this dual character, we must first take a look at the relation between the Spiritual party and apocalypticism in the thirteenth century.

Angelo was heir to a tendency within the Franciscans that understood the unique role of Saint Francis, the meaning of his special devotion to poverty, and the historical significance of the order he founded in terms of a theology of history based largely on the thought of Joachim of Fiore. The Calabrian abbot had not only predicted a key role for coming orders of *viri spirituales* ("spiritual men") in the imminent crisis of history, but had also looked forward to a millennial state of the Church on earth under the aegis of the most perfect form of the religious life. While Joachim's vision was bounded by his own monastic outlook, the pseudo-Joachite writings that began to be produced in the early 1240s vindicated these prophecies for the new mendicant orders, especially the Franciscans.

Disputes about the role of poverty among the Franciscans began before the death of Francis himself. In the Testament he wrote shortly before his death in 1226, the founder had given express orders that no glosses or modifications of his own practice of poverty were to be allowed, but the first papal bull regulating the Franciscan way of life, "Quo elongati" of 1230, declared the Testament null and void and began the process of accommodating Francis's poverty to the demands of a large and growing international organization.

The Spiritual Franciscans of the late thirteenth and early fourteenth centuries, such as Angelo, looked back on a long history of struggle within the order over the issue of poverty, though it is not correct to speak of a full-fledged Spiritual movement much before 1280. Angelo's major work, the *History of the Seven Tribulations of the Franciscan Order* written in the early 1320s,[3] placed the earliest trial in the Poverello's struggle with the laxists of his own time. While his *History* gives a partial and at times misleading account of the development of the order, it does reflect an ambiguity present from the beginning. How could the Franciscans both be completely poor in the manner of Francis and yet of service to the Church in the myriad ways demanded of them? Was poverty or obedience the greater good? Other religious groups in the history of Western Christianity have had to deal with similar problems; the Franciscan case was the more extreme at least in part because of their greater success.

From about 1240 on those in favor of the most rigorous observance of poverty within the order began to make use of elements of Joachite apocalyptic to further their case. Many of the treatises ascribed to Joachim but written in the thirteenth century probably originated in Franciscan circles. A distinctive Franciscan Joachite apocalyptic was developed whose basic elements continued to influence Angelo and the later Spirituals.[4] From the broader Joachite tradition these Franciscans absorbed not only the expectation of the imminence of the end of the present age, but also belief in a current confrontation within the Church between the agents of good and the Antichrist and his followers. Like Joachim, too, the Franciscan Joachites looked forward to the defeat of the dread Last Enemy and the establishment of the contemplative Church of the perfect in the third *status* or seventh age of history about to dawn. More distinctive of the Franciscan version of this scenario were three themes: the identification of the Franciscans and the Dominicans with the two groups of *viri spirituales* prophesied by Joachim, the specification of poverty as the special sign of the spiritual men, and the belief that Saint Francis was the Angel of the Sixth Seal of Apocalypse 7:2, whose advent marked the beginning of the critical period of history immediately preceding the coming of the Antichrist.

151

These hopes were shared in the highest circles of the order, as evidenced by the Generalate of John of Parma (1247–1257), a convinced Joachite, proponent of strict poverty, and later hero of the Spiritual cause. Unfortunately, some of the less balanced Franciscan Joachites pushed these apocalyptic ideas to a radical conclusion that predicted the collapse of the present Church in 1260 and its replacement by a totally new Joachite world order. This "Scandal of the Eternal Gospel" (1254–1255) resulted in perpetual imprisonment for one radical and the withdrawal of John of Parma from the Generalate. His successor, the noted Paris theologian Bonaventure (1257–1274), was not loath to use apocalyptic ideas in his theology of history, but always in a guarded way.[5] Bonaventure made a valiant attempt to preserve poverty of life, ecclesiastical obedience, and universal charity within the order, but the events following his death proved the effort to have been in vain. In the late 1270s definite groups of rigorists whose defense of the absolute poverty enjoined in Francis's Testament was buttressed by their apocalyptic understanding of history soon came into conflict with the majority sentiment in the order.

Angelo's Letter tells the story of one group of these, that from the Province of the March of Ancona, during the years from about 1275 to 1317.[6] What may not be obvious from his account is that, alongside the group under Angelo and Fra Liberato who were allowed to leave the Franciscans by Pope Celestine V, there were others, such as those around the noted Conrad of Offida, who held similar ideals but were not tempted to separate from the order. The extent of Angelo's adherence to apocalyptic ideas may be muted in this text, but his reference at the end to a sevenfold scheme of the persecutions of the true followers of Francis reveals an apocalyptic understanding of the meaning of his trials that is spelled out more fully in the *History of the Seven Tribulations*. The longer work shows that Angelo believed that the sixth persecution of the *viri spirituales* begun under Boniface VIII and now reaching its culmination with John XXII would shortly be followed by the final persecution, that of the Antichrist, and then by the reign of peace on earth.

Angelo's other writings include translations from the Greek of monastic classics, notably *The Ladder of Paradise* of John Climacus. During his lengthy exile in the East, the Italian hermit took the opportunity, unusual for the time, to become fluent in that language. This fact has led to an intriguing guess on the part of Herbert Grundmann, one of the foremost scholars of medieval apocalypticism. Early in the fourteenth century a new form of apocalyptic text spread through Western Europe, the *Prophecies concerning the Supreme Pontiffs*, consisting of brief illustrated predictions of coming popes, frequently ascribed to Joachim of Fiore. Grundmann showed that these texts were based on twelfth-century Greek imperial prophecies, the *Leo Oracles*, and that they appeared to be historical (according to the typical apocalyptic device of *vaticinium ex eventu*) up to about 1304, because Celestine V appears as a holy monk and Boniface VIII as an evil hypocrite.[7] These two figures are followed by predictions of coming holy popes, the *pastores angelici*, crystallizations of the positive side of the apocalyptic hopes for the papacy that had been developing since the days of Joachim of Fiore.[8] Grundmann went further and supposed that the Papal Prophecies, as well as another contemporary document reflecting on the apocalyptic role of the papacy, the *Book of Fiore*, were written by one of Angelo's group during the long papal conclave of 1304–1305 as propaganda for their own ideas of what future popes should be like. It is impossible to prove the claim, given the present state of our knowledge, but the intimate involvement of Angelo's Poor Hermits with Celestine V, the archetype of the coming Angelic Popes, and their Greek contacts give it a certain plausibility. Angelo himself does not make use of the Angel Pope in his known writings. He and his followers later laid more emphasis on negative apocalyptic notions of the popes, as well they might given their experiences. Many of his followers came to see John XXII as the prophesied false teacher sitting in the Temple of the Church, the papal Antichrist who condemned Franciscan poverty and persecuted its adherents.

On December 30, 1317, in the Bull "Sancta Romana et Universalis Ecclesia," Pope John issued his definitive censure of

Angelo's Poor Hermits and related groups as a part of his program to crush the Spiritual movement. Angelo, more fortunate than those Spirituals of Provence who were imprisoned or executed, was allowed to enter the Celestine Order and remained at Avignon in the house of his protector, Cardinal Jacopo Colonna. After the cardinal's death in 1318 he returned to Italy, taking up residence at Subiaco. In defiance of the papal bull, he devoted the last two decades of his life to the organization and guidance of his followers throughout Italy. These and like groups, usually called Fraticelli, were to keep the heritage of the Spirituals alive for almost two centuries. The hostility of the Roman Inquisitors eventually forced Angelo to flee south where he died at S. Maria del Aspromonte in the Basilicata on July 15, 1337. Angelo's later writings show that he never adopted the intemperate language of his Fraticelli followers. The letter that he wrote to Philip of Majorca sometime after 1329 gives us some idea of his views in the final years of his life.[9] It shows that he believed that John's condemnation of Franciscan poverty had been heretical and that he feared a coming false pope, but Angelo continued to counsel patient endurance of all trials. What is clear from his activities in Italy is that the aged hermit had refused to obey papal authority on an issue he thought openly sinful. As he claimed earlier in the *Letter of Defense*: "I have never despised or broken obedience with any prelate, although in the case of open sins I have been obliged to be disobedient."

The depth of Angelo's spiritual vision grows out of an almost unbearable tension between his allegiance to the structures of the medieval Church and his belief that these structures were no longer responsive to God's action in history.[10] In the *Letter* we find a desperate last appeal, based on four decades of struggle and suffering, to an unresponsive hierarchy. In his own way, and within the confines of his own vision, he had eventually to confront the perennial problem of the relation between conscience and authority that has taken a larger and larger role in Christian history since the fourteenth century. It is impossible to read the *Letter* and think that he found the answer he was forced to adopt after 1318 an easy solution.

THE FRANCISCAN SPIRITUALS

The Spiritual movement was especially strong in two other areas in the late thirteenth century, in the Province of Tuscany and Umbria, and in Provence in southern France. In Tuscany and Umbria Ubertino of Casale (c. 1259–c. 1330) was the primary leader, though other noted figures, such as the poet Jacopone da Todi (c. 1230–1306), were also involved. Ubertino was a noted theologian and preacher whose support of Angelo's group resulted in his suspension in 1304 and retirement to La Verna where Francis had received the stigmata. During this retreat Ubertino wrote his famous *The Tree of the Crucified Life of Jesus,* succinctly described by Decima Douie as "a prose epic of the life and passion of Christ, to which has been added a commentary on the Apocalypse bearing the unmistakable traces of Joachite influence."[11] Despite its length and digressive character, this work is one of the masterpieces of Franciscan apocalyptic spirituality and was widely read, by Dante among others. Ubertino was more radical than Angelo— he denied the legitimacy of Celestine V's resignation and saw Boniface VIII and his successor Benedict XI as together forming the Mystical Antichrist. Like Angelo, he looked forward to a coming period of triumph for the Franciscan spiritual men.

Ubertino was directly involved in the drama of the condemnation of first the Spiritual and then the Conventual position on Franciscan poverty. As the chaplain to Cardinal Napoleon Orsini, the protector of the Poor Hermits, he was the chief advocate of the Spiritual case before Pope Clement V during the years 1309–1312, and was largely responsible for Clement's bull "Exivi de paradiso," the last attempt at a compromise between the two parties within the order. He was also present at Avignon from 1316 to 1318 when John XXII, in cooperation with the Conventual Minister General Michael of Cesena, crushed the Spiritual party. Like Angelo, he had won the personal favor of the pope and was thus allowed to enter the Benedictines rather than remain under the control of his Franciscan enemies. Ubertino stayed on at Avignon and took part in the debates of 1322–1323 leading to John's condemnation of the Conventual view that Christ and the apostles had owned nothing and that the poverty of Francis and the order was modeled on this.[12] Finally, he too broke with John XXII. Accused of heresy, he fled Avignon in 1325 and appears to have spent his last years as a fugitive in bitter attacks on the pope.

Angelo and Ubertino, and indeed the whole Spiritual movement, were deeply influenced by the more complex and mysterious figure of the Provençal Franciscan Peter John Olivi (c. 1248–1298).[13] Olivi did not live to see the fate of the Spirituals. He remained loyal to the hierarchy of the order during his life, and even more than Angelo preached and practiced obedience to the papacy; yet more than any other figure he was the intellectual and charismatic center of the whole Zealot cause.

Olivi studied theology at Paris where he heard and was influenced by Bonaventure. Most of his life was devoted to academic concerns; he taught theology at Florence (1287–1289), where he met Ubertino, and at various houses in his native Provence. Denounced for unsound theological and philosphical views, he was condemned by the order in 1283, but vindicated in 1287. It is clear that he remained under suspicion in many circles for the rest of his life. Most of the issues advanced against him were highly technical theological and philosophical questions, but a number involved his interpretations of Franciscan poverty. Olivi was no radical. He defended the legitimacy of earlier papal bulls abrogating Francis's Testament and defining the nature of Franciscan poverty, but he took a clear stand for the *usus pauper* "poor use", that is, the most stringent observance of the law of poverty in everyday life. In September 1295 he wrote to Conrad of Offida condemning those Franciscans who denied the legitimacy of Celestine's abdication or who attempted to separate from the order, thus distancing himself from Angelo and his group. What was truly dangerous about Olivi's thought was the apocalyptic theology of history he worked out during his lifetime. His final book, the *Lecture on the Apocalypse*, written in 1297, summarized his apocalyptic theories and was the most important statement of the underlying theory of history common to most of the Spiritual party. Olivi maintained a division of Church history into seven periods, seeing his own era as that of the overlapping of the Fifth Age of laxity and the Sixth Age, inaugurated by Saint

THE FRANCISCAN SPIRITUALS

Francis, of evangelical renewal. The conflict between the carnal Church and the spiritual Church comprised of the adherents of true poverty would culminate in the onslaught of a double Antichrist, the first, Mystical Antichrist, a false pope who would attack the Franciscan Rule, and the second, Great Antichrist, who would openly slaughter the faithful. After Christ's defeat of these foes a spiritualized Church under the direction of the Franciscan Order and coming holy popes would rule the world in the millennial Seventh Age before the end of history. Olivi believed that these events were imminent. Though he did not identify any living ecclesiastical figure, even Boniface VIII, with the Antichrist or his agents, it was almost impossible for the later Spirituals not to see in his view of the future a prophecy of the activities of John XXII in persecuting the Spirituals and condemning the Franciscan interpretation of the Rule of Francis.

Olivi was not only an intellectual master for the other Zealots, but was also their spiritual leader as well. The radical Franciscans tended to be hero-worshippers, always prone to create a pantheon of charismatic servants of absolute poverty. In this pantheon Olivi ranked second only to Francis himself. To Angelo in his *History* Olivi had been foretold by Joachim and many other prophets; to Ubertino meeting Olivi had been the turning point of his life; among his Provençal followers Olivi's grave became a place of pilgrimage and miracle until it was destroyed by ecclesiastical authority. The influence of the *Lecture on the Apocalypse*, translated into the vernacular and eagerly read by the laity, was not quashed even by its condemnation by John XXII in 1326. It is difficult to determine what the nature of Olivi's personal magnetism was from his surviving writings. Undoubtedly, his qualities as a preacher and spiritual guide must have been great. One of the few documents where we can catch a glimpse of Olivi the master of souls at work is in a letter that he wrote to the imprisoned sons of King Charles II of Naples in May of 1295. Though parts of this document may strike us as rather formal today, the theme that burns through it was as precious to Olivi as it was to Angelo and the other Spirituals—the necessity of suffering in

157

order to enter into glory. Ernst Benz summarized the theology of history implied here when he wrote: "The essence of all historical occurrence is the rebirth which comes to pass through death and suffering."[14] Olivi's apocalypticism enabled him to endure and give meaning to his own trials; his ability to convey this message to others was central to the influence he wielded in the Spiritual movement both before and after his death.

ANGELO OF CLARENO
A Letter of Defense to the Pope concerning the False Accusations and Calumnies Made by the Franciscans[1]

Most Reverend and Holy Father. Your Apostolic Holiness and the Sacred College of Cardinals should know that the sentence of apostasy, heresy, and excommunication against me and my companions contained in the letters of Pope Boniface of happy memory and of the well-remembered Peter, Patriarch of Constantinople, was unexpectedly read out to me for the first time in the presence of Your Holiness and the College of Cardinals.[2] This condemnation is now fixed in your mind and has become completely believable to the extent that you seem to think that wild beasts have devoured us and that we are apostates from religion and faith and excommunicates from the law and the Church. Because unchangeable truth overcomes all things, it should be clear to Your Holiness and the Sacred College of Your Brethren that in God's truth we without doubt have a very different view of ourselves. We know that we are not and never have been apostates, heretics, or excommunicates, unless perhaps it be a heresy worthy of excommunication humbly and without regard to the opinion of those who think otherwise to believe, confess, love, and work for what Saint Francis believed and confessed about the observance of his Rule.[3] He taught this while alive and loved it as he was dying. He worked for it and commanded it to be kept. I confess that I have always held that heresy and that I hold it now. I stand ready for your judgment and I am ready to receive it with obedience.

In sound mind and good conscience we declare that the other things directed against me and my companions at the request of the Franciscans and contained in these letters are all lies coming from evil hearts and bad consciences. What was reported to the pope about us was false and mendacious. There is not and never has been nor ever will be, to the best of my knowledge, in me or in any of my companions a single one of all the faults contained in those letters or the petition of the Franciscans. These papal letters were procured not only by hiding the truth, but also by making false statements, wicked calumnies, and evil defamations. We did not and do not claim to observe the Rule of the Franciscans, but we live as Poor Hermits, just as Pope Celestine granted and desired. We did not at that time build any permanent dwellings, but lived in the houses of others like pilgrims and poor men. We did not preach to either the people or the clergy. We did not nor do we hear confessions, either by authority granted us or in any other way. The only exception was when a bishop we obeyed ordered it.

I would never doubt the existence of papal authority, even if angels and apostles supported by miracles claimed otherwise. The same holds true for such declarations as that Boniface was not true pope,[4] or that authority had long since left the Church and resided in us until the Church could be reformed, or that we and those like us alone were true priests, or that priests ordained by papal and episcopal authority were not truly ordained, or that the Eastern Church is better than the Western. I have never been so light-headed, foolish, or stupid as to allow myself to hear such things from anyone. I have always defended and will defend the contrary by my words and even by eager acceptance of death, though the whole world turn to the other opinion.

I am sure and I always have been sure of the faith of the Roman Church. I have never doubted it. There is only one Roman Church and no other, and the Eastern Church is schismatic and void. The unique, full, and perfect authority has always existed only in the prelates of the Roman Church, both the just and the sinful. True orders and the true power of the keys that leads to eternal life is found only in those ordained by them. I believe and have believed that papal decrees and decretals are divine and holy and that the rules and holy ordinances of the bishops and doctors are just and necessary. I have never thought otherwise, nor have I supported anyone who thought otherwise.

The things they accuse us of are more bitter than death because they lead to stain and error of the Catholic faith and to denial of Christ either from consent or from silence. Hence, I request Your Holiness and the whole Sacred College to send me each and every one of the accusations in writing, together with the names of the witnesses, especially the things that touch my person and denounce me as a heretic. I offer myself ready to respond in defense by word or deed. If need be, I will undergo poison, fire, any legal procedure, ecclesiastical judgment, or trial to clear me and my companions from the charge of heresy that has been wrongly and falsely placed on us.

Your Apostolic Holiness and the College of Your Sacred Brethren should know that I do not perceive or recognize myself to be or to have been an apostate or excommunicate from the law or from the Church. I have never despised or broken obedience with any prelate, although in the case of open sins I have been obliged to be disobedient. Because of this I suffered savage and inhuman persecution, although I believed that according to God it was lawful and advisable for me to disobey. The devil's envy could not bear that we were unwilling to turn back to what was behind and to ease off into what was inferior, but were ardently seeking to reach out to what was ahead and to ascend to what was above.

Gratuitously and completely without cause the Franciscans condemned us to perpetual imprisonment as schismatics and heretics when both Fra Liberato and I were quite ready to be completely obedient and when the stain of no refusal or other crime had been found in us.[5] They deprived us in life and death of confession and all the Church sacraments, and also conversation with all the Friars, even with the one who brought us the necessities of life. Under threat of like punishment they commanded that no one presume or dare to say that what was done to us was either unjust or wrong. A certain brother named Thomas of Castromili grew angry when he heard the sentence that was read once a week to the Friars gathered in chapter in order to frighten those who had a similar intent. When he declared that what had been done was displeasing to God and was wrong, they held him in prison until death because of it. There is testimony of this in the whole province. They cannot deny it or hide the facts.

Brother Raymond, the Minister General,[6] inquired and asked all the Friars of the province gathered in a provincial chapter about our unjust punishment and sentence. By the testimony of the Provincial Minister and all the other Friars he discovered that they had thus punished us not because of any offense or sin, but only because we were seeking to preserve the Rule in its vigor and rigor according to the will of God and of the founder. For this they had condemned us to the punishment of godless heretics. Then the Minister General strongly rebuked them about it, and absolved all who had been condemned to such penance and punishment. He sent Brothers Thomas, Angelo of Tolentine, Mark, Liberato and me to the King of Armenia with a special authority and permission that he would not have granted to heretics or schismatics.[7] The King was edified by our actions and our life. In the letters he sent the Minister General through his special messengers he made clear to all at the General Chapter of Paris how much thanks he returned to the General for sending such brothers to him and how much praise he gave us.[8] These letters gave joy to the General and glory and favor to the whole order. The King, the Princes, the clergy and religious all rejoiced in our actions and were edified to such an extent that the King himself decided to give up the throne and to live and die with us in the service of God. The Friars of Syria raised such commotion and anger against us that the Minister, with the consent or rather under the compulsion of those Friars who could not bear to hear of our name or our life, sent defamatory letters to the King and all the barons on his behalf and that of the whole order. He warned them to take care to guard themselves and their kingdom vigilantly and warily against us because we were apostates separated from the order, men who had once been imprisoned as schismatics and heretics. The King then held council with his wise men about the Friars' letters and summoned us. He was satisifed when he heard what we had to say about their letters and loved us more than he had before. But the rage of the Friars was growing ever greater. Perceiving this, we said goodby to the King and returned to Italy.[9] In weakened state we crossed through our own province. We were not able to ask Fra Munaldo the Vicar of the Province for a place to stay as long as we had not yet seen the Minister General. The response we got from him was that he would first rather take in and harbor more fornicators in the province than the two of us.[10]

Because of such persistent displeasure on the part of the Friars and because of their disobedience toward the General, it pleased Brother Raymond the Minister General that we should go to the Supreme Pontiff Celestine of good memory to beg from him assistance for the salvation of our souls and those of our companions. At his command we went to Celestine while he was in L'Aquila and explained to him our situation, resolution, afflictions, desires, and vows. He investigated everything he heard before all present, and invited us to keep our rule and way of life in his own habit.[11] After he heard from us about the differences regarding the vow of poverty and everything that Saint Francis commanded in his Rule, his Testament, and other writings, as well as how the Franciscans hated the Testament of their father,[12] he accepted our resolution and vow in the presence of all. He commanded us to preserve the Rule and Testament according to the will and order of Saint Francis faithfully and sincerely all the days of our lives, but to do so without the name of Friars Minor. We were even to add to the Rule and Testament if we could. Before all present he freed us from every tie and obedience to the Franciscans, saying: "My will is that you obey me alone and Fra Liberato in my place. I grant him the power this one time to absolve all your companions and brethren from penalty and fault. I give him the power to receive all those who wish to do penance and to lead the life that you have vowed." He recommended us to the Reverend Lord Napoleon,[13] and desired, as he said to us, that Napoleon should cherish us and care for us as a willing and generous promoter of pious causes. He ordered that we should respond

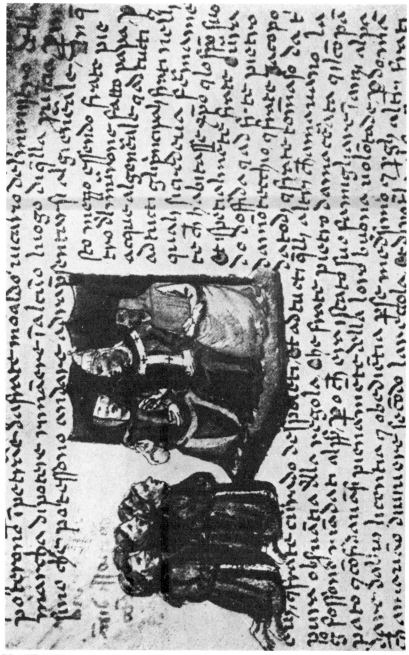

PLATE VIII:

POPE CELESTINE V APPROVES THE POOR HERMITS OF CELESTINE
Folio 57v of Cod. Vitt. Emm. 1167 of the Bibliotheca Nazionale of Rome. Reproduced
from A. Frugoni, *Celestiniana* (Instituto Storico Italiano per il Medio Evo. Studi
Storici, fasc. 6-7. Rome: Sede dell'Istituto, 1954), Plate V.

to those who asked us who we were with the answer: "We are poor men and brother hermits keeping the life and poverty we have promised in the desert and serving the Lord in the simplicity of faith." He recommended us in word and letter to the abbot of his own order. He wanted him to receive us and regard us as poor hermits, the same as his own brothers. He also desired that he provide us from his own hermitages with whatever was fit for such a life.

So up to the present day we do not perceive or acknowledge ourselves as apostates from any order. We believe that we really would be apostates before God and fugitives from the eremitical state if of our own will we were to abandon the way of life to which we have been called by the inspiration of God and the confirmation of the Supreme Pontiff. This would make us perjurers before Christ and worthy of damnation.

So we beg Your Holiness, after a legitimate dismissal of the charges made against us, to provide us with some way through which we can keep the vow we have given, a vow that was received and confirmed by the Supreme Pontiff. These reasons move us to believe and hold that the hearing of Your Holiness will show that we are not and never have been excommunicated. First, because we never defied any order given us by any official, and second, because no summons or legal action was ever sent us or given to us, or if sent, it was not delivered. Third, because for one year we waited and asked that what the pope had ordered should be done. Fourth, because we were unjustly cast out and the legal proceedings were held after our dispersal when it was impossible for them to be shown to us. (After the Patriarch's death, for many days we could scarcely come back to one spot and gather as a group.) Finally, because even if an excommunication done in that way had any effect, we have been absolved from it.[14]

If it is asked: "Why did you abandon those hermitages in that way?" the vehement persecution of the Franciscans is the answer. We could also cite the flight in the face of persecutors that Christ advised,[15] and the love of peace and quiet that is the end appointed before the final end of all the sons of God.[16] When the Franciscans heard that Celestine had freed us from their authority and order they straightaway came in arms to capture us, contemptuous of the fear of God and the dignity and command of the Supreme Pontiff. When Celestine renounced the papacy, Fra Liberato saw that for our safety and for the sake of peace with the Franciscans we should go to remote places where we could serve the Lord freely without the disturbance and scandal of men.[17] We crossed the sea and served the Lord on an island.[18] After two years news of us reached the Franciscans. As was their custom, they immediately tried to make trouble for us with the bishops and barons of that region.[19] In their false and evil suspicion they accused us of being Manichaeans, claiming that we did not eat meat and were not saying Mass. They said that we did not believe in the sacrament of the altar and that we had abandoned the Church, and many other similar things. Envy, that worst and most unjust of evils, taught them all this.

The princes, bishops, and clerics discovered that they said this about us out of envy and with great sin. Their wary agents came to the island unexpectedly and found that we did say Mass and made commemoration at Mass both for Pope Boniface and for the whole Church. We also said the canonical hours. Our rivals were quite disturbed. When the Franciscans saw that to purge the infamy placed on us the bishops and princes wanted us to sing Mass before the whole people, to eat meat with them, and to confess and preach before all the Catholic faith that we held they were not able to endure it. Upset and raging more bitterly against us than usual, they went to Pope Boniface. First they said how some apostates from the order had come to the province of Achaia and displayed a manner of life and a dispensation that came from Celestine. When they had spoken Boniface, as trustworthy men who were present have reported said: "Leave them alone; they act better than you do." Before this great man the Franciscans then advanced once more the lies against us already refuted. They said: "Holy Father, they are heretics and schismatics and they preach through the whole earth that you are not pope, that there is no authority in the Church, and similar things." These lies are clearly found in the Letters of Pope Boniface and of the Patriarch of Constantinople, as well as in the petition to You made by the Franciscan Minister General and the whole order. The great man was deceived by their falsehoods. Letters that I first heard read out in your presence were sent by Pope Boniface to three prelates of that province.[20] Rumor had reached our ears that very severe letters had been issued against us by the Supreme Pontiff. When we heard this, we all gathered together and decided that whatever they commanded, we would stand by the papal letters unto death and would obey them in everything. After the officials received the letters, we waited for one year, contrary to the will of the local lords who said they had the power from the bishops to expel us. We presented ourselves twice to the Bishop of Athens and more frequently to the Bishop of Patras.[21] He said that he would sooner allow himself to be deprived of his bishopric than to proceed against us, whose faith and innocence was certain, on the basis of letters obtained with such great lies. We asked the local lords to hold us prisoners somewhere and to write to the Supreme Pontiff about us, but we were not able to obtain either of these requests. Therefore we had to withdraw. Since we could not cross the sea, and since all human counsel and aid had been taken from us and the Franciscans were preparing traps on all sides to capture us, we entered the land of the Sevastocrator, which was quite near the island where we had served the Lord.[22]

The Patriarch of Constantinople returned from Venice when we had already scattered. The Franciscans immediately approached him in the person of a man as perverse as Torquatus in everything, named Brother Jerome, whom the Friars of the province had made their leader against us.[23] He came from the province of Catalonia, had left the Franciscans, and come into this area in clerical garb with several women, one of whom he said was his mother, another his sister. He carried books with him, which I afterward heard had been stolen or snatched. He lied that he had been sent to us by Brother Peter John of holy memory.[24] A few days afterwards, Henry, the parish priest, who had heard the womens' confessions, came to us with much sadness and said: "Brethren, beware of that man, because the one is not his mother and the other not his sister; the man is a liar and an imposter." When he saw that he was found out, he was not able to bear the reprimands and shame. He left us and entered the Franciscans, resolving to put all his own error on us in order to find favor with those who hated us. When he was discovered to be a liar, a perjurer, and a cad, he poured his poison of spite upon us. He entered as testimony against us eighteen erroneous articles he had thought up by himself or along with the women he had seduced, and which in his mad wandering from the faith he and a companion had written down. With violence he began to persecute and to defame for heresy the women he had known and had at one time cherished and commended as holy. They had disclosed his evil deeds and shown him to be an open liar, falsifier, perjurer, and ravisher. Later on the Franciscans, in the company of this vessel of iniquity and witness of falsehood, gained their aim from the Patriarch in the legal proceedings held against us when we were absent, expelled, and harassed.

Not being able to put up with Jerome and his mother, they sent him to the Tartars, cleverly hiding his evil works. The mother and daughter were thrown out of the area to remove the memory of such a great disgrace. He is the prime witness against us. He set wickedness in motion there and completed it here. Just as there he stole control of a province through false testimony, so here in the Roman Curia he received a bishopric as a fixed and evil witness to the spiritual death he gained through the deposition he gave the Inquisitors against us, though we were innocent.[25] The Patriarch, having completed what he thought was his task against us, died immediately.[26]

When he was dead, Franciscans, that is, the Vicar for the Orient and his eleven companions with their papal privileges, were sent from Rome to the infidels.[27] At the request of the Provincial Minister and all the Franciscans of the Roman Province they passed through our territory and stayed with us for six months. Brother Jacopo de Monte, the Vicar for the Orient, thought kindly of us when he heard from some Franciscans all the things that we had suffered. He was sad along with them, he cursed past mistakes, and the crimes of that evil man. He assured them about our faith and way of life. Although he believed that we were bound by no bond of excommunication, he came to us and absolved us conditionally by the authority of the papal privileges he possessed giving him power over all who lived outside the jurisdiction of the Roman Church in the lands of the infidels.

After they left us, we at once sent two brothers to Pope Boniface with letters from all of us, offering ourselves to his command and obedience. We also sent two others whom the Franciscans captured and detained so that they could not present themselves to the Pope.[28] Then Fra Liberato took a secret route and went to Perugia to see Pope Benedict of holy memory.[29] Soon after his arrival, the pope was taken from the misery of the present life and went to the Lord, and so Liberato was prevented from explaining in his presence his deeds and those of his companions.[30] When Pope Clement was elected,[31] he eagerly took the road to the Curia with Brother Paul as companion; but he took sick on the way and lay ill for two years. In the third year he was called to God and died.[32]

I labored for a full year before I was able to arrange the return of the brethren to Italy.[33] When all the brethren had already gone on ahead, I returned last of all. I found that Fra Liberato, along with all the companions he had in those parts, had been summoned by Fra Thomas of Aversa, the Inquisitor. He presented himself to him and was interrogated concerning the Catholic faith. He was detained for many days, but he and his companions were found to be most faithful Christians. Finally, Brother Thomas called him and all his companions together and said in the hearing of all: "Fra Liberato, Fra Liberato, I swear to you through him who created me that never had the flesh of one poor man been sold as dearly as I might have sold yours. The Franciscans would drink your blood if they could. Depart and hasten to the Pope with your companions because the tribulation that the Franciscans seek to bring upon you all is unbearable." On the same day Liberato left the Kingdom of Naples and went to the Curia, following the advice of the Inquisitor. But then he was called and went to another Court.

The same Inquisitor returned and seized all he could who wore the habit of a group not approved by the Church.[34] He seized many of our companions among them. They were led to Naples and kept prisoner for many months. Afterwards, he let go those born in the Kingdom of Naples. The Inquisitor immediately became ill and confessed with bitterness and sorrow that he had afflicted our companions unjustly at the incitement of the Franciscans.

When we had come to Perugia, I approached the Reverend Lord Napoleon and recalled our deeds to him.[35] He received me graciously and wished to take me with him, but I was stricken by sickness and was not able to follow. I remained in the Roman territory. The Franciscans defamed me and all my companions to the Curia with many false accusations. The Supreme Pontiff decided that we should be investigated on all those articles of which we are again accused. A careful investigation was made by Patriarch Isnard, then Vicar of the City,[36] the Bishop of Rieti,[37] Peter de Capocci,[38] the Penitentiaries of the Dominicans and Franciscans,[39] and four other Dominican Inquisitors. An inquiry was also made concerning the brethren living in other places in the Kingdom of Naples, and all were found to be faithful and Catholic Christians.

I came to the Curia in the year the Council of Vienne was celebrated.[40] Through Patriarch Isnard my business and that of my companions was presented to Pope Clement. He decided that we should serve the Lord in the state in which we were, but my heart was not put at rest by this. Although I have always hated to be at the Curia with my whole heart (more than any other pain I have thus far felt in the world), and although I would not dwell anywhere except as a poor little pauper, a stranger and not a member of the household, nevertheless, because of God's will, I put off my return to my companions in order to bring our business to a definite conclusion.[41] I know that it was God's will that I was unable to return, since he arranges all things for the best.

Now, in the security in which I have been held by Your Holiness, my heart has grown joyful and my soul has rejoiced in God more fully and more perfectly because it is guarded under the hand and command of the Pastor. The witness of the Spirit of Christ, which I think is in me, gives testimony to my spirit that I am not an apostate,[42] a heretic, or an excommunicate. I have never turned away from the life-giving love of Christ and from his sanctifying worship, and I have never wavered in the faith of the Holy Roman Church and have not spurned its sacred authority. On the contrary, I have preferred and honored it, and have always been prepared to die for the confession of its holy faith and authority. Despite all this, I do not seek what to believe by my own testimony, but as a suppliant I ask what the investigation of me and my companions looks like, and what is going to happen this second time. I also ask that whatever the Franciscans say can be fully proven against me should be given me in writing. Your Holiness and the Sacred College should make your judgment on the basis of what you find out through men who are not enemies and subverters of the court. The Franciscans have not only assailed my righteousness[43] and that of my companions, but also first of all that of Saint Bernard of Quintavalle, the earliest companion of Saint Francis, and then Fra Cesarius of Spira, who was struck with a club and died, and of all their companions. I have seen some of them and heard from them what they saw and suffered.[44] Second, they assailed the righteousness of that most holy man Simon of Assisi and Fra Simon of Comitissa and all their companions. They were hampered by fraud, were scattered by apostolic authority, and defamed as heretics throughout the order. Many of them became famous for miracles.[45] Third, they afflicted Brother John of Parma and his companions, who were stained with the reputation for heresy, the same Brother John whom Almighty God has made famous with apostolic miracles.[46] Fourth, they persecuted the holy man Peter John and all who followed and favored his way of life and teaching. They abused him during his life as someone who held errors about the faith, and they oppressed those who loved him both during his life and now after his death, although God has glorifed him with many miracles. They seek to destroy and slaughter them all like schismatics, heretics, and apostates in faith and morals.[47]

So it is no wonder that they boldly persecute and devour me and mine, simple and abject men. They indict us as bereft of all human aid, like heretics and excommunicates. They have learned to gain their desire with this sword and to complete their revenge to the damnation of their own souls and the abuse of God and his Church. The Supreme Pontiff and the Sacred College of the Roman Church has never known how to destroy men with judgment, but rather how to free the poor man who has no one to help him from the powerful man.[48] Thus, I beg Your Holiness to free me and my companions from the anger and fury of the Franciscans and to show us how and in what way we may be able to keep the vow that we made. Otherwise, God himself will judge and require our blood at your hands.[49]

PETER JOHN OLIVI
Letter to the Sons of Charles II[1]

Greetings in the special love of Christ Jesus to the Lords Louis, Robert, and Raymond Berengar, revered sons of the famed King of Sicily,[2] from the poor little man called Brother Peter John Olivi. In life I am a sinner, in dress a Franciscan who ever gazes on the great deeds of Christ's Cross and glories triumphantly in his Passion. You are distinguished beyond all others and particularly endowed in a marvelous manner because of your royal and Catholic ancestry.

When we look at the order of the universe, the sacred law that Christ solemnly promulgated presents itself in many and admirable ways—"Unless the grain of wheat falls dead upon the ground, it will remain alone; if it has died, it will bear much fruit."[3] This law is the foundation of the whole process of natural change and movement according to which the corruption of one thing is the generation of another.[4] By means of this law the potency of matter passes from the unformed to the formed state; even more remarkably, the very lack of form itself serves at the same time as the stable source and foundation of forms. In imperial fashion, every external act of God has its beginning from this law. The fundamental preamble of creation is that God make his work out of nothing and that works already created be subject to the rule of Almighty God in such a way[5] that they may be changed from one thing into another as he wishes and at his simple pleasure. This is why the root of all grace, both in the celestial and the terrestrial Church, stands in the center, that is, in humility. If I may so speak, it receives its foundation and its increase in the central nothing. From this divine law comes that hidden and ineffable mystery of our redemption by which the Only-Begotten Son of God the Father, equal to Him in all things, emptied himself and took the form of a servant, suffering the death of the cross for the just at the hands of the unjust.[6]

We confirm this law in many ways in our whole manner of living and dying. As John says, the seeds or fruit from whose eating we live are not life-giving unless they first die.[7] Unless these seeds are separated from their chaff and hulls through many kinds of threshing, cleansed by being passed through different sieves, pounded fine by millstones, presses, and threaded filters, and finally transformed through cooking and the heat of digestion, they cannot refresh our bodies with their flavor. After they have been swallowed, they do not become our flesh unless they have been despoiled of their own forms. The first stage in our own making is reception into a mother's womb as into a kind of prison burial, so that we can then go forth into the light as if rising from the tomb and being given liberty from the confines of a cell and dark penitentiary. Infants' limbs are bound with bonds and swaddling clothes so that they are not bent from the proper straightness by twisting. The ignorant and crude levity of youth, always prone to evil, needs educational discipline, as the apostle says: "As long as the heir is a youth, he does not differ from a slave, although he is the lord of all that his father has."[8]

By means of this wonderful law Christ's Church was conceived in the Synagogue's womb, burst out with bitter labor, and departed from it. Christ spoke to his disciples about this birth at the Last Supper: "A woman has sadness when she bears; when she has given birth, she no longer remembers the pains because of her joy at the offspring who is born."[9] According to this form and law the people of Israel went forth from the iron furnace and hard slavery of Egypt. They split the Red Sea by God's strong hand and crossed it dry-shod. So, too, the whole army of the elect ascend the path of bodily death, as through the midst of the Red Sea, hastening from the exile of this world and the devil's tyrannical power to the Kingdom of Heaven.

Thus, the meaning of Christ's word is clear—"It was necessary for Christ to suffer and so to enter into the glory of his kingdom."[10] The same is true for the apostle's saying that we have to enter the Kingdom of Heaven through many tribulations.[11] Listen to the Lord's brother James telling us: "Hold it all joy, my brothers, when you fall into various temptations, knowing that the proof of your faith creates patience, and patience possesses a perfect work."[12] He adds, "Brothers, take up the example of the patience of the prophets. We bless them who endured. You have heard of the endurance of Job and you have seen the purpose of the Lord."[13] For this reason in Hebrews Paul challenges us to the difficult and triumphant struggle:

> Since we have such a great crowd of witnesses over us, let us put aside every weight of earthly things through patience and hasten to the struggle before us, gazing upon Jesus, the author and finisher of our faith. Because he had joy set before him, he endured the cross, putting aside all shame. For this reason he sits at the right hand of God. Think upon him who bore such insult from sinners against himself so that you may not grow weary and lose heart. God punishes those whom he loves; he corrects every son he receives. God offers himself to us as to sons. Who is the son whom his father has not corrected?[14]

From this he then draws a consequence that is even more noteworthy: "But if you are without the discipline in which we all share (that is, all God's sons), you are illegitimate and not sons."[15] From this the *Gloss* concludes that anyone who does not suffer chastisement is not in the number of God's sons. The apostle says it again: "In the present all discipline seems to be a matter of grief rather than joy, but afterwards, to those who have been tried by it, it yields the most tranquil fruit of peace."[16]

So that no one should think this arrangement unreasonable, a triple law and the threefold teaching of the practical arts also repeat it. The law of justice proclaims it, for it is just that the sinner who is conceived in evil does not return to the fullness of grace without some paying of penalties. For this reason, one who is zealous for justice ought to wish that the rule of equity be fulfilled in himself, so that at least in this he might be a friend of justice and thus justified. The law of grace also proclaims it, not only because the source of redeeming grace was crucified for men, but also because the realization of the highest and dearest friendship is proven and manifested in undergoing tribulation and death for a friend. As Christ said: "Greater love than this no man has, than to lay down his life for his friends."[17] In approval and support of the supreme act of love we ought to long for and to prefer eagerly and joyfully every form of pain and death for the love of Christ who loved us so much and redeemed us so dearly. The law of the glorious victory and crown also proclaims it. The apostle testifies that no one will be crowned who has not fought the good fight.[18] Anyone who triumphs without a good fight has really lost. By giving us contests that are real and difficult battles, God provides a greater merit and crown for us. Then these words can be sung of us as well as of the martyrs:

> These are those whom the imprisoning world despised,
> They completely scorned its aridity and sterile flowering,
> O Christ, Good King of Heaven, they followed you!
> These were the ones who for you trod upon
> The furies, savageness, and cruel blows of men.

And further:

> What voice, what tongue is able to disclose
> The gifts you are preparing for the martyrs
> Shining with laurels amidst the blood's red flow?[19]

The art of medicine, purgative, preservative, or conservative, proclaims this too. Why do we use corrosive powders, burning cauteries, and bitter medicines on various illnesses, except that the art of purgation demands it? Why do the sick and even healthy people diet in various ways, if not to be preserved from illness and kept in good health? What wise man doubts that spiritual ills, the wounds of passion, the abscesses of bodily lusts, are less in need of the smart of medication and spiritual plasters? The art of warfare and of military pluck and skill proclaims this. You cannot be a real soldier without daily experience of difficult encounters and terrible dangers. You must endure blows and strokes in many ways. Ecclesiasticus says, "What does he know who is not tempted?"[20] as if to say, "nothing." No wonder, because Paul says of Christ in Hebrews that he learned obedience from the things that he suffered.[21] He gained an experimental knowledge of difficulty unto death through the experience of the Passion. This is the reason why the whole arrangement of an army in battle demonstrates no little wisdom and beauty—shadowy and carnal in the things of earth, divine and celestial in the things of heaven.

The art of building, the art of agriculture, and, in general, every mechanical action shows the same thing. Why are silver, gold, and other kinds of metal cast, hammered, and forged, except that one cannot make the artificial form of a container otherwise? Stonecutters hammer rocks this way and that so that a beautiful image can be carved and portrayed. Farmers make furrows with a plow, dig with hoe or mattock, pull out thorns, cut away brambles, and cut off and root out anything superfluous according to Christ's statement: "Every branch in me that bears no fruit will be taken away, and everyone that does bear fruit will be cleansed so that it can bear more."[22]

Come then, noble knights, gird yourselves for battle! The time of pruning has come and the voice of the turtledove sighing with a groan rather than a song is heard in the land.[23] It is necessary that at the full opening of the sixth seal the sun and the moon will be deeply darkened, the stars will fall from heaven, and there will be an earthquake so great that all the mountains and the islands will be moved from their places.[24] When the sixth angel blows the trumpet, the four angels that are bound in the great river will be freed so that a mounted force of twenty thousand times ten thousand horses and riders will go forth against the battle line of Christ our God.[25] The sixth vial is poured out by the sixth angel into the great river Euphrates so that its dried up waters can be a road for the kings coming from the rising of the sun, and the three unclean spirits can go forth to the kings of all the earth and gather them in battle on the great day of the Judgment of Almighty God.[26] Just as the fountains of the great abyss burst and the cataracts of heaven were opened in the six-hundredth year of Noah's life so that no one could be saved unless he was in the ark made at God's command, so must that whore Babylon be sunk in the depths of the sea. It will happen under the sixth head of the beast, the one carrying the prostitute, when the ten horns that are like kings will seize power for an hour. They hate the whore and will make her desolate. They will also battle the Lamb, but the Lamb, like the King of Kings and Lord of Lords, will conquer them, just as the ark overcame the flood and rested on the highest mountains.[27]

Then the dove that was sent out will bring back an olive branch in its beak, that is, it will preach evangelical peace to all. This will take place according to the passage in which as the sixth angel blows the trumpet, John receives and devours the book once closed but now open. The angel with a face like the sun holds the book and says to him: "You must prophesy again to many peoples, nations, tongues, and tribes." He is the angel of the sixth seal ascending from the rising of the sun, having the sign of the living God marked on him in order to sign the twelve tribes of Israel and to call together and sign with the sign of the cross a great and innumerable crowd from every nation and tongue and people so that with white stoles and palms of triumph they may stand before God's throne in the sight of the Lamb, serving him day and night. The Lamb who is in the midst of the throne will rule them and lead them to the fountains of the waters of life. He will wash away all lamentation and sickness from them.[28]

I have provided a foretaste of these things in succinct and typological fashion so that amidst the trials of this world your royal hearts may not be oppressed, but rather lifted up. It was certainly not from any lack of desire or of love that I have not yet come to see you nor written a letter of response to your very humble letters and petitions. There was a threefold cause. First, some might be displeased by the sudden rumor (coming not from me but from others) and try to substitute another person for the visit because it seemed to smack of some kind of future honor or promotion. As soon as I understood this, I decided to abandon the idea of visiting and to keep silence.

Although the world is not as worthless to me as it should and ought to be, nevertheless, I truly acknowledge that I do not enjoy the company of anyone save a person I perceive eagerly longs for the world's contempt and Christ's embrace now or in the future. I would consider it much more honorable and precious to me to visit you in your humble state and to serve you in a familiar way than to attend you when you are exalted in the glory of your Kingdom with formal ceremonies of any kind. In this latter kind of meeting, the glory of our little brotherhood[29] would be darkened and endangered, and an unedifying appearance of ambition and lust for gain would be shown to the whole world unless the meeting took place before a retinue of the most virtuous and noble bystanders. In the former case, humility, piety, and faithful gratitude would be evident at once, although there could be the possibility that I was deceiving you in hope of future gain.

The second reason is that in the Minister General's letter to me about this I was given permission on that occasion to visit you under certain conditions. Among these was that unless you expressly guaranteed that I would be able to see you freely without any impediment or prohibition, my journey would not be a service or a consolation on either side. I did not want to obtrude myself in an ambitious and presumptuous way by requesting this from you, so I decided to write nothing to you then, but to keep telling you and others that I was personally prepared to go whenever you would simply command it or recommend it. The third reason is that although I would never urge anything against anyone, especially the lords and princes of the earth, I was still afraid to reveal even trivial matters in writing. Things written in complete simplicity are frequently perversely interpreted.[30] A trustworthy man told me that even your father the King feared that you would be made beguines,[31] or, to speak more properly, that you would be made fools of in religious matter through my fine words. If he believed that it would happen according to the way the apostle describes when he says, "We are fools for Christ,"[32] or, "Whoever wishes to be wise in this world must become foolish in order to be wise,"[33] or "The foolishness of God is wiser than men,"[34] that is, than the human wisdom of the world, then I do not have the wisdom and power to fill you with this supremely wise foolishness. If he spoke about the opposite kind of foolishness, far be it from me to want to pour back my foolishness or that of others into you or anyone through silly talk or advice. If I have received any real gift from God, I know that this is the most important: to be faithful to the truth of his faith and to the sound advice of our neighbor. And so I almost always choose and have chosen to condemn my own miserable life in public and private so that the radiance of the life of Christ is not obscured by the darkness of mine. Despite all this, if it is your pleasure to have me come to you, please have the Lord of the territory remove the obstacles, command me through a messenger, and I am ready to agree without delay.

May Jesus Christ, the Son of God, strengthen and confirm your hearts through the overflowing excess of his consolations, which are taught by the Spirit's anointing and the joyful shout of psalmody, the key of David that unlocks the secrets of the house of God. We enter this house through the asceticism of prayer and tribulation, just as David himself entered through the many attacks that Saul and others inflicted on him, as he makes known so beautifully in all his psalms. Recall how he advanced to the Kingdom under God's tutelage through hardships and persecutions of many types so that he learned the art of ruling before he taught it. Joseph, too, gained the prudence of a ruler through being sold and cast into prison. By means of this prudence he later was the ruler and savior of Egypt, his brothers, and the whole house and family of his father. Jonah did not preach saving penance to the Ninevites until he had been sunk in the sea, swallowed by the whale, imprisoned in its belly, and wonderfully delivered by being vomited forth. I do not doubt that the time will come when you will say in praise of God: "The Lord slays and gives life, He leads down to hell and back again; He injures and restores."[35] He strikes, but his hands will heal. He frees us from six tribulations, and in the seventh surpassing peace will come after every evil has been removed.[36]

I humbly ask you to greet Brother Peter, your companion

and by your leave your lector.[37] If you deign to order or provide anything for my arrival, please command me at once, because if I do not come to you, I perhaps will have to hurry somewhere else.

May the surpassing sweet memory of the Most Delightful Jesus and the redolent fragrance of his name make your souls drunk with his unspeakable joy and peace that surpasses all understanding.[38] Given at Narbonne on May 18, 1295.

PLATE IX:

THE PREACHING OF THE ANTICHRIST
Antichrist stands on a pedestal with the devil whispering in his ear. Behind to the
right are clerical supporters centered on a prominent Dominican. From the fresco in
the San Brixio Chapel in the Orvieto Cathedral. Reproduced from *Gli Affreschi del
Signorelli ad Orvieto* (Milan and Geneva: Fabbri and Skira, 1965), p. 15.

Part V
SAVONAROLA

On the walls of the San Brizio chapel in the cathedral of Orvieto stands the most powerful portrayal of the career of the Antichrist in the history of Christian art. Painted by Luca Signorelli about 1500, the story of man's Last Enemy unfolds in epic proportion and fascinating detail. Several incidents in the large fresco are puzzling, notably the prominence of a group of Dominicans among the religious being seduced by Antichrist's preaching and miracles. Why this emphasis on the Preaching Friars? Indeed, why so monumental a treatment of the Antichrist at all since the subject was not a usual one in Christian art? A plausible answer has been given by André Chastel, who suggests that Signorelli was giving visual form to the views of those, like the eminent humanist Marsilio Ficino, who saw in the recently executed Dominican Friar Girolamo Savonarola the immediate forerunner of the Antichrist.[1] Signorelli's fresco then was in part a polemical attack on the most famous apocalyptic preacher of the end of the Middle Ages.

Like Joachim of Fiore and many other apocalyptic thinkers, Savonarola was a sign of contradiction both during life and after death. The attacks of Ficino and Signorelli can be contrasted with the extravagant praise of Giovanni Nesi whose *Oracle of the New World* of 1497 saw the Dominican as a messianic initiator of the mellennial age of history. Savonarola's sense of his own mission was also an exalted one, though expressed more modestly in terms of the roles of preacher and prophet, the first a traditional one for any Dominican, the second less usual, but one he defended on the basis of the theology of the great Dominican Thomas Aquinas.

The drama of Savonarola's life and death needs no emphasis here. In order to understand the significance of his ideas, the source of his appeal, and the reason for the intense opposition he aroused, one must glance at the role of apocalyptic thought in the later Middle Ages, because while apocalyptic spirituality during the period 1300 to 1500 shared a common dialectic of hope and fear with expectations of the end found in any age, it also possessed its own character, both from the content of its special hopes and fears and from the manner of their application to current events. There is no room here to follow the rich variation in the use of apocalyptic themes during these two hundred years,[2] but some broad generalizations will help to understand the kind of apocalyptic prophet that Savonarola became.

The fears for the future that loomed over the people of the later Middle Ages were not totally different in kind from those of previous ages. They may have differed in degree, though this seeming intensity could be the result more of the relative abundance of our sources than of any statistical increase in terror. As in other times, pressure from external foes, particularly the continuing success of the Turks, was a factor in expectations of an imminent crisis of history. There were, of course, variations in the details of the coming crisis resulting from expansions of the traditional apocalyptic scenario,[3] but perhaps the most distinctive characteristic of the pessimistic pole of late medieval apocalyptic thought was its obsession with the state of the Church. Corruption in head and members of Christ's Mystical Body was the most evident sign that evil was mounting to a point of culmination. Key stages in the history of the recent papacy, such as the Avignon Captivity (1309–1377), the Great Schism (1378–1418), and the worldly Renaissance papacy, all fed an intense sense of gloom for the future.

The hopes that balanced these pressing fears were even more distinctive and original. Not only were they also largely ecclesial in setting—a desire for the renewal, reform, and renovation of the Church—but they were also usually intraworldly and millenarian, centered on the triumph of the Church Militant in this world after the defeat of the Antichrist and the forces of evil. Joachim of Fiore had had an unmistakable impact on the history of Western apocalypticism. Without reducing the history of late medieval thought about the end of history to the story of Joachim's influence, the abbot of Fiore's myth of the coming third *status* of the Holy Spirit was the catalyst responsible for the new optimism of the later Middle Ages.

This optimistic side took different forms of expression. Although the work of reforming the Church could be done only by God, in the later medieval apocalyptic scenario it was commonly thought that he would make use of three special agents. Two of these originated with Joachim; the other antedated the abbot but was soon absorbed into Joachite apocalyptic by his followers. We have already noted the early history of the figure of the Last World Emperor and remarked on his absence in Joachim; but it has been shown that by the middle of the thirteenth century the Joachite script also began to call for a good Last Emperor who would chastise the Church in order to reform it.[4] This final ruler's destiny included universal dominion, the conquest and conversion of the enemies of Christianity, the recapture of Jerusalem, and the establishment of an era of peace.

After 1300 the ally and superior partner of the Last Emperor was frequently seen as a coming holy pope, the *Pastor Angelicus*. The creation of an important role for the papacy both at the time of the attack of the Antichrist and in the coming *status* of the Holy Spirit had been Joachim's work. The development of the distinct hope in a future Angel Pope or Popes during the thirteenth and fourteenth centuries was the result of a dialectical tension between negative judgments of current unreformed popes and intense but frustrated commitment to the institution of the papacy. These hopes seem to have reached their apogee in the fifteenth century.[5]

The third key role in the hopes for the renewal of the Church on earth was that of a group or groups of spiritual men (*viri spirituales*) who would suffer persecution under the Antichrist but be vindicated in the renewed Church. Joachim viewed them as two monastic orders; later thinkers frequently identified them with the two major mendicant orders. The most crucial question regarding the *viri spirituales* concerned their relationship to the coming millennial age. Where a particular religious order, such as the Franciscans, or a new spiritual movement, such as the Apostolic Brethren of late thirteenth-century northern Italy, came to be seen as the present historical realization of the coming more perfect state of the Church, conflict with ecclesiastical hierarchy became inevitable.[6]

The late fifteenth century was rife with apocalyptic speculations, most notably in Germany and Italy. The prevalence of such ideas in Renaissance Italy should come as no surprise—the optimistic side of late medieval apocalypticism could blend quite well with Humanist hopes for a returning Golden Age,[7] and the darker side of the Renaissance world with its concern for magic, astrology, and demonic forces could thrill with delicious terror at rumors of the Antichrist. In these years Italy was a prey to uncertainty. The delicate balance among her five chief powers—Milan, Venice, Florence, Rome, and Naples—led to frequent political crises. Great wealth and a remarkable cultural flowering not only had produced a sense of moral crisis in the minds of many, but also had attracted the rapacious interest of the powers beyond the Alps. The peninsula was about to enter a troubled century when she would become the battleground for the ambitions of other lands. It is no wonder that wandering preachers of gloom filled the land in the late fifteenth and early sixteenth centuries.[8] Girolamo Savonarola began his prophetic career as one of these.

Savonarola was born at Ferrara in 1452 and entered the Dominicans at the age of twenty-three. He was at San Marco in Florence between 1482 and 1486 before being sent on a preaching mission in northern Italy. Recalled to the city in 1490 at the request of Lorenzo de'Medici, his preaching grew in popularity and influence during the next four years. The content of the friar's sermons during this time was largely one of apocalyptic pessimism. Based on visionary experiences that seem to go back as far as 1484, his message was simple: The Church and Italy must be scourged severely and soon before they could be reformed.[9] Events were to bear out this message of doom and to give what seemed to be miraculous confirmation to the prophecies.

The young and foolish Charles VIII of France (1483–1498) was in the midst of planning a major expedition to Italy to vindicate French claims to the Kingdom of Naples. Charles's crowning in his fourteenth year matched the initial details of the most famous of late medieval imperial prophecies, the "Second Charlemagne Prophecy," which had it that:

> Charles, the son of Charles, from the most illustrious nation of the lily will have a lofty forehead, high eyebrows, wide eyes and an aquiline nose. He will be crowned at about thirteen years of age, and in his fourteenth year he will gather a great army and destroy all the tyrants of his kingdom.... He will make war until his twenty-fourth year.... He will destroy and burn with fire both Rome and Florence. He will gain the double crown.[10]

Originally created for Charles VI in 1380, a revised vernacular version of this oracle was issued in 1494 by a Guilloche of Bordeaux.[11] A number of other prophetic texts appeared at the same time in both France and Italy.

In the fall of 1494 the powerful French army drew near Florence. Fear of siege and sack reduced the population to despair. Piero de'Medici, the ruler since his father's death in 1492, fled in terror to Charles and made concessions suicidal to the safety of the city. At this juncture Savonarola and several others were sent by the Signoria, the council of the chief men of the city, to treat with the French king. While they were absent the city rose against the Medici. Charles entered Florence on November 19 in an atmosphere of hope and fear. Despite some tense moments during his brief stay, there was no sack; instead, a treaty was signed and Florence's great peril was averted. Savonarola's key role in the almost miraculous events that saved the city—first the bloodless revolution against the Medici, and then the leniency of the "Last-Emperor-Elect"—cannot be denied, nor can his importance as a force in the creation of the new republican form of government in the following months. Though the picture he paints of his own role is doubtless exaggerated, his was certainly the single most influential voice in Florence. But if the prophet led the city, the city in turn decisively changed the prophet. Donald Weinstein in his penetrating study *Savonarola and Florence. Prophecy and Patriotism in the Renaissance* (Princeton: Princeton University Press, 1970) has shown how during this time strongly optimistic millenarian hopes centered on Florence as the harbinger of the renovated Church came to dominate the friar's preaching and writing.[12] The Kingdom of God on earth was about to begin on the banks of the Arno.

This dramatic new stage in Savonarola's preaching found its fullest expression in the text entitled *The Compendium of Revelations*. The friar began it in the spring of 1495 as a defense of his prophetic message against his Florentine enemies. Soon more pressing reasons for such a defense became evident. The army of Charles VIII, after considerable initial success, suffered a series of reverses and began an inglorious retreat from Italy during the middle of the year. Pope Alexander VI, one of the least savory occupants of the Chair of Peter in any age but a leading member of the league of Italian states that had banded together to oppose the French invasion, summoned the friar in late July to come to Rome to explain his prophecies. Pleading ill health and his duties at Florence, Savonarola said he could not come, but promised to send his forthcoming *Compendium* instead. On its publication in August, the work was a nine-days' sensation—five Italian editions and three in Latin were published during the course of a year.

Not quite three years remained in the stormy career of Fra Girolamo, years marked by continued proclamation of his message on the one hand and increasing opposition from two quarters on the other. Savonarola's attacks on corruption in the Church gradually came to focus more and more on Rome and the Roman Curia—his observations of evils here scarcely demanded prophetic insight. It is not surprising that the final years of his life were dominated by his increasingly bitter relations with Alexander VI. But within Florence itself opposition also grew, fueled by the political, financial, and economic difficulties of the new republic on which the Dominican had staked so much. Suspended from preaching by Alexander in September of 1495, Savonarola was obedient until the following spring. After intricate legal maneuvering, he was finally excommunicated on May 13, 1497. Further fruitless negotiations with the pope followed, and in 1498 the friar took the radical step of preparing letters asking the secular powers to summon a General Council to depose the unworthy pope, elect a suitable candidate, and undertake the work of reform.

Threatened by papal interdict for their harboring of the excommunicate prophet and given ammunition by the increasing troubles that Florence had endured under the new government, Savonarola's enemies tightened the net around him. Hatred of the friar came to a head in the spring of 1498. A foolish proposal of an ordeal by fire between a Dominican adherent of the prophet and a Franciscan opponent was a fiasco, and despite the ardent group of *Piagnoni* (the hard-core supporters of the Dominican) that were still in the city, the vindictive Signoria arrested Savonarola and with papal approbation had him put to the torture. Under repeated torments he broke down and at first confessed that his prophecies had been self-serving lies. Soon, however, he regained his composure, renounced the confession extracted under duress, and continued to maintain his innocence until his execution as a heretic and schismatic on May 23, 1498. His death can scarcely have been an unexpected one. In 1496, in response to an offer of a red hat made through the procurator of the Dominicans, he had thundered: "I want no hats, no mitres great or small. I only want the one You, O Lord, gave to your saints, death. A red hat, a hat of blood, that is what I want."[13]

Modern historians have not always found it easy to appreciate *The Compendium of Revelations*,[14] but this combination of apology and vision gives us much insight into late medieval spirituality. The text falls into two unequal parts, an account of Savonarola's early revelations up to 1495 and the sermon that he gave for the Octave of the Annunciation on April 1 of that year. Weinstein has shown how the prophet interpreted his early career to fit the delicate situation in mid-1495, though this was done with no intent to deceive. Despite the polemical context, the apology provides an immediate and convincing portrayal of the prophetic consciousness of its author. The lengthy sermon, a highly allegorical account of a journey to heaven, is more difficult for the modern reader to appreciate. Almost one half of this sermon is taken up with a debate with the devil, a section that forms a theological defense of the prophetic role of the friar parallel to the personal apology at the beginning. Savonarola makes use of his solid knowledge of Thomistic theology, especially the treatment of prophecy in the IIaIIae of the *Summa*, to rebute a series of attacks that doubtless reflect those that had already been made and would continue to be made against him.

The description of the heavenly court—the ranks of saints, choirs of angels, and the presentation of the ornate crown representing the prayers of Florence to the Virgin—must be visually imagined in order to be appreciated. Works of art frequently helped shape the religious imagination of the late Middle Ages.[15] Savonarola is painting a tableau, similar to a large Quattrocento altarpiece, centered on the Madonna surrounded by carefully orchestrated registers of saintly and angelic intercessors. In a similar fashion, the involved allegory of the gems and colors of the crown was meant to appeal to the visual imagination of the hearers, many of whom would also have been acquainted with the ancient traditions of the allegory of colors and precious stones on which the descriptions are based. The friar was calling on a battery of resources designed to move his audience as much through visual as through verbal means, and we have to try to picture the heavenly vision if we would try to understand the popularity of this sermon.

The apocalyptic content of the *Compendium*, especially when compared to other key texts such as the *Sermons on Haggai* preached during the Advent of 1494, shows how much the broad lines of the Dominican's predictions fit the general scenario previously described. Savonarola held a seven-age theory of history that he found revealed in the Apocalypse. He saw his own time as the end of the fourth age, that of indifference, soon to be followed by the fifth age of the persecution of the Antichrist, whose defeat would usher in the sixth age of renovation when the pagans would be converted and there would be one flock and one shepherd.[16] While the Dominican was not primarily an apocalytic theorist as such, but rather essentially a preacher of reform, he gives much attention to the three key *dramatis personae* of the forces of good of late medieval apocalyptic beliefs. The coming Cyrus who would scourge the Church seems to have been a part of his preaching even before the rumors concerning the invasion of Charles VIII. The *Compendium* gives a full account of his moderate conception of the imperial role in the coming renewal. It also stresses the importance of future holy prelates (in one place spoken of as "angelic"). Other texts, such as the *Italian Sermons to the Florentines* and a letter written during 1495, show that he also believed that "in this renovation of the Church, which is a supernatural thing, there will be a holy and good Pope."[17] As the Dominican Friar came into more direct conflict with the papacy, undoubtedly the dialectic of Angel Pope and Papal Antichrist exercised a greater influence on his thoughts. It was to end in his explicit break with Alexander VI and his appeal to a General Council.

At first glance, it might seem that there is no place in Savonarola's thought for the *viri spirituales*, and it is true that they do not appear, at least in the traditional form. But it may be regarded as Savonarola's most dramatic innovation to have replaced the customary notion of a religious order as the carrier of ultimate apocalyptic significance with the *populus Fiorentinus*, the entire population of the city of Florence, purified of vice and conceived of as the vanguard and model of the millennium to come. It is true that Joachim of Fiore had envisaged a monastic utopia composed of oratories for all the classes of Christian society for his third *status*, but this was but a distant preparation for Savonarola's bold transformation of Florentine civic patriotism into a new kind of apocalyptic vision. In this, as in much else, the friar takes his place as one of the most notable apocalyptic prophets of the Christian tradition.

GIROLAMO SAVONAROLA
The Compendium of Revelations[1]

For a long time by divine inspiration I have predicted many future events in various ways. But because I remember that Our Savior Jesus Christ said, "Do not give what is holy to dogs or cast pearls before swine, lest they trample them underfoot and the dogs turn and tear you,"[2] I have always been sparing in speech and not gone further than what seemed necessary to men's salvation. Therefore, my proposals were limited, although the exhortations, persuasions, and proofs I made were many. I never disclosed the manner and great number of the visions and many other revelations I had, because the Holy Spirit did not inspire me to, nor did I think it necessary for salvation. I did not think that men's minds were ready to accept them. Now necessity compels me to write down the coming events I publicly preached about, especially those that are more important and of greater weight. Many who tried to write these things down as I spoke from the pulpit have not expressed the full truth, but given one butchered and much mixed with error since the pen cannot keep up with the swiftness of the tongue. Some people, either through lack of understanding or wrong interpretation and malice, have spread my words among the crowd with additions, subtractions, and many distortions.

Therefore I will try to gather whatever I have publicly preached up till now about the future into a brief *Compendium*, leaving out the special manner in which each of the revelations was made and the scriptural proofs I used when I preached.

I do intend to introduce a full account of the vision I preached on the Octave of the Annunciation of the Blessed Virgin Mary because many took it down imperfectly and corruptly and sent it to various parts of Italy.[3] I must write, because I cannot and will not for God's honor allow his mysteries to be derided or profaned, particularly by those who say

192

that our predictions, collected faultily and with many errors by some, should be spread abroad by the printers. I have taken care to publish these prophecies in both Latin and the vernacular so that they cannot be corrupted or distorted in any way and that they may be equally available to everyone.[4] I beg all whom this *Compendium* reaches that if they have ever heard that I said something that was different from what is contained here, they should not believe it in any way. Our lukewarm friends,[5] that is, those wise in the ways of this world, have fabricated many things against me inside the city of Florence and more outside it. I know that there will be those who will interpret these writings in various ways, as Daniel puts it: "Many will pass by, and knowledge (that is, opinion) will be varied."[6] Many will mock these ideas. Nevertheless, I hope that devout readers and the simple of heart will gain much from reading this under the illumination of Truth Itself. It is written: "His conversation is with the simple";[7] and again: "You have hidden these things from the wise and prudent and have revealed them to the little ones."[8]

Before I begin what I have to say, the character of prophetic revelation must be clarified in order to understand these matters. Each one can then understand how God teaches prophets the things they preach to the people. Because it is written in the ninth chapter of the First Book of Kings, "One who today is called a prophet was at one time called a seer,"[9] he is properly said to be a prophet who sees things that are beyond the natural knowledge of every creature, even though by means of the light of prophecy he also sees many other things that are not beyond human knowledge.[10] Since that light can attain divine things, it reaches human matters even more easily. Future contingent acts, especially those that depend on free choice, are far beyond the natural knowledge of any creature; neither man nor any other creature can know them in themselves. They are present to eternity alone because it embraces the whole of time. The rational or intellectual creature cannot know them in their causes, because the causes are balanced between producing or not producing contingent effects of this kind and the created intellect cannot discern which side they will come down on. Therefore, all arts of divining, of which "judicial" astronomy is the chief, have been condemned by the divine scriptures and the ecclesiastical canons.[11] Knowledge of future contingents is proper to divine wisdom before which everything that is past, present, and future stands open at the same moment, as it is written, "All things are naked and open to his eyes."[12] Future contingents cannot be known by any natural light; God alone knows them in his eternal light. Those to whom he deigns to reveal them receive them from him alone.

He does two things in a revelation of this kind. First, he infuses a supernatural light into the prophet, a form of participation in his eternity. From this source the prophet discerns two things in the revelations—that they are true and that they come from God. This light is so effective that it makes the prophet as certain of these two things as the natural light of reason makes philosophers certain of the truth of the first principles and makes any man certain that two and two make four. Second, God sets before the prophet in a clear way whatever he intends him to know or to predict, and he does this variously, as is written in Osee: "I have spoken over the prophets and have multiplied the vision, and I have been revealed in the hand of the prophets."[13] Sometimes he inspires what he is to predict in the prophet's intellect without any images, the way he gave wisdom to Solomon and the way David prophesied; other times he imprints in the imagination different figures and images that signify what the prophet is to understand and predict. From the power of this same light the prophet himself clearly understands the meaning of these visions, otherwise he would not be able to say, as is written in Daniel, "There is need of understanding in a vision."[14] In such visions he frequently perceives various words pronounced internally by different persons within his mind. He knows that God forms these words from the same light through the ministry of the angels. Sometimes God sets forth things to the exterior senses that signify what is to be revealed. This is especially true of the eyes, as in the fifth chapter of Daniel we read about the hand that wrote on the wall before the eyes of

King Belshazzar, "Mane, Thecel, Phares", which Daniel saw with his bodily eyes and interpreted by means of an internal light.[15] Note that God makes these external apparitions and images through the ministry of the angels, as Saint Denis says in his book *The Celestial Hierarchy*.[16] Whatever comes from God proceeds in an orderly way, as the apostle says: "The things that are of God are ordered."[17] The order of divine wisdom is to arrange the lowest things through those in the middle and those in the middle through the highest. Since the angels are in the middle between God and men, prophetic illuminations from God are presented through the angelic spirits who not only internally illumine and move the imagination to various apparitions but also speak to the prophets from within. Very frequently they even show themselves to the prophets externally in human form, predicting future events and teaching them the many things they must do. Through the light mentioned above the prophets clearly know that these are apparitions of angels and that the things the angels speak are true and come from divine wisdom. In these three ways, sometimes one and sometimes the other, I have grasped and known future events. In whichever way these matters came to me I have always grasped them as completely true and certain through that light's illumination.

As Almighty God saw the sins of Italy multiply, especially in her ecclesiastical and secular princes, he was unable to bear it any longer and decided to cleanse his Church with a great scourge. And since, as the prophet Amos says, "The Lord God will not work his word without revealing his secret to his servants the prophets,"[18] he willed that the scourge upon Italy should be foretold for the sake of the salvation of the elect, so that thus forewarned they could prepare themselves to bear it with greater firmness. Since Florence is located in the middle of Italy, like the heart in a man, God himself deigned to choose her to receive this proclamation so that from her it might be widely spread through the other parts of Italy, as we have seen fulfilled in the present.[19] Among his other servants he chose me, unworthy and unprofitable as I am, for this task, and saw to it that I came to Florence in 1489 at the command of my superiors. That year, on Sunday, August first, I began to interpret the book of the Apocalypse in public in our Church of San Marco.[20] Through the whole of the same year I preached to the people of Florence and continually stressed three things: first, the renovation of the Church would come in these times; second, God would send a great scourge over all Italy before that renovation; and third, these two things would happen soon. I worked at proving and establishing these three conclusions by firm arguments, by figures from the Holy Scriptures, and by other likenesses or parables formed from the things that are now happening in the Church.[21]

I urged the case at that time only with these arguments and kept secret the fact that I had also received knowledge of them from God in another way, because it seemed that the state of souls was not then ready to receive that mystery. In the following years, finding minds more ready to believe, I sometimes introduced a vision, not disclosing that it was a prophetic vision but setting it forth to the people only in the manner of a parable. Indeed, I suffered great opposition and every form of mockery on the part of all kinds of people. In my discouragement I had firmly and frequently decided to stop and to preach something else. But I was not able to. Any reading or study I began faded and brought on disgust, and whenever I thought of other things or tried to preach them, they became so empty to me that I was displeased with myself. I remember in 1490 when I was preaching at Florence in Santa Reparata. I decided to supress a sermon on these visions that I had already composed for the Second Sunday of Lent. I had determined that I would abstain from them thereafter. As God is my witness, I dragged through the whole preceding Saturday and the entire following night until dawn without sleep. Every possibility was closed to me and every message except this one unavailable, so that I literally did not know where to turn. Finally at daybreak, worn out by the long watch and in the midst of prayer, I heard a voice that said to me: "Fool! Do you not see that God wants you to announce these things in this way?" And so the same morning I gave a terrifying sermon.

My faithful listeners know how fittingly my expositions of

the scriptures always agreed with the present times. One that especially caused admiration in men of great intelligence and learning was that from 1491 to 1494 every Advent and Lent (with the exception of one spent at Bologna) I undertook continuous sermons on Genesis, always beginning from the last point of the reading of the previous Advent or Lent. I was not able to reach the chapter on the flood until after the tribulations began. I thought that I would be able to expound the mystery of the building of Noah's ark in a few days, but so many and such important things about its making struck me every day that I spent the whole Advent and Lent of 1494 on its mystery and construction. With God's will and prompting, I left off where it says "Make it with second and third stories."[22] In the following September, on the Feast of Saint Matthew the Apostle, I began from the following text, that is, "Behold! I will bring waters upon the face of the earth." Since everyone knew that the King of the French had entered Italy with his forces, when I started my sermon with the words "Behold! I will bring waters upon the face of the earth," many were immediately astonished and acknowledged that this passage of Genesis had been gradually prepared by God's hidden inspiration to fit the times.[23] Among them was Count Giovanni della Mirandola, a man unique in our times for his talent and broad learning.[24] He later told me that he was terrified at these words and his hair stood on end.

To return to the subject. In those first years I used to predict coming events only by means of scripture, rational arguments, and various parables, due to the lack of readiness in the people. Then I began to hint that I had knowledge of future events by another light than the understanding of scripture alone. Finally, I began to disclose it still more clearly, now making known the words divinely revealed to me frankly and exactly.[25] Among them I often repeated: "Thus says the Lord God—the sword of the Lord will come upon the earth swiftly and soon."[26] And again these others:

Rejoice and exalt, O you just; but prepare your souls for temptation by reading, meditation, and prayer, and you will be freed from the second death. And you evil servants, filthy as you are, stay filthy still; let your belly be filled with unmixed wine, your loins rotted with lust, your hands defiled with the blood of the poor. This is your part and your lot. But know that your bodies and souls are in my hand and after a short time your bodies will be destroyed by scourges and I will hand your souls over to everlasting fire.[27]

These words were not taken from the sacred scriptures, as some thought, but newly come from heaven at that time. Since in any one vision sent from heaven there were many words of this kind, I revealed only a part then. I concealed the vision itself lest it be mocked by unbelievers. I thought it necessary at that time to reveal only this part so that the order of the words I publicly proclaimed then could be understood.

In 1492 on the night preceding my last Advent address in Santa Reparata I saw a hand in heaven with a sword on which was written: "The sword of the Lord will come upon the earth swiftly and soon." Above the hand was written, "The judgments of the Lord are just and true."[28] The hand's arm seemed to proceed from three faces in a single light. The first face said, "The iniquity of my sanctuary calls to me from the earth."[29] The second responded, "I will visit their iniquities with a rod and their sins with stripes."[30] The third added, "My mercy I will not take away from him, nor will I suffer my truth to fail, and I will have mercy on the poor and needy."[31] The first one spoke again, "My people have forgotten my commandments countless days."[32] The second responded, "Therefore I will destroy and crush them and not have mercy."[33] The third added, "I am mindful of those who walk in my precepts."[34] Then a great voice from the three faces thundered out over the whole world:

Hear, all you who dwell on earth, thus says the Lord. I the Lord am speaking in my holy zeal. Behold the days are coming and my sword will be unsheathed against you. Be converted unto me before my fury is fulfilled, for at the

PLATE X:

THE SAVONAROLA MEDALLION
Above the profile of the friar; on the reverse Florence under God's scourge.
Reproduced from D. Weinstein, *Savonarola and Florence* (Princeton: Princeton
University Press, 1970), Plate 4 (Alinari photograph).

time when distress has come upon you, you will seek for peace and you will not find it.[35]

When the words were finished the whole world was present to my sight. Then a multitude of white-robed angels came down from heaven to earth carrying countless white stoles on their shoulders and red crosses in their hands. They went through the whole world offering everyone a white stole and a cross. Some accepted the gift offered and were clothed; others refused, but did not prevent people from accepting; some both spurned it for themselves and prevented others from taking it. These last were the tepid and those puffed up with human wisdom. They made fun of the gifts and sought to persuade others not to take them.

Then the hand lowered the sword toward the earth and soon the air was seen to be darkened with dense clouds. It rained swords and hailstones with dreadful-sounding thunder, as well as arrows and bolts of fire. On earth war, pestilence, famine, and countless tribulations arose. I saw the angels walking through the midst of the nations giving cups of pure wine to those clad with stoles and bearing crosses. When they had emptied them they said: "O Lord, how sweet are your words in our mouths!"[36] The angels brought the dregs left at the bottom of the cups to those who did not want to drink, but seemed to want to do penance though unable, saying "Why have you forgotten us, Lord?"[37] They wanted to raise their eyes to look on God, but they were hindered by the severity of the tribulation. They were like drunken men; their hearts seemed to be taken from the midst of their breasts. They sought the comfort of human pleasures and did not find them; they carried on like the senseless and insane.

Then I heard a very powerful voice from the three faces saying: "Hear the word of the Lord. I have waited for you in order to have mercy on you. Come to me because I am kind and merciful, bestowing pardon to all who call upon me. But if you do not, I will turn my eyes away from you forever." Then the voice turned to the just and said, "Rejoice, you just, and exult, because when my brief wrath has passed I will break the power of sinners and the power of the just will be exalted."[38] And immediately the vision vanished and this word came to me: "Son, if sinners had eyes they would certainly see how hard and difficult this plague and sharp this sword can be." The Spirit said that the hard plague and sharp sword signified the rule of evil prelates and those who preach human philosophy. They neither enter the Kingdom of Heaven nor allow others to enter. By this he indicated that the Church had fallen so far because their spiritual attack was much worse than any corporeal tribulations that could happen. The Spirit told me that I should exhort and beg the people to beseech God to send his fear on the earth, to renew the love and memory of the benefits of the Passion of his Only-Begotten Son in the hearts of men, and to give the Church good pastors and preachers of the divine word who would feed his flock and not themselves.

After that, again at the God's inspiration, I predicted that someone would cross the Alps into Italy, like the Cyrus of whom Isaiah says:

> Thus says the Lord to my anointed Cyrus, whose right hand I have grasped to subdue the nations before his face, and to turn the backs of kings and to open the doors before him that the gates be not closed. I will go before him and will humble the great ones of the earth; I will break the bronze gates and will burst the bars of iron. And I will give you hidden treasures and the mystery of hidden places so that you may know that I am the Lord who calls you by your name, the God of Israel, for the sake of my servant Jacob and Israel my elect.[39]

I also said that Italy should not trust in citadels and fortresses, since he would overcome them without any difficulty. I predicted to the Florentines, especially to those who then controlled the government, that they would choose a plan and course of action contrary to their safety and profit, that is, they would join the weaker side that would be beaten. Like drunken men they would lose all their judgment. Even when these events were already breathing down their necks they did not believe it, though I frequently said they would be fooled by human wisdom. I omit the private and personal predictions that I made; to avoid scandal it is not right to reveal them in public. But at that time I did make known to some of my friends the time set for the deaths of Innocent VIII and of Lorenzo de'Medici.[40] I also predicted the revolution in the government and state of Florence that was to come when the King of the French first approached Pisa,[41] and many other things that, were I to enumerate them now, might not be believed at all because they were not then made public.

As the French King approached and the Florentine revolution loomed, even though the sword had appeared to me over Florence, as well as much bloodshed there, I reflected that God had especially chosen this city in which to announce these things and I strongly began to hope that the prophecy was conditional and that if the people did penance the most merciful God would withdraw his judgment at least in part. On November first, the Feast of All Saints, and the two following days, I spared neither voice nor lung. As everybody knows, I declaimed from the pulpit so strongly that my body grew weak and I almost fell sick. I proclaimed a fast on bread and water alone and frequent prayers from the whole people. I often shouted out words that came from the same source as the others cited above: "O Italy, adversities will come upon you because of your sins. O Florence, adversities will come on you because of your sins. O clergy, this tempest has arisen because of you." I frequently repeated that Italy, especially Rome, would be destroyed, and I called out the following words revealed to me by the same Spirit:

> O nobles, men of learning, and common folk, the strong hand of the Lord is upon you and neither power nor wisdom nor flight can resist it. Therefore I the Lord have waited for you in order to have mercy on you; be converted to the Lord your God with your whole heart, because he is merciful and kind. If you do not, he will turn his eyes away from you forever.

Then, when the most Christian King of France drew near, I was asked by the Signoria of Florence to undertake a legation to his Majesty along with some other citizens. I quickly consulted with my fellow Dominicans and other citizens and was unanimously advised to undertake the journey. I was forced to accept the burden even more by charity than by their advice, and therefore set out with the chosen ambassadors for Pisa. There I set forth in the vernacular before his Royal Majesty the divine warnings as follows.[42]

> Most Christian King and Great Minister of Divine Justice, know that Almighty God, in whose hand is all power and rule, gives and bestows his goodness on his creatures in two ways: through mercy and through justice. Through mercy he attracts the creature to his love and converts it; through justice he often casts the creature from him because of its faults. These two ways are so connected that they always accompany each other in every work and every creature, as is written, 'All the paths of the Lord are mercy and truth.'[43] He exercises justice on the damned by inflicting punishment for sins on them; He also brings them mercy because he afflicts them without regard to what they deserve and punishes them more mildly than they should be. He shows mercy to the blessed by giving them more abundant glory than their works and labors deserve, and preserves justice by bestowing glory on them according to the greater or lesser merits done in life.[44]
>
> Because what is in the middle partakes of the nature of the extremities, what we said about the blessed and the damned can be easily imagined to be true of other creatures, that is, that mercy and justice always accompany each other, although they have different conditions and different effects. Mercy's job is to bear sins patiently, with long suffering to wait for sinners to come to repentance, to call to them pleasantly, and when they are sweetly attracted to draw them to herself, to embrace them when they are drawn in, to forgive them with gentleness, justify them with kindness, give them great increase in grace, and generously fill them with the infinite treasures of heavenly glory. This is justice's task: after the sinner has been endured with

patience, awaited with long-suffering, sweetly and frequently called, but has still completely rejected all this, to deprive him of grace, strip him of virtues, remove the light, darken his intellect, and permit him to fall into any pit of sin so that all things may work together for ill in his case and he may be finally punished forever in hell. The immense goodness of God, the lover of men, had endured the grave sins of Italy most patiently, and now these many years had waited with long-suffering for her to do penance, and had sweetly and frequently called her through his many servants. But because she did not wish to open her ears, nor to acknowledge the voice of her Shepherd, nor to do penance for her sins, God, Almighty and Supreme, decided to let justice follow its course and to exercise judgment upon her lest his patience be consumed by her pride. Otherwise, her sins would multiply and grow worse day by day because she completely disregarded God's mercies, and rejected baptism and the Blood of Christ, prefering a harlot's face and stony countenance.

Mercy and justice always go together in every divine work, as I said before. So great was God's goodness that in order to show mercy and justice to his people he revealed to one of his unprofitable servants the mystery that he intended to reform his Church for the better through a great scourge. The unprofitable servant began to preach this in the city of Florence four years ago under divine inspiration and command. From that time until this he has never ceased to call the people to penance with loud proclamations. The whole city is the witness, nobles and commoners, old and young of both sexes, town folk and country folk. A few believed; others did not believe at all, and others mocked. But God, who cannot lie, made everything that up to now had been foretold on his orders to follow perfectly, so that mortals cannot doubt that what remains unfulfilled from the predictions will also take place. All of the listeners mentioned above are witnesses that this is the way it was. Even though the unprofitable servant never put forth the name of your Majesty because God's will did not yet permit him, nonetheless it was you he was describing and pointing to in hidden fashion in his preaching and you whose coming he awaited.

SAVONAROLA

So you have finally come, O King. You have come, Minister of God. You have come, Minister of Justice. May your coming bring good luck everywhere! We receive you with happy heart and joyful countenance. Your coming has gladdened our hearts, lifted up our minds, and made all the servants of Christ and lovers of Justice and a holy life burn with joy. They hope that through you God will put down the proud, lift up the lowly, overthrow vice, magnify virtue, straighten what is bent, renew what is worn, and reform what is hideous. Come then joyfully, fearlessly, and triumphantly, seeing that he who sends you is the one who triumphed on the wood of the cross for our salvation. Nevertheless, Most Christian King, listen to my words attentively and take them to heart. The unprofitable servant to whom this mystery was revealed by God, that is, the Most Holy Trinity, Father, Son and Holy Spirit, and by Our Savior Jesus Christ, true God, God's Son, and true man, King of Kings and Lord of Lords, and also by the whole heavenly court, exhorts and warns you who are sent by God that in imitation of him you should show mercy everywhere. This is especially the case for his city of Florence, which even though it labors under a heavy weight of sins still has many servants of God, both seculars and religious of both sexes, for whose sake you ought to leave that city unharmed. Thus with tranquil minds they may be able to beseech God to be propitious to you and to aid you in this expedition. The same unprofitable servant exhorts and warns you on God's behalf that you should use all care to protect and defend the innocent, widows and orphans, and all who deserve mercy. You should especially protect the chastity of the spouses of Christ in religious houses, lest because of you sins be increased. If this happen through your fault the solid strength of the power given you from on high will be weakened. Also on God's behalf he exhorts and warns you to forgive offenses freely, that is, mercifully to pardon whatever has been done against you either by the people of Florence or by others. It was done in ignorance because they did not know that you had been sent by God. Remember your Savior who when he hung on the cross mercifully forgave those who crucified him. If you give heed to this, O King, God will increase your earthly king-

205

dom, will grant you victory everywhere, and will at last reward you with the Kingdom of Heaven. He alone is blessed and powerful, King of Kings and Lord of Lords. He alone has immortality and dwells in inaccessible light which no man sees nor can see, to whom is honor and dominion through infinite ages. Amen.[45]

With these words I fulfilled the commands of the people of Florence, which there is no need to put in here.

In the meantime the Florentine state had gone through a revolution. I returned to the city and began again to preach that everyone should be intent on prayer and penance. It was quite clear that divine mercy had freed the people of Florence from the greatest dangers through these means. Continuing to preach the saving message, I said that the Florentines still had to cross many perilous shoals, that they would be shaken by other tribulations, and that all Italy, particularly Rome, would be disturbed. (I never disclosed by whom, when, or how.) I said there was no remedy left for the rulers of the Church and the princes of Italy aside from penance—neither heaps of money, nor armies, nor fortified places and castles could help them. Even if they had an infinite treasure, the strongest and largest possible army, iron walls and adamantine fortresses, not only would this not be enough, but they would even flee like weak women. God would blind them and at the same time deprive them of strength and good sense, as is written in Job: "He brings counselors to a foolish end and judges to stupidity. He loosens the belt of kings and binds their loins with a cord."[46] I also added that one barber would not be enough to shave all of Italy, but that others would come. This will certainly happen.

I foretold many things in the same vein, although from time to time in different words. I added that the Turks and Moors would be converted to the Christian religion in our time, saying "Many of you who are standing here will see this."[47] The revelation regarding this had come to me a long time before. In 1492 during Lent when I was preaching in the Church of San Lorenzo in Florence I saw two crosses on the night of Good Friday. The first one, in the midst of Rome, was black. It touched heaven and spread its arms through the whole world. On it were written the words "The cross of God's wrath." When I saw it, the air at once grew dark and turbulent with swirling clouds all mixed with winds, bolts of lightning, arrows, hailstones, fire and sword. A countless multitude of people were destroyed so that very few were left on earth. Afterward I saw a peaceful and clear time come and a golden cross in the midst of Jerusalem, the same height as the other, and so shining that it lit up the whole world and filled it with new flowers and joy. Its inscription was "The cross of God's mercy." Without delay all the nations of the earth, men and women, gathered from all sides to adore and embrace it. I received many other much clearer visions on this theme, as well as on the other things I predicted, especially about the renovation of the Church and the scourge. I have been strengthened by many visions and proven illuminations at different times.

I further predicted that the city of Florence would be reformed for the better. This was God's will and the Florentines would have to do it. On God's behalf, I also foretold that by this reformation the city would become more glorious, more powerful, and richer than it had been up till now.[48] The fact itself has proven that this was God's intention. A reformation of this sort that seemed a contradiction (because anyone would have thought it completely alien to the behavior and custom of the city) had an effect that would have seemed impossible to human judgment. This contradiction and the bad will of many was the reason for the delay of the universal peace and the suspension of the graces divinely promised us. Hence I roused the people to prayer and fasting, which made them become devout and well disposed, and so peace itself was finally obtained. The "Appeal against the Six Beans" of the Signoria to the General Council, which I advised for the greater security of the citizens and the stability of the whole city, was established in the correct order and with the right statutes.[49] As hope grew I labored with the most urgent prayers to be reconciled with God so that he would restore the graces once promised to the Florentines. This is clearly stated in the sermon for the Octave of the Feast of the Annunciation of Mary, which we set down in the following form just as it was preached.

Blessed be God, the Father of Our Lord Jesus Christ, the Father of mercies and God of all consolation, who consoles us in our every tribulation so that we too can console those who are in any distress through the exhortation by which God has also exhorted us.

Dearly beloved in Christ Jesus. A living faith with constant prayer and long-suffering patience has so much merit with God that there is nothing so great that it cannot be obtained from him by this means. This is proven not only by the authority of the Old and New Testaments and the experience of our fathers of old, but also in these dangerous times by the frequent touch of our own hands, so to speak. By means of these three weapons we have often been miraculously freed from the greatest perils that threatened our city of Florence and the whole populace. In the midst of the deepest opposition we have also obtained the reform of the city, peace, and much else besides—things that went against the expectations of human wisdom and the views of almost everyone. It is fitting that these three virtues joined into one should be worthy to be heard by God in the case of great matters that surpass the ordinary course of his other works. First, because faith is a virtue that extends and strengthens the intellect in those highest truths that natural reason cannot prove. Among the other virtues it rests in a special way on the divine omnipotence, which it believes can do all things. Because of faith the faithful man lets go not only of sense knowledge and imagination, but also of natural reason. Believing in God with a simple heart, he is worthy to attain splendid things that surpass nature's course, every created power, and all sense knowledge, imagination, and human wisdom. Second, because God is the first mover of spiritual and corporeal things, our every thought and good resolve come from him before they come from us, as the apostle says: "We are not able to think something on our own as if it came from us."[50] Since any natural cause and mover looks to a preordained end for whose sake it produces its effect, so much the more does the cause of causes, God the Supreme Good, move the souls of the just to long for, hope for, and beg for great things from him, especially those that contribute to the common welfare of the Church, as Paul says, "The Spirit pleads on our behalf with unspeakable groans."[51] He will lead all such longing, hope, and petition to the desired goal. Therefore do not wonder that faith asks for great things through constant prayer, especially because God so frequently and firmly promised in the scriptures to hear our prayers. He even taught us to pray with a certain importunity. Discouragement in the midst of tribulations produces many evils, such as anger, hatred, indignation, and other unjust works. Patience, on the contrary, drives discouragement away or at least lessens it in view of Christ. It restrains the one who has it from many sins and strengthens him in virtues. And so it is written: "Patience possesses a perfect work."[52] A person who bears the adversities of this world with equanimity for God's sake deserves to be consoled and to get his wish from God. Paul says, "Tribulation produces patience, patience endurance, and endurance hope. Hope does not disappoint because the charity of God is poured out in our hearts through the Holy Spirit who has been given to us."[53] And so no one should be amazed that after having patiently borne so many tribulations and having been devoted to frequent prayer with living faith, from him who is good through essense and not through accident we have attained lofty things that surpass what is usual in our time. We will speak of these clearly and in order, first asking that you put human wisdom completely aside and in the simplicity of a pure faith hear us with cleansed ears.

Beloved citizens, when I saw that the revolution of the state and government was near and knew that so great a change could not take place without great danger and bloodshed unless divine mercy brought aid because of the penances, fasts, and prayers of good people, under God's inspiration I decided to encourage the people by constant preaching to do penance in order to obtain mercy. On the Feast of Saint Matthew, September 21, 1494, I used all my power to arouse the people to confession, fasts, and prayers. They did this gladly, and God's goodness changed justice into mercy. On November ninth by a divine miracle the state and the government were changed without bloodshed or scandal of any kind.[54]

People of Florence, when you had assumed the new form of government I called you together in the Duomo, without the presence of the women, before the Signoria and all the magistrates. After I spoke at length about the correct government of cities according to the traditions of philosophers and theologians, I then set out what should be the natural government of the Florentine people.[55] I continued to preach on the following days, proposing four courses of action. The first was the fear of God. The second was to prefer the common good of the republic to one's own private concerns. The third was to make common and full peace with those who had shortly before governed the city. I added to this the "Appeal against Six Beans" so that by means of this no one could make himself head of the city in the future. The fourth was to set up a full General Council like the Venetians, so that the benefits of the city could be restored to the whole people and not kept by any individual, and so that no one could make himself too powerful.[56] I maintained that it was God's will that these four counsels be fulfilled and that he had decided that the people of Florence were to be ruled under this form of government in the future. I added that no one could resist his will because God would turn the white beans into black ones, that is, he would change the hearts of those who were in opposition and would cause those who had firmly decided to resist it in the Council by voting no to approve and consent to it.

That was the way it happened, as everyone in your city knows. Many of those who in the beginning were opposed to the measures confessed that they had undergone such a change of heart. I not only recommended these four items to the people by the authority of God's will, but I also demonstrated their truth by firm arguments and showed that no other form of government would be advantageous to you, people of Florence. I promised on God's behalf that if you adopted them your city would be more glorious than ever in its temporal and spiritual government. It would also be stronger and richer.

Because of the lack of faith, the foolishness, and the malice of many who opposed the peace and the "Appeal" when the Great Council had been set up, I was afraid that God had been provoked to anger because his advice had been spurned. I feared that he had so withdrawn his protecting hand that the promises he freely made to you, Florence, were revoked and invalidated. Nevertheless, having taken account of the greatness of God's goodness, we increased our prayer and fasting. After a short while, as we predicted, the peace and "Appeal" won approval, to the great surprise of all. Considering this, I realized that God's promises were withdrawn for a time rather than lost by our fault. Hence when your prayers were renewed, I offered myself to undertake the role of ambassador to God in your name to regain these graces. After continual prayers and fasts I did not presume to approach immediately to the high throne of Infinite Majesty ("under which those who bear the world bow down")[57] but went to the Glorious Virgin, Mother of God, on the day of her Annunciation, which is for you the beginning of the year, begging that due to the joy of the feast she might deign to become our advocate with the Most Holy Trinity. She most graciously accepted. On the same day, my people, I brought you the joyful news in San Marco. As we kept on praying during the Octave of the Feast, I announced to you that I had been told that a positive response would be given on the last day of the octave. I urged you to complete the prayer and good resolve you had begun so that these promises would overflow with every manner of grace.

On the night before the octave's last day, as I was about to set out to receive the hoped-for response, I thought that I ought to have fit companions and the correct garb. While I was thinking about the kind and number of companions I should choose, many women presented themselves. Among them Philosophy first promised her services, declaring that great wisdom was fitting for an embassy to such an exalted place. Rhetoric also presented herself, recommending the highest eloquence in this affair. But I responded to them and to the rest of the daughters of human wisdom that since their knowledge begins from the senses it does not surpass sensible things. Even

211

if sensible things afford some knowledge of God, yet it is so small that it can be considered almost nothing. It is covered by three veils: the veil of accidents by which the human sciences come to know corporeal substances; the veil of corporeal substances through whose imperfect understanding we rise by intellect to a consideration of the soul and spiritual substances; and the veil of the substances of the soul and of spiritual beings through which, much more imperfectly known than bodily things, our intellect strives to rise to the knowledge of God, who infinitely surpasses everything else. Therefore, the knowledge of God gained through reason is very weak.

The knowledge of the saints is incomparably more perfect and greater than natural knowledge. They see God face to face and through him they also behold all things in the opposite way from philosophy. Faith holds a middle place between these two kinds of knowledge, more perfect than the knowledge of philosophy and inferior to the knowledge of saints.[58] Because we name things insofar as we know them, philosophy and rhetoric, which depend on the light of natural reason, are too lowly and childish to have a place with the Divine Majesty and the saints. Therefore I rejected philosophy, rhetoric, and the other human sciences as unfit for this legation, and I chose simplicity of faith, of wisdom, and of the eloquence of the sacred scriptures. I put it on within and without with all my strength and in every way—in believing, understanding, speaking, setting out, contemplating, and even in my attire. I would do all things in simplicity. I diligently meditated on that saying of Solomon's, "He who walks in simplicity walks confidently. And his conversation is with the simple."[59] Having taken Simplicity as a companion, and accompanied also by Faith, Prayer, and Patience, we directed our journey to the threshold of paradise.

Lady Simplicity bore a very beautiful and precious covered gift to offer the Supreme Majesty. We shall unfold its mystery below. When we had just begun our journey, the cunning Tempter of the human race, pretending to be an aged and bearded hermit, met me and drew near. After he had saluted me he said: "My son, for many years I have done penance in the neighboring hermitage you are passing. By the revelation of the Holy Spirit I have at this moment understood the fruit of your preaching and your good intention toward God and the salvation of souls. At the same time, however, it was revealed to me that you have been led into error in your simplicity, for, in order to call the people back from vice to virtue, you have predicted many tribulations and at the same time promised good things as well. This is not at all permitted, because God who is Truth wishes his preachers to be completely filled with the truth." I answered him: "I am not a little surprised at these words, Father. The Holy Spirit reveals only what is true, but your objection to me is false because I never have used such deception. I am not so ignorant that I do not know that God, who is of the most simple nature, places the highest value on simplicity and hates duplicity, which in any way it exists, whether in word or work, is a lie. It is written: 'You will destroy all who speak lies; evil is not to be done that good might come.'[60] This is especially true because the sacred doctors think that every lie spoken in seriousness by a preacher from the pulpit is a mortal sin. It cannot be possible that I should bear fruit in preaching by means of lies; the fruit itself shows that I have not been a deceiver. Indeed, as I often testified before the people and now again testify and swear on my soul: may God erase me from the Book of Life if I have ever used deception in my preaching. And so this inspiration of yours cannot have come from the Holy Spirit."

The Tempter then spoke. "Granted that you did not lie about them, you still foretold unusual and unheard-of things. Many thought that you made them up and proclaimed them under the influence of a melancholic spirit. Or perhaps they came from your dreams or wild imagination." I responded: "Father, I do not sense such a spirit in my heart, but rather the highest joy, a light that is not natural, and the revelation of images that are beyond nature. Since I spent a good deal of time studying philosophy, I understand well how far the natural light of reason and the power of imagination go, and I know that they do not reach what has come to me, especially regarding future contingent acts. I know this both because of the precise order I have always maintained in speaking, and because of the insight and perfect harmony I have had in applying the sacred scriptures to the course of the present life. I have done this without distortion or violent wrenching or dissonance, as my hearers know. Anyone of mediocre intelligence knows that this cannot come from a melancholic spirit or from dreams or wild imagination."

He said: "Then some constellation under which you were born or the influence of some planet or star has caused you to meditate, propose, and predict these future events." I said: "Father, it is extreme folly to believe that the influence of the heavens allows knowledge of the future.[61] As the Philosopher says, 'There is no determined truth about future contingents; about such matters there is neither science nor art.'[62] There is no leading philosopher, Greek or Latin, ancient or modern, who followed divinatory astronomy, even though some falsely claim certain writings composed by others for Albert the Great in order to have authority for their errors.[63] If you look at this art carefully—if art it can be called—you will understand that it has no foundation or proof for its claims. You may want to pay attention to those things; I would rather follow foolish old wives' tales than something of such little weight and science! Anyone can deny such things just as easily as they are senselessly affirmed. If I had time, I would show that this superstition belongs to fools and dolts rather than men of sense and intelligence. But now for us who profess Christian teaching it should suffice that astrology is condemned in many places in sacred scripture. In the forty-seventh chapter of Isaiah the Holy Spirit speaks against Babylon and says: 'Your wisdom and your science have deceived you.'[64] And later: 'Let the diviners of the heavens stand up and save you, those who contemplate the stars and compute the months so that from them they can tell you what is coming upon you. Behold, they have been made like straw, the fire has burned them up, they did not free their souls from the flames.'[65] And in the tenth chapter of Jeremiah: 'Do not learn according to the ways of the Gentiles, and do not fear the signs of heaven that the nations fear, because the laws of the people are vain.'[66] In brief, the holy books show that knowledge of future contingent events is a property of God. God alone knows them, and he to whom he deigns to reveal them, as Isaiah says: 'Announce the things that are to come in the future and we will know that you are gods.'[67] Therefore, those who pay attention to these superstitions sin gravely because they claim for themselves what is proper to God. Hence all the doctors and sacred canons detest this art. Those who pursue divinatory astronomy are not only fools and men of weak mind and no judgment, but also bad Christians. The heavens do not act without the mediation of lower causes in the disposition of matter. For example, it is not within heaven's right to produce a vine from an olive seed. Even though the heavens influence man's senses, they cannot dispose them to phantasms other than what nature allows. Father, knowing my nature for a long time, I have recognized much more excellent phantasms in my senses than those which nature affords. Further, the heavens cannot act directly on the intellect,[68] because the corporeal cannot act directly on the incorporeal. Therefore the heavens are not able to influence the supernatural light I perceive in myself. And again, the heavens and nature do not make artificial things. They construct neither clothes, nor homes, nor the like. Because the significant sounds and the order of the words and sentences which I often heard inside me and outside me in both Latin and Italian belong to the realm of art and reason, what I heard and preached in this manner can in no way come from the heavens or nature."

The Tempter then said: "This could be done by the power and work of the devil, for he is able to fashion artifical things and to make something that is superior to bodily nature. Therefore you have surely been deceived by diabolic fraud." I answered: "Father, I have been through the sacred scriptures and the lives and teachings of the saints from beginning to end and thus I understand well enough all the marks of diabolical as well as divine apparitions. I grasp how much they differ not only on this basis but also from experience. For a long time I have known that my visions could in no way have come from the devil, particularly because the things I understood and

215

foretold were much more certain to me than the first principles of the sciences were for philosophers. It is clear that a light of such certainty cannot have come from the devil. Furthermore, even the devil cannot know future contingents. I see and always have seen everything happen just as I have known and predicted that it would for many years. Not even an iota fails. I have not been mistaken in the smallest detail. Besides, the devil is virtue's enemy and so it is unbelievable that when so much fruit has come from my preaching he would not have left me. At least he would have openly deceived me so no faith would be placed in me any longer and the trust that had been given to me and other preachers would be wholly destroyed. In Florence, where I preached for a long time, all, or nearly all, who live a good and pious life follow my teaching. Those who are openly known to be evil and not living a Christian life attack it as enemies. They try to defame me and even to kill me. Nonetheless, my teaching has always increased and borne richer fruit, so that the number of my disciples has continually increased, while my adversaries have decreased. At the same time my deeds have prevailed and those of my enemies have been weakened and almost destroyed. So, Father, this teaching and work is not the devil's, but Christ's, who desires always that his teaching and work grow in the midst of supreme opposition."

The Tempter again spoke. "Whatever you say, my son, I will never be persuaded that Christ has spoken to any mortal after his Ascension into heaven." I answered. "Father, you are very much against the witness of the Bible, for in many places we read that after his Ascension he appeared to many, among others the Apostle Paul as he affirms in the First Epistle to the Corinthians.[69] By your claim the stories of the saints would lie, and Saint Francis, who said he received his Rule from Christ, would have deceived the world. There are many other saints who claimed they had spoken with Christ. If Christ was crucified for sinners, what wonder is it if he himself or his angels address a sinner for the good of Holy Church? If Christ daily does not shrink from the ministry and touch of countless wicked priests in the sacrament of the altar, why do you think it unworthy that he speak to sinners? Men today are blinded by so much darkness that what is very easy in God's sight seems impossible to them. They are not in awe at the greater deeds, but the rarer. It is greater to justify a sinner and to dwell in him by grace than to speak to someone. They believe in the former and are not surprised at it; the latter, they cannot believe."

The Tempter said: "I acknowledge that in the earliest times Christ spoke to many. But now it is not necessary for salvation since there is a large fund of scripture and doctors." I answered: "Holy scripture and the doctors are completely sufficient in themselves to instruct men in the way of salvation by exterior teaching. Nevertheless, unless a person has the interior light of grace, he gains little from Catholic teaching. It is necessary for God to infuse the light of grace within, a light common to all who wish to live in an orthodox manner. Beyond this, a more specific and particular light is often needed, especially for those whose task it is to enlighten others. They need it because of the details and numberless circumstances that come from diversity of men's ages and conditions and from the variety of their states. Because of all that there is very often doubt about what to do or to choose in the present or the future. Unless a person were specifically illumined by God, he could not be sure from scripture and the doctors what was the more useful course. It is not possible to put these details in books, because the world itself could scarcely fit so many volumes. Therefore Plato ordered anyone who talked about details to be still.[70]

"Since a change in the Church Universal never takes place without serious spiritual and bodily tribulation, there is need to prepare God's elect and strengthen them in the life of goodness so that they are not found unprepared. If we carefully consider the Old and New Testaments, we see that Almighty God has always foreseen these changes and through the mouths of his servants has forewarned, comforted, consoled, and illuminated them about what to do. The Prophet Amos in his third chapter says: 'Will there be an evil in the city that the Lord has not done? For the Lord God will not do his word unless he has revealed his secret to his servants the prophets.'[71] Since the present Church has reached the dregs and God plans to renew it through many tribulations, it must be that he will foretell the scourges to his elect in these days through his servants. Thus they can be prepared and not be taken unawares by the coming evils."

The Tempter: "How can you know the time of the renovation of the Church when it is written: 'It is not yours to know the times nor the dates which the Father has placed in his own power'?"[72] I responded: "Pay more careful attention to the words, Father. It says, 'It is not yours to know the times nor the dates,' not all times and dates but only 'those which the Father has placed in his own power,' such as the day of judgment when Christ will restore the kingdom of Israel and about which the apostles were speaking though they did not yet understand what kind of a restoration it would be.[73] Certainly Noah had been told the time of the flood,[74] Jeremiah the seventy years of the captivity of the people of Israel,[75] and Daniel the seventy-two weeks of the coming Christ.[76] Thus many prophets had the times told them and predicted to them clearly."

The Tempter: "Why did God choose you for this task rather than another, since there are many better than you are in the Church?" I answered: "And I would like to know this from you, Father: Why did God choose Peter who had denied Christ three times and Paul who had persecuted him as the princes of the apostles rather than those of their era who were better than they? Why did he make Luke and Mark evangelists, preferring them for this ministry over many others who were more holy or at least equal? Why did he choose the idolatrous and wicked Balaam to whom to reveal great mysteries of the Church and Christ and to show angelic visions and speechs rather than the many others more just or less evil than he? No explanation can be given of these cases, but only the divine will, as Paul says to the Corinthians in speaking of the graces of the Holy Spirit: 'The one and the same Spirit works all these things, dividing to everyone as he wills.'[77] Writing to the Romans about predestination he says: 'He has mercy on whom he will, and he hardens whom he will.' You will then say to

218

me, 'Why does he still find fault for who can resist his will?' O man, who are you to reply to God? Shall what is created say to him who formed it, 'Why did you make me thus? Does not the potter have the power from the same mass of clay to make one vessel for honor, another for dishonor?' "[78]

The Tempter: "Then you are holier than others?" I answered: "The grace of prophecy does not sanctify a man, indeed it is often given to sinners, as in the Book of Numbers we read of Balaam who even though he prophesied was a wicked man.[79] As Our Lord says in the Gospel: 'Many will say to me on that day: Lord, Lord, have we not prophesied in your name, and in your name cast out demons, and in your name done a great many works of power?' Then he will say to them: 'Because I have never known you, depart from me, all you workers of iniquity.'[80] These charismatic gifts[81] are bestowed for the advantage of others rather than for one's own. It is better to have the lowest measure of charity than to possess every charismatic gift, as Paul says, 'If I speak with the tongues of men and of angels and have not charity, I have become like sounding brass and tinkling cymbal.' "[82]

The Tempter: "I have heard that you depend on the visions of some women and preach what they dictate to you." I responded that that was neither true nor likely. "As is publicly known in the city, I very rarely speak to women, and even then do so briefly. My fellow Dominicans know how unwillingly I go to visit them, and I have never heard a woman's confession. Further, since women are fickle and not able to keep a secret, you can believe that a thing like this could not have been hidden for so many years. I know that their testimony is rarely included in the scriptures, although some prophetesses are read.[83] I think that God has done this so that we will not depend on their testimony very much, though it is not to be completely rejected, as it is written, 'Spurn not the prophets.'[84] The reason is that women lack experience, are poor in judgment, fickle, and very weak, susceptible to vanity, and thus easily fooled by diabolical cunning. Since I am sure of this, you should not believe that I would have trusted in their prophecies, nor would I have affirmed them constantly before so many people. If what was foretold did not take place, the result would have been great danger to the faith, contempt of God, and shame and grave danger to me."

The Tempter: "Some say that you have used your friendship with rulers and knowledge of their secrets to preach what they have decided to do." I answered: "I know how great the instability of man is, especially the hearts of rulers, which often change as the seasons do. It would be foolish for me or for anyone else, even if we knew their secrets, to base our words on their plans, especially since they are mortal and can die at any hour. There are also the various hindrances to their schemes, either from opposition of other rulers, or weakness, or human fickleness. These can happen at any day or hour. Therefore, what will happen to them or through them is so uncertain that neither the angelic nor the human intellect is able to know and foretell it infallibly, because it would have to know all the circumstances and the impediments that could happen and to be sure how they turned out. God alone knows this, he who calls the things that are and the things that are not, to whose eyes all things are present.[85] It would be complete insanity to base the future on so weak a foundation."

The Tempter: "Others say that many citizens have told you the secrets of the government of Florence, and thus you know many hidden matters and the intentions of other rulers. You then put these together to guess the future by insight and clever reasoning." I answered: "This is not worthy of a response, Father, because it comes from simple men of small judgment who do not understand that such things cannot be affirmed with certainty through an inquiry like this. The response made before should be sufficient for them."

The Tempter: "Others think that you invented those predictions with the deepest connivance and cunning of public officials and magistrates. You then announced them with such craftiness that when they did not happen you would still have an excuse." I answered: "It is now five years since I began to predict the war and those many individual matters that are now partly fulfilled. Those who speak thus sang another tune then. They claimed I was a simple man deceived by my own simplicity. Now, because a part of what has been foretold has been fulfilled and manifest signs and clear indications show that the part that remains to come will be fulfilled, they have changed their tune to cover their confusion and announce that I am a crafty man who puts his words so cautiously that he can never be caught. They know that I foretold that someone would come who would cross the mountains and the plains, and who would overcome defenses, fortresses, and cities 'with rotten apples' as the saying goes. I prophesied that the Florentines would follow advice contrary to their best interests and would lose all prudence and good sense like befuddled drunks. They heard many things like this. Once again I hope to have many particular events revealed to me from on high. I will preach them just as openly and directly to the whole people. They will not be given varying explanations. If the preceding predictions had failed, I would not have been able to defend them by any interpretation. So now, if these things do not take place, I will be unable to escape confusion."

The Tempter: "I understand that you have the revelations of Saint Bridget, Abbot Joachim, and many others from which you foretell coming events by divination." I responded: "Father, I testify that I have never delighted in this sort of reading, and that I have never read the revelations of Saint Bridget and rarely, or almost never, those of Abbot Joachim. The reading of other prophecies of this sort has never been my pleasure. I own none of them, as my fellow Dominicans and friends know. They are witnesses to how much the reading of the Old and New Testaments delights me, because for many years, I have used almost no other book or form of reading. I shrink from other reading, so to speak, not because I condemn other writings or because the books of the doctors displease me, but because in comparison with scripture anything sweet seems bitter. If you do not believe this, at least do not think that I am so light-headed that I would have asserted the things I so firmly predicted as certain and so often repeated as confirmed if I had no other foundation than the one you mentioned. Because these prophecies are not numbered among the canonical books, I could not find internal conviction to believe and to foretell them. Furthermore, as already appears above and will be clear below too, in my preaching I descended to details I think are not present in these prophetic writings. Even stronger, were I to grant that I took them for a foundation, this ought to be enough to induce faith in me so that men might do penance for their sins. The objection comes to nothing more than this— 'You are not a prophet, but preach the prophecies of others.' To which I answer, if I announce the truth, whatever the way, that is enough for me, as long as men are converted to the good. I do not wish to be held for a prophet, for the name is a grave and dangerous one. It renders a man quite disturbed, and arouses many persecutions against him, although for Christ's sake they are freely borne. For this reason I do not agree that I have ever depended on the prophecies of others, except for the canonical ones. As I said, I have not read them. If at the instigation of a friend I looked at some, I gave them back after having scarcely read them once. I neither condemn them nor approve them, but leave them to God's judgment 'to whose eyes all things are naked and open.'"[86]

The Tempter: "Son, the things that you say you received from God should be kept in secret. This is what the writings of the holy fathers advise." I answered: "If this were the truth, it would follow that Moses, Isaiah, Jeremiah, and the other prophets of the Old and New Testaments did not act correctly by preaching their revelations to the people and by putting them in writing. Many hermits have likewise not acted correctly. So too Saint Benedict, Saint Vincent Ferrer, Saint Catherine of Siena, Saint Bridget, and countless other saints whose prophecies and divine revelations we read in various books have all erred in publicizing them. I acknowledge that such matters ought not to be divulged unless God commands it or love of neighbor and God's warning urge it. For this reason the whole populace of Florence knows that I have spoken only in public about these sorts of things. I have not gone beyond what I was conceded or commanded. In private I never or rarely talked about them, except for what was said under seal of faith to some of my close friends. Believe me that I have many things hidden in my heart that I have never manifested and will never manifest unless God inspires me to do otherwise."

The Tempter: "Whoever prophesies future things ought to confirm them with miracles in order to be believed. Otherwise, heretics could do the same. So the Canon 'Cum ex iniuncto extra de haereticis' can be invoked against you, the one that seems to indicate that those who preach such things confirm them by some sign or miracle.[87] Some say that in not doing this you have acted in a heretical manner and are to be judged as a heretic." I answered: "These men are either ignorant or evil. They either do not understand the sacred canons from lack of careful examination, or else they have spitefully twisted them. You will not find what they say written down anywhere! On the contrary, few of the prophets are known to have been famous for miracles. When Ananias opposed Jeremiah, as found in the twenty-eighth chapter of his book, the prophet did not prove his word by miracles, but said: 'Hear this word that I speak in your ears and the ears of the whole people. The prophets who existed before me and you from the beginning have prophesied battle, affliction, and famine upon many lands and many great kingdoms. As for the prophet who prophesied peace, you will know him as a prophet whom the Lord has truly sent when his word comes true.'[88] When Jonah the prophet preached the overthrow of Nineveh, he showed no miracles to the people. Of those who prophesied in the times of the kings of Israel, very few proved their prophecies with miracles. Why ask about others when the prophet of prophets, Saint John the Baptist, completely lacked miracles? It is written in the tenth chapter of John, 'Many came to Jesus and said that John had worked no sign. All the things that John had said about this man were true, and many believed him.'[89]

"The text of the decretal brought against me above is not to the point, because it speaks against those who usurp the office of preaching without the permission or command of prelates, claiming that they have been invisibly commissioned by God. The canon says that they ought to prove this by signs, as did Moses, or by the testimony of the sacred scripture, as did

John the Baptist, who said, 'I am the voice of one crying in the desert, as Isaiah the prophet says.'[90] As I have demonstrated, according to their interpretation this canon would be contrary to sacred scripture. Therefore I have rightly called them either ignorant or else wicked perverters of the canons. There is no need for me to prove my mission by signs or scriptures, since all know that my superiors commissioned me to the office of preaching. I do not say that I have been sent by God alone and not by them. They are not in justice able to call me a heretic. A heretic is one who has obstinately chosen to follow some teaching contrary to the holy scripture or to the teaching of the Holy Roman Church. I do not recall having said or written anything that did not agree with the teaching of Christ and the Church. I desire that everything I have said or written up to now, and will say or write in the future, be ever subject to the correction of the Holy Roman Church. I am prepared to receive reproof gladly from it or from any man wherever I have been in error."

The Tempter: "In a nutshell, I do not wish to believe too hastily, for it is written, 'He who believes hastily is light-headed.' "[91] I responded, "It is also written, 'Charity believes all things.'[92] Since the Holy Spirit, the author of these two sentences, cannot contradict himself, it should be noted that there are some things that should be believed with difficulty, such as detractions, murmurings, and abuse of one's neighbor; others that should be believed with ease, especially those whose belief helps men to live well. Even if what our faith preaches were not true—which is impossible—I would try to believe it, because these beliefs lead to a life so excellent that a better cannot be imagined or found. Some other matters can be believed or not indiscriminately and without sin, such as the histories of the pagan races and the like. Since the things that I predicted are not opposed to faith, or morals, or natural reason, and since they are plausible, as I have shown by many arguments at various times, and since they also persuade men to live piously as experience has shown, it follows that the charge of levity cannot be leveled against anyone who believes them with ease. Our ancient Fathers, such as Saints Jerome, Ambrose, Augustine, and Gregory, and many others who were very skillful in every science and very prudent in human affairs, believed such things with ease, even when they came from the uneducated, as long as they were men or women of approved life and reputation. They not only received them with pure trust, but they also immortalized them by setting them down for the others' profit, as appears in Jerome's *Lives of the Holy Fathers*, Gregory's *Dialogues*, some of Augustine's short works, and in many writings of different saints.[93] We are certainly not holier or wiser than the ancient Fathers who wrote down countless things of this kind for our benefit in the Old and New Testaments and in other books that have been approved and received by Holy Church."

The Tempter: "If we were to believe all the visions told us, we would certainly find ourselves often deceived. Hence it is written, 'Test the spirits to see whether they are from God.' "[94] I answered: "In this area something is hidden that not everyone can grasp, but I will try to make it clear to all by means of a comparison with natural things. In nature we see that whatever has the same form also has a tendency and way of acting that corresponds to that form. Thus heavy things move to the earth's center, light things move upward. A similar explanation holds in supernatural things, so that beings that have one kind of supernatural form possess the tendency and way of acting that comes from the form. Since the light of faith is the same supernatural form in all who believe, though some possess it more intensely than others,[95] and since this light has a native tendency toward the truth as its proper object, it is not possible for anyone who is informed by this light to adhere firmly to a falsity contrary to the faith without the corruption or loss of the light of faith. Whenever a faithful and sincere person hears something that is above the capacity of his intellect, if he is acting according to the light of faith, he will never firmly adhere to the false side, but will always surrender everything to God and to the teaching of the Church. Note that anyone who lives correctly and walks in the way of God is illuminated by a special light above the common light of faith. It exists for the sake of joining charity to faith and for uprightness and simplicity of mind, as it is written, 'A light for the pure of heart has arisen in the darkness.'[96] By means of this light they can discern revelations and divine operations without any error. Just as God directs nature so that it does not err, for the Philosopher says that the work of nature is the work of an intelligence that does not err,[97] so too he directs the faithful and simple to know his works and revelations without error. He who does not want to be deceived in these questions should live piously in simplicity of heart and should be directed by God into the truth itself without any error. Thus the Fathers we mentioned above were not mistaken in believing and writing down such things. Only some proud men were fooled, especially those who thought that they were wise when they opposed and scoffed at such things. They not only never prayed (except perhaps with their lips), but they did not even know what the word 'prayer' meant."

The Tempter: "Nevertheless I see that many very wise men of great and keen genius and impressive prudence, most skillful in all human affairs, scoffed at those visions. I am moved by their authority." I answered: "Did I not say that in order to understand these things pious living and walking in God's sight alone were required? Human wisdom is totally unequal to these matters. Rather, because of its pride, God leaves it in darkness as unworthy of so precious a light. It is written: 'You have hidden these things from the wise and the prudent and revealed them to the little ones.'[98] The apostle says: 'Where is the wise man? Where the scribe? Where the investigator of this world? Has not God made foolish the wisdom of this world? Because in God's wisdom the world did not have knowledge through God's wisdom, it has pleased him to save believers through the foolishness of preaching.'[99] Isaiah says, 'Where is the learned man, where the doctor of the law who ponders its words, where the teacher of the little ones? You will not behold the shameless people, the people of profound speech, so that you will not be able to understand the eloquence of his tongue, in whom there is no wisdom.'[100] Let those wise men answer whether what I foretold was possible or impossible for God's power and wisdom. If they are wise, they will confess that such things are not only possible for God, but also quite easy to do. Since the wise man's role is not to speak foolishly and without reason, I want to know why they were moved to mock these matters. If you look at it carefully, they are not able to put up any argument against our predictions, certainly not a demonstrative one. The material does not allow it, because we foretold contingent things to come, and demonstration concerns necessary things, not dialectical and probable ones. The latter arguments lead to opinions that, even though they do not make the intellect absolutely sure as demonstrative arguments do, still incline the mind more to one side than to the other. From the viewpoint of natural causes the things I foretold are indifferent. They could either happen or not. From the viewpoint of the divine will God is freely able to do them or not. If he does not reveal them, no one can know where his inclination and decision rest. Therefore, these predictions can neither be proved nor disproved by means of natural arguments because a foundation in nature is lacking.

"Furthermore these predictions cannot be rejected on the basis of signs, because of the two kinds of signs that have the greatest power of disproof, neither works in this case. The first is when a prior condition contrary to the things predicted is manifest in the world. This does not interfere at all in this case, but rather proves the opposite, because when God intends to show his glory he does great things at unexpected times. He causes them to be foretold long ahead when no prior condition is apparent, as can be seen from the prophets of the New and Old Laws. So too in my case when everything seemed peaceful I foretold that war would soon come; and now when the world is in turmoil I predict the greatest tranquillity and peace will immediately follow. When the Florentines thought they were very fortunate, I prophesied evils to them; now, when they are in great difficulties, I announce that supreme happiness will soon be theirs. Therefore, the first sign has no power of disproof.

"The second sign, that is, the reprehensible life of the prophet, might seem to be valid, but this too holds no water. As I have mentioned, evil men have prophesied things to come from the power of the prophetic light, for this is a charismatic gift that can be possessed even by someone in mortal sin. And, so, I do not see the basis for this mockery of the wise, except in their own pride. They ought to note that they could be justly put to shame by this pride. We have shown that none of these things is impossible, but they are likely and fitting. Therefore, whenever anything we predicted takes place, the wise will be subject to no small danger of ridicule and loss of the glorious distinction for which alone they labor in everything they do. I am not at all surprised at their ridicule, since Christ has said: 'I have come into the world to do judgment, so that those who do not see may see, and those who see may become blind.' "[101]

The Tempter: "Those who believe in you are quite rare in comparison with those who ridicule these predictions. It seems hard to follow the judgment of so few." I responded: "This is a very frivolous argument. We see that very few men have correct judgment and that very few are wise in comparison with the multitude of fools, as is written, 'The number of fools is infinite.'[102] So, too, few live justly in comparison with those who live unjust lives, because many are called but few are chosen.[103] In both Testaments we read that they were few in number who followed the prophets, Christ, and the apostles, in comparison with those who persecuted them. There is also a great difference between those who hear these things from the author's mouth and those who receive information from the account of the hearers or from others. If you speak about my audience, the number of those who believe cannot be compared with the number who do not; rather, almost none of my hearers is a nonbeliever. But if you are talking about the others who have not heard me, I grant that the number of nonbelievers is much larger than that of believers. It is one thing to listen to a man who has an interior perception of all these things in the fullness of his spirit, and to hear the sound of his living voice, his arguments and their order, the force of his words and their agreement with scripture. It is quite another to hear someone who does not personally feel them or who lacks their spirit repeating them. He will have a weak voice, halting disordered arguments, and dry ill-chosen words, without spirit and almost dead, with all the life breathed out. So Saint Jerome rightly says: 'The living voice has I know not what hidden energy; it resounds more strongly as it passes from the speaker's mouth to the ears of the listeners.'[104] It is written: 'I will give you a mouth and wisdom so that all your adversaries will not be able to resist or contradict you.'[105] We read concerning the holy Protomartyr Stephen that when so many wise men gathered together and argued with him, 'they were not able to resist the wisdom and the spirit which spoke in him.'[106] It is no wonder that many who do not hear the original speaker never believe, especially since the teaching of Christ has always undergone contradiction from the beginning of the world to the present. Therefore, detractors in various places have easily corrupted the minds of the simple. Without hearing the source, the simple are easily led astray."

The Tempter: "Many claim that a number of the things you foretold have not happened, and for this reason they do not believe the other things you predicted." I answered: "Whatever I have publicly preached about things to come has either already taken place or certainly will take place. Not one iota will fail. But note that when I spoke apart and privately, because I am a man and then spoke as a man, perhaps I let slip something that was less true, though I have no consciousness or memory of such a thing. I always try to speak the truth. If it ever happens otherwise, it will come either from a slip of the tongue or from speaking about the future not in the spirit but in a human way, as is usually the case. I have often warned in the pulpit that I should receive no more faith than other men in any private conversation, except in the case of those coming particular events known through heavenly illumination of which I have spoken to some of my close friends. Part of them are already fulfilled; the rest will doubtless also be completed. I know that the divinatory spirit is not always at the service of the prophets themselves, but comes and goes at the will of the Holy Spirit. When it is present it does not reveal everything, but discloses more or less according to its wishes. Thus Nathan the prophet speaking from his own spirit persuaded David to build the Temple when he said: 'Go and do everything that is in your heart, because the Lord is with you.'[107] But afterwards, at the command of the Holy Spirit, he revoked his word.

"Some stupid people who have spoken to me have boasted that while we talked I did not know the secrets of their hearts, as if to infer that any prophet should be equal to God and know everything. 'They are in error, knowing neither the scriptures nor the power of God.'[108] The great prophet Elisha when the Sunamite woman whose son had died came to him said, 'Her soul is in bitterness and the Lord has hidden it from me and not revealed it to me.'[109] Many came to tempt me, because in my preaching they heard me say that their cunning could not deceive me. They did not understand that I meant to signify that they would not be able to make me preach things that were unsuitable by their frauds. Whatever I said in the pulpit I was first accustomed to weigh in the balance of prayer and scripture, as well as by natural reason, experience and trustworthy witnesses. I did not say this because the secrets of their hearts could not be hidden from me. Only God can read them. Even though many thought that they had deceived me in matters of some import and weight, their frauds were not hidden from me. I often heard of them before they spoke. Other times I heard of them afterwards, as some of my acquaintances to whom I told this in secret can testify, and even some of the liars themselves who recognized that their licentious schemes and frauds were found out.

"I know that this objection came partly from some religious (though few) whom I warned and reproved in charity about hidden faults. Some of them were unrepentant and always denied things that became evident from clear signs and indications in the passage of time, even though they still persisted tenaciously in their wickedness. Some confessed to their friends that I had spoken the truth about them, although before others they were still ashamed and denied it. This error also came from falsifiers who made up many lies by additions or subtractions to my words according to their wishes, thus making me the author of their errors. It also could have come from those who heard me preaching, but who did not receive my words in the sense in which they were spoken. For this reason it was often necessary for me to repeat the same things. Therefore, I decided to write down whatever I had publicly preached about the future so that they could understand everything that I had predicted and would no longer ascribe things to me that I had not even thought of. And, so, Christ's teaching might be defended from so many calumnies."

The Tempter: "I think that the fact that you have become a conversation piece for the Florentines and for the whole of Italy should be enough to keep you quiet." I answered: "My concern is to please God and not men, because as the apostle says, 'If I would please men any longer, I would not be a servant of Christ.'[110] I am not so stupid that I do not know that anyone who preaches such things is held for a fool by the wise men of this world. Along with Paul I say to them, 'We are fools for the sake of Christ, you are wise men.'[111] But in the time when the just will stand in great constancy against those who persecuted them,[112] I hope to hear the voices of these wise men as they say: 'These are they whom we at one time held in derision and as an image of reproach. We fools judged their life to be madness and their end without honor. Behold how they have been numbered among God's sons and their lot is with the saints.' "[113]

The Tempter: "If you were only made a fool of, it would not count for much. But you are also hated and your life is in serious danger. It would be better if you considered stopping right now." I answered: "As I said, I am not so insane that I do not know that everyone rebukes me and that every human state of life has grave hatreds raised against it. But the more I see my teaching, undertakings, and works to be like the teaching and works of Christ, the apostles, and the holy prophets who were mocked, hated, and persecuted because of the truth, the stronger I become. This is a sign of divine predestination, as Christ says: 'Blessed are you when men hate you, persecute you, and speak every lying evil against you for my sake. Rejoice and exult because your reward is great in heaven. Thus did they persecute the prophets who lived before you.' "[114]

The Tempter: "I now know quite well that you do not sin from ignorance or from foolish simplicity, because you have answered my objections in a way that shows that you are seriously moved to make these predictions. Although a host of other objections could be advanced, you would easily be able to refute them since you have answered many more difficult ones. Therefore, if you do not preach those things from ignorance, it follows that you make them up with deceit in order to gain glory, dignity, and wealth, as many hold. That, my son, is detestable." I answered and said: "Although it is not right for me to justify myself, nevertheless, I will respond with what modesty I can manage so that Christ's teaching does not suffer blame. I said before that the light of prophecy does not justify a man in any way, and I acknowledge that I am a sinner in need of divine mercy. But mark God's word to Samuel the prophet: 'Men see what appears on the outside; God beholds the heart.'[115] And whatever my life may be, good or evil, only God, no one else, can judge me. Everyone must be presented before the judgment seat of Our Lord Jesus Christ so that each can report what he did while in the body.[116] Those who think that way about me in my judgment have no basis, because they cannot investigate my heart's secret and the final intent of my preaching except from external signs. Those who think ill of me have no foundation in such things, at least insofar as human judgment can grasp. If, as they say, my aim is not a good one, then because every agent acts for the sake of an end,[117] the end of my preaching must be some temporal good and God is rejected.

"Temporal goods are of three kinds. Some are external to man, such as riches, honors, glory, power, and dignity. Some are in man's bodily part, like strength, health, beauty, and pleasure; some in the intellectual part, like knowledge, eloquence, and other special gifts. Since these men cannot see what is hidden in my heart, in order to make such a judgment about me they have to base their argument on an evident external sign from which they can prove that I have desired one or all of these things. I do not think they can report any such sign. They cannot say that I am after money. It is well known that my brothers and I are reduced to the moderation and scarcity of a simple way of life according to the rule of our order so that the citizens of Florence can testify that we have never bothered them about anything beyond the bare necessities of life. I have not been friendly and familiar with the powerful and the rich, but in my preaching I have always resisted their unbridled desires. Following the judgment of flesh and blood, they would have much to complain about in me, although according to the Spirit they ought to thank God for the works that he has done for them through me.

"It cannot be said against me that I am hungry for honor and glory, because as I said above and have learned by experience, proclaiming things to come gains one derision rather than honor, especially in the case of the important people with whom unspiritual men and the worldly-wise seek to gain reputation and glory. Anyone who would put his goal in glory and honor and seek them from the weak and lowborn from whom no profit can be expected, and who is hated and ridiculed by the powerful, would be completely insane.

"You cannot reasonably say that I aspire to ecclesiastical dignities, for in our times we know how they are acquired. I have always taken the opposite course in my sermons, forever speaking in a general way about public matters. I have never marked out anyone in particular by name or in such a way that one person could be censured. Nonetheless I have aroused against myself the hatred rather than the good will of those who have the power to grant these dignities. I have not for that reason been led to try to reconcile them or flatter them, as do those who are interested in dignities.

"My attackers cannot have a foundation for their view with regard to bodily goods, for I could not give myself up to pleasures without its being openly known, especially by my brethren who as eyewitnesses of my daily life know my labors of mind and body very well. If you knew how much work it is (leaving other things aside) to preach continuously so many years in the same city, especially with the intention of bearing fruit and the desire of saving souls, you would think quite differently. Even though it may seem unfitting for someone to speak about himself and his own style of life, I have been given permission for now. Let this suffice for an answer—nothing can be discovered about me that would allow the judgment that

I organized my sermons to gain bodily goods. Therefore, they speak like fools.

"Further, my enemies cannot base my sermons on the goods of the intellectual part of man by claiming that their goal is the parading of wisdom and eloquence. Everybody knows how simply I preach and how completely I avoid any pretense of wisdom and eloquence. I have not said all this to praise myself, because in God's sight I am not justified in this,[118] but in order to show those who falsely accuse our teaching, rather Christ's teaching, that they are without foundation and that without evident signs they usurp the judgment of the heart that belongs to God alone. If I seem to have fallen to praising myself, I answer with Paul, 'I have spoken in foolishness,' and 'I have become foolish; you have forced me.' " [119]

The Tempter: "I am surprised that you would deny that there are clear external signs of your wickedness when all know that you left the Congregation of the Lombard Observance, and also withdrew from San Marco in Florence, San Domenico in Fiesole, and other places joined to them so that you would not have to remain obedient. Like a Lord you arrogated the priorate for life and thus obtained a fine state for rejoicing."[120] I answered: "I could not have made this withdrawal alone, without the consent of the brothers of those houses. More than a hundred of them agreed (though not all at one time, since San Marco went first), as is evident from the published document. They cannot all be thought so foolish or evil that they were unable to judge whether this withdrawal would be good or bad, particularly since for more than six months they gathered and prayed to God about the matter four or five times a day. As the result has shown, the separation was clearly done not for the sake of relaxation but for that of strictness. This is not a falling away from our professed obedience. Its form is a promise of obedience to God, the Virgin Mary, Saint Dominic, and the master general of the whole order, or prior, or whoever presides in the place of the general. Our profession binds us to obey the general, not the Lombard Congregation. When we withdrew we were still obedient to the general. According to our constitutions the Province of

Tuscany was divided from the Province of Lombardy, and neither naturally rules over the other. One time when the Convent of San Marco was deprived of the correct number of brothers due to a terrible plague it could not stand on its own and freely committed itself to the control of the Lombard Congregation. Now with the aid of divine grace the number of brothers is such that it is well able to govern itself and so it is suitable that it legitimately return to its proper state, because when the cause ceases so should the effect, especially when the customs of the Lombards and Tuscans differ so much.

"It is not true that I made myself prior for life. Even the Pontifical Brief of Separation was so procured by my efforts that it laid down that the prior a year from the day of his election would be free and void of all responsibility and that it would be in the power of the brothers to choose whom they preferred. This is annually observed. This year a biennial vicar, the head of our whole congregation, has been established. When two years are over he will yield to another and like the rest of the brothers be a subject once again, at least through the whole following two years. Things will follow this order and there will be no opportunity for domination. Anyone who abandons obedience out of desire for domination does not bind himself with stricter rules, but seeks a freer life. He devotes himself to excess in eating, drinking, and dressing, and has a good time. None of this is seen in our congregation, but rather the greatest harmony and charity, which do not agree with ambition, as is written: 'Quarrels always are found among the proud.'[121]

"Since it would be far too drawn out to bring up all the reasons that led me to the separation, let this alone suffice for the present, that is, as long as it is believed. Whether it is believed or not, I will by no means leave it out since I know that before God I speak the truth and am not lying. No ambition or desire for the pleasure of bodily comfort pushed me to this separation; the brothers of Lombardy know that I had no lack of honor and comfort there. But it was God's will that I should do this. I was moved to the separation by the same light by which I predicted the future. God willed it, inspired it, and urged it because he had decided to do many things through us in Tuscany, and especially in Florence. Some of these we have already seen accomplished; the others we will soon see done. None could have come about had not that separation come first."

The Tempter: "If you knew it was God's will, what need was there to get the aid of worldly human power to obtain a papal brief for the separation?" I answered, "When God wants something done, he still wishes fit means for the conditions of the times to be used. The present situation required that it be so. God also wanted us to face very great opposition from those against us in order to show that he was the author of this affair, not men. My brethren will testify that at the height of the dispute I used to exhort them and often assure them that if the whole world were against us we should still be sure of victory, because it was God's will. As indeed it happened."

The Tempter: "One thing mars your responses—that you are grasping at the state and government of Florence and looking to seize the highest position so that you can drag the people where you want." I answered: "Those who knew me recognize that up to now I have never been involved in public affairs with the exception of this one time. In the new situation and great danger of Florence it seemed to be my duty to advise how the city ought to be governed. With divine inspiration I recommended things that were necessary and useful for public safety to the citizens, but I did not compel them. After a good form of government had been adopted, everyone knows that my last message was to fear God always and above all, to pray before taking up any serious matters, and not to come to me for advice any longer. My desire is to pursue peace and quiet, but God in the meantime inspired me to do otherwise and charity urged it. When asked, I did not cease giving advice.

"No one can justly complain about what I have done up to now by saying, 'Nobody fighting for God gets involved in worldly concerns so that he may please him to whom he has committed himself.'[122] In things of such importance, and even those of lesser weight, many holy men have dutifully taken up the charge of political power over both lords and commons as the readers of the sacred histories know. Saint Catherine of Siena, despite her female sex, often intervened in public affairs for the common good. She undertook an embassy for the Florentines to Pope Gregory XI at Avignon and not long after one for the same pontiff to the Florentines. Therefore to treat of public affairs for the sake of universal peace and in order to lead men to justice and to good actions and for the common salvation of souls is not to be involved in secular affairs, nor are Paul's words to be understood in this way. Rather it is to gain the people things spiritual and divine. According to Aristotle, it is just to designate each thing from its end."[123]

The Tempter: "This excuse could be admitted if you had exhorted the people of Florence to some good form of government, but you advised a form of government that seems dangerous to prudent and practical men. To put something of such importance at the discretion of the people and to snatch it from the hands of the powerful cannot be done without grave danger." I answered: "If you look at this government correctly, it is right and natural for the people of Florence. All good government is divided by philosophers into three types. The first, when one person with full power rules the multitude, is the best, if the ruler is just. The second is the administration of a few powerful and wise men, which is called aristocracy, that is, the rule of the best. The third is when a city or province is governed by the whole people; this is called a polity. This belonged to the Florentines from of old, and they call it a 'popular regime.' Ancient custom shows that one quarter of their magistrates, especially those who really govern the state, should come from the artisans. This government is not merely of the crowd, but of the whole people, that is, of all those who can hold office because they have been citizens for a fixed time.[124] Because it is easy for the powerful to push the crowd where they want, we gave the city a style of government like a polity, or a popular one. If it is kept, after this no one powerful man will be able to gain a tyranny by reason of riches or connections. Only the virtuous will be exalted. The citizens will dwell in their city free of trouble, and no one will be permitted to oppress another unjustly. This type of government will give the greatest unity and peace. As I have often explained and as experience has taught, only three kinds of people will complain about it—the ambitious, the wicked, and the foolish. This is because, unless they improve, they will no longer be able easily to obtain the positions they unworthily desire.

"It is not true that this government is dangerous, for it is not entrusted to the crowd at all, nor absolutely to the people or the magnates, but to whoever obtains his power and authority from the Great Council where what is to be considered will be pondered maturely. The nobles and the prudent men used to governing will attend the council. In such a large gathering there can be only rare error, especially when this form of government will have grown stronger and more elaborate through use (nothing is immediately perfect), and when all the fit citizens meet in Council, not just a third as now. The citizens intend to set it up this way, but it has not yet been decreed because there is no public place large enough for such a big crowd. The fullness of power will always remain in this council, and such a large group will not be easily corrupted or perverted by those hungry for tyranny. To corrupt so many would be difficult and in a way impossible, especially because the judgment and examination of other prudent and proven citizens will have been invoked before the council takes up anything. This will take place first through a consideration made by their colleagues summoned by the Signoria, and then by the 'Consiglio de'Richiesti' composed of eighty men, almost always from the first rank, who will be charged with the examination of whatever is coming up. This will be set out in the new reform of the government.[125]

"The more this new government advances, the more it will cleanse the city from the infection of the evil and the foolish and force all citizens to pursue honest life and virtue. Through the Great Council administrative offices suitable to its character will be set up, and when only worthy men of sense have been admitted to these offices the city will be ruled well and happily in things spiritual and temporal. Florence will not labor constantly under the different quarrels of the citizens, which everyone knows are so harmful to the Republic. The citizens can remain quiet and safe at home and make the city flower with virtues and riches. No one will be compelled to foster injustice, but all will be able to embrace a life that befits good and perfect Christians."[126]

The Tempter: "In summary, your excuses do not square with many people because hypocrisy has learned how to conceal its ideas with care." I answered: "I know that it is impossible to satisfy everyone because a servant is not greater than his master.[127] Even though Christ could not be in error, nevertheless, the Scribes and the Pharisees could not believe that he was not a seducer. It is enough for me to show that the verdict and complaint of those who presume to judge my inner intention completely lacks any foundation in exterior indication and that their words do not come from a good intention. Although I acknowledge that I am a sinner, I can show from valid reasons and arguments that my deeds have not come from ill will, as they lyingly claim. I have already shown that they do not proceed from ignorance.

"First of all, God cannot consent to evil and give it assistance. He always condemns it and diminishes it. Two things stand out from my predictions that can only be done by God. They prove that my teaching is from him and not from human malice. One is that the greater part of what I foretold has already been fulfilled and verified exactly, down to the last jot; the other is the change in the people of Florence. Anyone would openly confess that never in the recent memory of man has there been such a change in men and women and a holiness of like proportions as when Florence passed from vice to virtue and to a decent way of life. The reformation of the city (something everybody thought was impossible) was brought off by the admonitions in my sermons. I could here introduce many almost miraculous events that happened in the city through my activity by the grace of God. For the sake of brevity I will leave them out. It is fitting and true that God, the just and best Parent of all, should enlighten the good rather than the evil with his light and should permit the evil rather than the good to fall into error. Since all the good people of Florence follow this teaching, and all who lead lives that are blameworthy and unchristian attack it, it is consistent that it has its origin in God and not in error and cunning.

"It is unlikely that such deceitful malice would not have been detected during the many years I lived at Florence, especially because the Florentines are the shrewdest of men and the most inquisitive spies of others' lives. Even more, in my case evil men, priests and religious as well as laity and men of every station, drew up many attacks and false accusations against me, to the point of making up letters of excommunication and criminal accusation. If there were error or deceit in my preaching, I say that it absolutely could not have been concealed until today. Truth always grows in the midst of difficulties and gets stronger in conflict because it then shines forth more brilliantly. It has conquered everything. Becoming successively greater, it now has more strength than ever before."

The Tempter: "Finally, to speak the truth, it seems to me that you talk about vice and virtue the way other preachers do. You follow their usual style and do not come off as original. This prediction of the future bears no fruit for souls and looks like ostentation rather than true modesty." I responded: "Causes are known by their efforts. Since all know that very great service for the salvation of souls has come from this message and this kind of preaching, it can scarcely be, as you claim, that my preaching and predictions are useless. Rather, they are especially useful and fruitful. They bring men to penance and prepare God's elect to bear coming tribulations with calm, because 'Darts foreseen make lighter wounds.'[128] Even though not everyone turns to God, the elect for whom these things were foretold have profited greatly from them, as it is written: 'You have shown your people hard things; you have given us the wine of compunction to drink. You have given yourself as a sign for those who fear you so that they might flee from the bow, so that your beloved ones may be delivered.'[129] Even if others did not believe, the elect surely did. These things were given to me for their profit, as is written: 'All who were destined to eternal life believed.'"[130]

When I had already taken up a good deal of time in

arguing like this with the Tempter, I finally looked back at my companions and saw them talking together and laughing at me. I turned to them and said, "What are you saying to each other and why are you smiling?"[131] They answered: "You do not seem to know who you are talking to." I then drew near Lady Prayer and asked her to tell me who he might be. She said: "You have become involved in an argument based on human wisdom, the kind that is foolishness to God. So you have not recognized who he was who was disputing with you till now. Go join Lady Simplicity, since she well knows every cunning of the Enemy. She will teach you what you want to know." When I joined the Lady my eyes were immediately opened and I knew that he was not a hermit, but mankind's Tempter. Then I collected my four companions and said: "Foul Satan, the craftiness and arts by which you try to pervert the hearts of the simple and to lead them away from the faith have gained you nothing. God's strong hand is with us; it makes his work grow. You and your angels have been put to confusion." When I said this he disappeared at once, filling the air with great cries.

From that point on we peacefully pursued the journey we had undertaken and came to the gates of heaven, which were surrounded by a very high wall of precious stones and seemed to encircle the whole universe. On the top of it angel guardians sat round about, sweetly singing what is written in Isaiah: "Sion is the city of our strength; the Savior will place a wall and a bulwark in it." We knocked on the gates without delay. They then responded, "Open the gates and let in the just nation that upholds the truth." My companions lifted up their eyes to heaven and responded: "Let the old error depart. Keep the peace, because we have hoped in you." The angels replied with melodious voice, "You have hoped in the Lord for endless ages, in the Lord God who is strong forever. Let fear be far from you. Your desires will be fulfilled and human pride will be confounded, because God has cast down those who dwelt on high and humbled the lofty city. He will humble her to the very earth, drag her down as far as the dust. The foot of the poor man, the step of the needy will tread her under." In the midst of these words we saw the gates opening and heard them sing from within: "The just man's path is correct; his way is right to walk upon." We turned toward God and responded: "We have waited for you, Lord, in the way of your judgments; your name and your memory are the desire of our soul." When I heard this I became much more fervent and lifted up my voice and said, "My soul has desired You at night, and in the depths of my heart my spirit has kept watch for You in the morning. When You judge the earth all those who dwell on the globe will learn your justice."[132]

The gates were opened right after these words and under a light of immense brightness we saw indescribable things. I will speak of part of them as the sermon goes on.

Before we went in, Saint Joseph met us, he who is the spouse and guardian of that Immaculate Virgin to whom we were going for a response to our embassy. Before he introduced us he said, "The Lord be with you." We responded, "May the Lord bless you." We then added: "Holy Father, because your Spouse, the Virgin Mother of God, on the Feast of her Annunciation took up the task of pleading on behalf of the Florentines for the restoration of the promises lost by their sins, and because we were told within the octave that a good answer would be given us on the day of the octave itself, we have returned tonight, all ignorant of the details of the response, so that we can learn what good news we can announce to the Florentines tomorrow morning. We therefore brought along this beautiful present."

At that moment we uncovered the very luxurious crown that Lady Simplicity was carrying. It looked like this. Three circlets or crowns of unequal size were joined together and arranged so that the higher were smaller than the lower. The first or lowest crown was the largest and was linked together with twelve precious gems green like jasper and cut in the form of human hearts. The hearts were upside down with the narrow ends like the points of a crown. Along the lower edge of the hearts the Canticle of Zachary, "Blessed be the Lord, the God of Israel,"[133] divided into twelve verses, one for each of the hearts, enclosed the whole like a small band or fillet. On the side of each heart running from the base up around the top and down to the other base the Hail Mary was inscribed. In the middle of each heart the name of Jesus shone forth most splendidly. Above the point of each heart a single pearl gleamed; over the pearls were twelve little green banners on which were inscribed the twelve privileges of the Virgin with their intercessions. Two related to the Eternal Father: the first, "True Spouse of God the Father," because she and God the Father have the same Son; the second, "Admirable Spouse of God the Father," because as the Father begot the Son from all eternity in heaven without a mother, so she begot the same Son on earth without a father. Two others concern the Son: first, "Mother of God," and second, "Mother of her Father," for the Lord Jesus Christ is her Son, and as God and Creator of all he created her. Two relate to the Holy Spirit, that is "Special Sanctuary of the Holy Spirit," since she was filled with all graces by him in a singular way, and "Ineffable Sanctuary of the Holy Spirit," because he made her worthy to be the Mother of the Creator of the universe. Two concern her virginity: first, "Virgin of Virgins," because no other virgin can be compared to her who had no strain of mortal or venial sin; and second, "Fruitful Virgin," for she alone is virgin and mother. Two relate to the Church Triumphant and the whole universe. The first is "Sole Queen of the World," since she is the true spouse, mother, and sanctuary of the King of the whole creation, who is God three and one. The second is "Queen to be honored above all creatures." To God alone is due the honor of adoration since he is the First Principle and Ruler of all things. To the saints only the cult of honor is given, fitting for those who share in God's beatitude or who because of some other dignity act in God's stead. Because beyond all this the Glorious Virgin is the Mother of God and far surpasses all the other saints in honor, she is venerated with "hyperdulia," that is, superior honor.[134] The two final privileges refer to the Church Militant. The first is "Sweetness of the Hearts of the Just," because through her they beg abundant graces from God, and also because her love is sweeter than honey and the honeycomb and miraculously makes souls and bodies chaste. The second is

"Hope of Sinners and Those in Misery," for because of her prayers and merits they can hope for God's mercy. These twelve privileges were inscribed on each of the little banners in this way: "True Spouse of God the Father, pray for us," "Admirable Spouse of God the Father, intercede for us," and so forth.

Above this first crown there is a second smaller one composed of ten hearts of gleaming pearls arranged like the lower ones. The Canticle of the Virgin, that is, the Magnificat, was inscribed at the bottom, divided into ten verses to match the number of hearts. Around each of them one of the ten commandments was written. In the midst of each was a ruby; at the top there was a chalcedony on which sat a small white banner for each heart. These ten banners contained inscriptions of the ten petitions made by us and by the city of Florence. The first was: "In all things may God's will be done." The second, "We desire the honor and glory of God before all things." The third, "We seek the renovations of the Church." The fourth, "We hope for the salvation of all the faithful." The fifth, "We pray especially for the salvation of our souls." The sixth, "We beg for the forgiveness of the sins of the people of Florence, which have interrupted the promise God once made them." The seventh, "We pray that the scourges the people have deserved may be averted." The eighth, "May abundance of graces and full gifts of the Holy Spirit be given to this city." The ninth, "We beg for an abundance of riches and an enlargement of our power so that these graces may be spread to other peoples too." The tenth and last, "May whatever God promised up to now be fully restored to the Florentines."

A smaller third crown placed atop the second shone with four hearts of flaming carbuncles. At the bottom of the hearts was written the Canticle of Simeon, "Now do you dismiss your servant, O Lord,"[135] similarly divided into four verses. Around each was written the name of one of the four evangelists; in the midst of each was a glowing cross, and on top a topaz with a flaming little banner superimposed. On the first of these it said: "We ask for angelic protection for the city of Florence." On the second, "We earnestly entreat a rule of perfect bishops and prelates." On the third, "We request the teaching of holy preachers;" and on the fourth, "We beg for a multitude of fervent clergy, priests, and religious." Finally, above this small crown shone one heart composed of many small hearts of different colors wonderfully joined together. Around it was that saying of the Lord: "This is my command, that you love one another as I have loved you. In this all men will know that you are my disciples, if you have love for one another."[136] At the heart's peak glowed a very beautiful emerald inscribed with the words: "They have one heart and one soul in the Lord."[137] A small crucifix was fastened to the emerald with a little banner thus inscribed: "May there be peace in your strength and abundance in your towers. For the sake of my brothers and my neighbors I will speak peace concerning you. I have sought good things for you for the sake of the house of the Lord our God."[138] Rods of the purest gold wound about the three crowns and bound everything together in a beautiful way. This is the gift that we decided to offer to the Majesty of the Eternal King through the hands of the Glorious Virgin Mother in order to obtain divine mercy and to complete the restitution of the graces promised us.

Joseph asked us what the mystery of the crown signified. I answered: "I realize, my father, that you know it, but that for our greater consolation you want me to describe it briefly. The people of Florence consecrate this crown to the Virgin Mother of God, your Spouse, in order to regain the graces once promised them. Every day they have devoutly prayed first the Canticle of Zachary, or, if they did not know it, the Apostles' Creed in its place, then twelve Hail Marys, then the Magnificat, the Canticle of your beloved Spouse, and finally the Canticle of Simeon. They have completed this crown not only with tongue but also with heart and deed. The first circle of green hearts signifies the beginnners who have recently started to do penance in the verdure of faith. The joining at the top denotes the purging of their conscience.[139] Desiring to advance in spiritual things, they offer their hearts to God and beg for themselves and for the whole city what appears on the titles of the little banners.

"The second circle of the pure white pearls designates the advanced who are not only cleansed of consciousness of guilt but are also free of earthly desires. They keep the divine commandments most diligently. The ruby fixed in the midst of the hearts shows their charity. The chalcedony placed at the top points to works burning with love and the good example they give their neighbors through which many remorseful sinners are thus led to penance, just as straw is attracted by chalcedony when it is heated by the sun or by rubbing. And so the petitions on their little banners are worthy to be heard. The third crown of hearts made of carbuncles that light up the night like a flame is that of the perfect. Although they are very few, they are all lit with divine love and burn most ardently, keeping both the commandments and the counsels of the Gospel. In the middle of the hearts they bear a cross red with longing for the martyrdom they greatly desire for the name of Christ. The topaz placed above the hearts has the color of the purest gold and a heavenly brightness. It surpasses the splendor of all other gems as long as it is lit by the sun's rays. It signifies the deeds and teaching of the perfect who are lit by Jesus Christ, the Sun of Justice. They ask only for things splendid and spiritual. The heart made out of many hearts at the very top of the crown represents the concord and charity of all the just, and at the same time the public peace recently established among the citizens. When they neglected this earlier, God grew angry and withdrew the graces destined for them. Now that they have agreed upon the peace pleasing to God, they are asking him to restore these benefits completely. The emerald located above the highest heart points to the hope of gaining from God the flowering of life everlasting and in this world the promised graces. The golden rods that connect and organize everything witness to the agreement and order in work and prayer of the beginners, the advanced, and the perfect."

Then that most holy old man Joseph joyfully grasped my right hand and brought us in when the gates had been shut. He said, "May your journey be a fortunate one. Rejoice, for you will receive pleasing new gifts, as you were told." We lifted up our eyes and saw a very broad field, covered with delicious flowers of Paradise. Live crystal streams flowed everywhere with a quiet murmur. A vast multitude of mild animals, like white sheep, ermines, rabbits, and harmless creatures of that sort, all whiter than snow, played pleasantly among the different flowers and green grass alongside the flowing waters. There were leafy trees of various kinds decorated with flowers and fruits, in whose branches a crowd of varicolored birds flying here and there in a wonderful way sang a sweet melody. In the middle I saw a high throne like the throne of Solomon described in the Third Book of Kings:

> King Solomon made a great throne of ivory and covered it with much yellow gold. It had six steps and the top was round in the back. Two hands on either side held the chair, two lions stood beside the hands, and twelve small lions stood on the six steps. No such work had been made in any other kingdom.[140]

On this throne there sat a most beautiful and gracious Lady holding in her lap an infant brighter than the sun. Above them, almost in the middle between heaven and earth, shone a wonderful light with three faces that lighted up the whole world. The triple face seemed to take the greatest delight in the sight of that wonderful Lady, and to fill her with light more than any other thing that could be seen. It smiled joyfully upon her and her son with such high delight and gaity that mortal tongue could not express it. The whole joy of the three faces seemed to be turned toward the mother and the son. A countless array of ministers stood in ranks about the throne—something marvelous to see! Astonished at this wondrous sight, and not able to bear the light because of human weakness, I immediately fell on my face.[141] My guardian angel and Joseph our leader revived me and lifted me up on my feet. I asked Joseph to reveal to me the mystery of so great a sacrament. He graciously replied thus: "This is the mystery of the renewal of the Church throughout the world that you have foretold to mortals for these many years. The walls made of precious stones are the doctors, preachers, and prelates filled with virtues who will protect the Church in that time. The angels who are arranged on the walls signify the coming communion between prelates and angels. The prelates will be illuminated and guarded by their protection.[142] The gate signifies the scriptures of the Old and New Testaments. Every believing Christian enters the Church through faith in the scriptures. The flowers on the field are the different virtues that will fill the world. The streams of water are the divine graces that will be plentiful at that time, as is written: 'Come all you who thirst to the waters;'[143] and again, 'Let him who thirsts come to me and drink;'[144] and, 'He who wishes, will freely receive the water of life;'[145] and, 'He who drinks from the water I will give him, will never thirst. But the water I will give him will become a fountain welling up to eternal life.'[146]

"The harmless animals are the Christians engaged in the active life, who at that time will lead such simple lives that they will hold wealth and temporal goods for little and will exult in Christ's virtues and in his special graces. The birds signify Christians and religious who are devoted to contemplation and sing God's praises on the branches of the trees, that is, at the summit of the virtues. They will contemplate divine things continuously on the wings of the intellect through the mysteries of the Church and of the scriptures. The marvelous throne with the orders of ministers about it is the Church Triumphant, which will rejoice to such a degree in this renewal that when she sees Christians living the angelic life she will deign to bend down and join with them not only invisibly, but even visibly, as we read of the early church.[147] The light shining out from the three faces is an image of the Holy Trinity, which lights up the whole world but has especially filled Christ's humanity and after it that of his Glorious Mother with greater gifts and more singular prerogatives. You saw her seated on the throne representing Christ's Incarnation. The Feast of the Annunication is a sign of this. The throne itself shows the special decoration of virtues given to his Mother by her beloved Only-Begotten Son. The ivory refers to the purest whiteness of her virginity, because of the chastity of the elephant[148] and the whiteness of his bone. And so it is written, 'Solomon made a great throne of ivory.' Solomon is interpreted as 'the man of peace,'[149] and this agrees with Our Savior who brought true peace on earth. The great charity of the Virgin is shown from the mass of gold about the throne, and so the text says, 'And he covered it with much yellow gold.' The round top of the throne points to the contemplation the Virgin has of the Godhead that is without beginning and end. 'In the back' is added, because while this Mother was in the flesh she did not see God face to face, but contemplated him through creatures, as God said to Moses, 'You will see my back parts, but you cannot see my face.'[150] (This is so even though we are entitled to believe that at one time he did see the divine essence while still alive, but we are now speaking according to the common condition of human life.)[151] The seat of the throne signifies humility, which is the foundation of all the virtues. The two hands holding the chair are the twin forms of knowledge, that is, of God and of self. By means of these hands we hold fast to humility. The two lions alongside the hands betoken fortitude in good and bad times, something that humility gives to men. The steps that lead to the throne are the merits of the saints, far above which is the Glorious Virgin. The twelve little lions on the six steps are the saints of the Old and New Testaments, which praise and magnify her together. I will describe them to you in their orders as we proceed. You will see that 'nothing like this has been made in any other kingdom.' "

As we were speaking, I drew nearer the throne and saw coming a countless multitude of infants in white with fragrant little pale flowers in their hands. Around their temples the flowers were so small and bright that they seemed to be pearls and gems. With great happiness they were singing, "Praise the Lord, children! Praise the name of the Lord! May the name of the Lord be blessed!"[152] I asked Joseph who they were and he answered, "Have you not read in Zachariah, 'The squares of the city of Jerusalem will be filled with children and infants playing in her squares?'[153] These are the infants who have been saved either through their parents' faith and sacrifices in the time of the natural law, or else through circumcision in the time of the written law beginning with Abraham, or finally through the power of baptism in the time of the law of grace. The special ones that are adorned with glowing wounds and red flowers are the Innocents who were slaughtered by Herod for the sake of Christ." I saluted them as they drew near and said: "May the Lord look upon you, O holy children, that is, upon the glory of your bodies and those of your brethren."[154] They answered: "You are blessed by the Lord who made heaven and earth."[155] Then they said, "Why have you mortals come to visit us who are immortals?" I responded that I was the spokesman of the Florentines and exposed the whole business and my part in it. They said: "Unless you shall be converted and become like little children, you will not enter the kingdom of heaven."[156] I answered "Every good and perfect gift comes from above.[157] Pray for us then that it may be so." Then with full hands they scattered white flowers over our crown saying: "These are our prayers that will help you to obtain the graces you desire. We also pray that in the city of Florence under God's leadership children may be well instructed in the Christian religion and in the love of Jesus Christ who for our sake has deigned to be an infant himself because of his ineffable goodness." Having left some of their number with us, the rest departed, turned their faces to the Holy Trinity, and made supplication on bended knee.

We advanced and came to the steps of the throne. Before the first step we saw a large group of men and women, encircled with tiny violets like gems, sitting in a circle around the throne among the fresh grass and pleasant flowers. I asked Joseph, "Who are they, my Lord?" and he answered, "They are married men and women who lived piously and chastely and so are adorned with violets. Though they were involved in earthly cares and hence could not fly as high as those who lead the celibate life, their sympathies were still far removed from earthly things. They gave the world a heady fragrance of virtues like the sweet-smelling violet, which even though it does not grow tall is still pleasing and fragrant.

"Those you see sitting on the right and left sides next to the first step are very powerful advocates for your cause. They will speak to you in the name of the others." On the right were Saint Joachim and Saint Ann, the parents of the Glorious Virgin Mary; on the left, Saint Zachary and Saint Elisabeth, the parents of John the Baptist. When I saw them I saluted them with great reverence and said, "May the Lord look upon you, upon you and upon your children." They answered, "May you be blessed by the Lord who made heaven and earth." I told them the reason for my journey and explained the mystery of the crown. After a pleasant conversation, I asked the aid of their prayers. They immediately fastened two beautiful little garlands made of violets to the bottoms of the first two hearts of our crown and said: "These are the tokens of our prayers that will help you. We will also ask that God grant abundant graces so that marriages in Florence will always be chaste and pure in reverence for the great sacrament that signifies the union of Christ and the Church." From that band these four followed us to help us with their favor. Their companions gave themselves up to very devout prayer.

Having ascended the first step, we saw a group of men and women more exalted then the first group. They were adorned with small white violets shining like gems, which because of their fragrance many call carnations. To my request, "Who are these, my Lord?" the holy companion and father Joseph said: "These are men and women who lost the flower of virginity but preserved without stain the holy duties of widowhood or chastity, and hence they are adorned with white violets but not lilies. The first on each side are the widow Saint Anna, the daughter of Phanuel, and Mary Magdalene, your special advocates, selected from this band for your special assistance." I saluted them, begged their prayers, and gave the same explanation I had before. They offered us two garlands of white violets, which were fixed to the next two hearts. They said: "These are the prayers by which we beg God that in Florence the gift of chastity may be given to widows of both sexes and to all who in any way have lost the lily of virginity." Saint Anna and Saint Mary Magdalene left their companions in prayer and followed us.

On the second step a higher order of men and women

smelling of white lilies were seen about the throne. I turned to Joseph and said, "Who are they, my lord?" He answered, "These are the virgins of both sexes. On the right sits the martyr Saint Catherine, on the left, Saint Catherine of Siena, your special advocates." I saluted them and asked their help in the usual way. They tied on two garlands of very small lilies of marvelous odor, promising that they would beseech Almighty God that the virgins of Florence preserve their chastity completely unharmed and dedicate it to Christ. Both Catherines accompanied us while the others prayed.

Saint Zenobius and Saint Antoninus, bishops and pastors of Florence, held the first places on the third step. This step was dedicated to the holy doctors of the Church. They were all crowned with hyacinths (called "alisii" in the vernacular), which signify heavenly contemplation by their color. We begged their prayers, and after a pleasant talk they likewise added two garlands of the same flowers to two hearts of the crown, praying that holy pastors, doctors enlightened from above, and fervent preachers might be given to Florence. On the fourth step we saw a vast number who looked like they were slain but nonetheless were alive. They were marked with brilliant wounds glowing like stars and were garlanded with very beautiful red roses. In awe at this victorious army of saints I asked Saint Joseph, "Who are these?" He said, "These are the ones who have come through great tribulations and have washed their garments in the blood of the Lamb."[158] The first one sitting on the right was Saint Stephen the Protomartyr; on the left was Saint Sebastian. We saluted them and made our request in the usual way. They joined two garlands of red roses to the next hearts of the crown. They said: "These signify the prayers of our chorus. We also all beg that the promised graces be restored to you and that divine love may so enflame the hearts of the Florentines that they will not refuse to undergo martyrdom for Christ's name."

On the fifth step there were rather few people, but they were of such glory and dignity that they seemed to surpass the others in power. To my "Who are they, my Lord?" Joseph answered: "These are the holy men whom God chose in unfeigned charity[159] and to whom he gave eternal glory. The Church shines by their teaching, as the moon does by the sun. They are whiter than snow, more gleaming than milk, more ruddy than old ivory, more beautiful than sapphires.[160] They are the holy apostles and evangelists. The particular supporters of your cause are Saint John, the beloved disciple of the Lord Jesus, on the right, and on the left Saint Mark, the patron of your friars' house." They were all decorated with very delicate roses of a flesh color betokening the whiteness of innocence, the redness of divine love, and the sweet odor of all virtues. When they heard our salutation and request, like the others they added two garlands of these roses to the crown and prayed that God would give so much grace to the Florentines that they might renew the apostolic life and perfection of the primitive Church. In this way the twelve green hearts were all decorated with garlands of different colors. Do not think that the flowers of these garlands are comparable in size or thickness with those here below. Because they signify deeply spiritual prayers they are so light and graceful and the garlands made from them are composed with such artifice that they would not cover the forehead if placed on a head like a diadem. Indeed, like a delicately woven cloth perfectly joined to the edge of the crown, they increased its decoration.

Climbing the sixth stair we saw a venerable group adorned with palms. Asking who they were in our usual way, we were told they were the patriarchs and prophets of the Old Testament. On the right side, John the Baptist, the Lord's precursor and chief patron of Florence, presided; on the left, David the Prophet with his harp singing, "Let us sing to the Lord for he is good, for his mercy is forever. Let Israel now say that He is good."[161] After our salutation, on either side of the crown they fixed two excellent little branches of palm bright as emerald and adorned with tiny dates like precious gems. They said, "We will beseech God for you that just as the palm fixes a short root in the earth but lifts a full thick crown to heaven, so too God will inspire the Florentines to strive after heavenly things in such a way that they will pay no attention to earthly things without necessity."

We had now climbed all the steps when a most beautiful chorus of youths met us. In their hands they carried small crowns surrounded by short written documents bound with golden strings. From these crowns flames seemed to shoot out on all sides. When I saw them I turned to Joseph and said: "Who are they, my lord?" He responded: "These are the guardian angels of the men and women of Florence whose legate you are. In the prayers they said for this cause they have completed a crown of twelve Hail Marys, and for this reason each angel is coming to offer the crown of the soul entrusted to it to God. The written documents are the words and promises of each soul; the golden strings are their charity, and the sparks of flame and their fervent prayers." Among them, one angel that seemed friendlier to me than the others drew near and smilingly said to saintly old Joseph: "What fellowship can we have with this man, a mortal and a sinner?" When Joseph gazed at me happily, I took courage and said, "Who is this, my Lord?" "Don't you know who it is?" he answered. "I do not know, my lord." Then he smiled and said "You are confused because of his words, and that is why you do not recognize him." Then I recovered my spirits and looking upon him knew him to be my faithful guardian angel and director. He said to me, "How do you a sinner dare to walk among heaven's citizens and the spotless choruses?" I said, "I would not have dared had not your Lord and mine been crucified for us. You angels are not able to glory that God became an angel the way we can glory that he became man, as it is written, 'He never saved the angels, but he has saved the seed of Abraham.' "[162]

During these happy conversations I had a constant desire to draw near to the throne to salute the Glorious Virgin Mother. Since I knew that I was a sinner, I first knelt down upon the earth with bended knee and with my companions made this prayer to God to beg for mercy and the forgiveness of my sins. "May God have mercy on us and bless us; may his face shine upon us and may he have mercy on us. Let us know your way upon the earth, and your salvation among all nations."[163] Then all the angels and the saints who accompanied us, along with the others who assisted at the throne, even the blessed infants, bent their knees and sang in sweet harmony and devout love: "Let the peoples give praise to you, God; let all the peoples praise you. Let the nations rejoice and exult, because you judge the peoples in justice and guide the nations upon the earth. Let the peoples praise you, God; let all the peoples praise you; the earth has yielded her fruit."[164] Then I and my companions added, "Let God, our God, bless us, and let all the ends of the earth fear him."[165] They concluded with joy, "Glory be to the Father, the Son, and the Holy Spirit." We joined in, "As it was in the beginning, is now, and ever shall be. Amen."

When this prayer was finished, I saw the Virgin's throne lifted up and raised so high that it soon vanished from my eyes, while I (I know not how) remained in the midst of the field completely stunned and half-dead along with that numberless company of saints. I thought that this happened because of some error or sin of mine. Joseph saw this, took my right hand and bade me be of good cheer. "Do not fear. You must ascend higher where your guardian angel will lead you." He then left me to the angel's care, saying that answers would be forthcoming from a higher source. Continuing to pray and gazing at heaven, I burned with desire to see that Blessed Lady on whose intercession all our hope is placed. Suddenly heaven opened and wonders appeared to my eyes that would be utterly impossible to explain.

Men believe that there is a great difference between knowing something by seeing it and knowing it from the account or writings of someone else. For example, if someone had seen Florence with his eyes and someone else had only an idea of it from the account and description of another, would you not judge that there would be considerable difference in their knowledge? This is especially true in the case of heavenly visions, where countless particular circumstances appear to the eye that are above man's power to write down or speak about. Although they are spiritual, they are presented to us through bodily appearances that are full of mysteries. Because it would be impossible to describe all of them, I will recount a part, as much as seems sufficient for the task I have undertaken.

Looking up to heaven, I saw nine choirs of angels arranged in individual circles that gradually increased in beauty and size.[166] Even though the lowest choir encompassed the world in which we live, the one above was larger and more beautiful, and so on until the highest, just as in the case of natural bodies, like the elements and the celestial spheres, where the higher surpass the lower in size and perfection. The first choir, that closest to us, was clothed with thick and dark green garments, adorned with emeralds. The second had a red color and a decoration of carbuncles, the third was blue with sapphires, the fourth was a clear white like water lit by the sun, along with a decoration of beryls. The fifth was like the whitest linen and adorned with onyx, the sixth like woven gold with chrysolites, the seventh was clear green with jaspers, the eighth was sprinkled with heavenly light and decorated with the purest gold and topazes. The ninth and highest choir was red in color with a gorgeous flame and a decoration of carnelian. Although all these gems imitated the color of the garments, they could be very clearly distinguished from them and from each other, both by their live shining brightness and by the different ways they were attached through excellent and admirable art and arrangement. The elegance of the art increased as the orders grew higher.

This mystery is described in the twenty-eighth chapter of the prophet Ezekiel, where beginning with the highest choirs he says, "Every precious stone is your garment, carnelian, topaz and jasper, chrysolite, onyx, and beryl, sapphire, carbuncle and emerald."[167] Above all these choirs I saw the Virgin Mother seated on a throne, clothed with the sun and covered from head to foot with precious stones of the same kinds. She bore the Infant Jesus on her lap in memory of the Incarnation. He was brighter than the sun and was adorned with countless gems of all kinds unknown to mortals. Above all this the wondrous light of the three faces poured down so much light on the throne of the Virgin that had one not seen that supreme brightness he would doubtless have thought that the Virgin was God. Rays proceeded from there like streams of water brighter than any crystal in the midday sun. They spread down through the choirs of the blessed angels. (Because words fail, I am comparing the rays to streams of water.) Illuminated by these rays, and, so to speak, recreated in wondrous fashion and heated in the sweetness of love, the nine choirs gazed upon the threefold face with such great rejoicing and gladness and with so ardent an attachment that no human tongue could tell it. They could not stop praising God as they sang together in an indescribable harmony of sweet voices, "Holy, holy, holy, Lord God of Hosts. Blessed is he who comes in the name of the Lord. Hosanna in the highest."[168] Then they turned to the Virgin and said: "You are the glory of Jerusalem, the joy of Israel, the honor of your people. Because you have acted manfully, your heart has been strengthened; so the hand of the Lord has strengthened you, and you will be blessed forever."[169]

I grew weak at such an abundance of the sweetest harmony and awesome light. Again I fell on my face, but my angel strengthened me and lifted me up. I asked him what these wonders were and he answered: "These are the orders of the celestial hierarchies to whom God has given the government of the world. The first hierarchy is closest to God and beholds the order of government in God himself. The second knows the same order in the causes and universal ideas; the third in particular things. And so the first order meditates the goal of the whole arrangement, the second sets out what is to be done, and the third carries it out.

"In the meditation of the goal three things are necessary. The first is to examine the goal and above all else to keep it before you. This belongs to the Thrones who have the name Thrones or Seats because in their purity and sublimity they are open to the Eternal King and his illuminations. Hence they are clothed with clear green as if filled with the fruitful verdure of eternal fields. They are adorned with precious jaspers which are colored like flowers to signify their purity. Second, it is necessary to have perfect knowledge of the goal. This belongs to the Cherubim, who are named from the fullness of wisdom. They are full of light and pierce the glow of the Godhead with a penetrating and lively eye. They are clothed with heavenly brightness sprinkled with gold because of contemplation and of wisdom. They bear topazes of the same color because of their knowledge of many things. Third, it is necessary to love the goal to perfection, and this is ascribed to the Seraphim who are interpreted as 'fire.' They burn with the fire of love. They are dressed with flames of fire and adorned with glowing carnelians. This is the mystery of the first hierarchy.

"The second hierarchy arranges what is to be done in the entire world. In this arrangement the first task is to order things, and this is the job of the Dominations. They are called Dominations because they are free from all servitude. They do not depart from justice either from love or hatred, the way that temporal lords do who are slaves to their passions. Hence they gleam with woven gold and chrysolites, which have a golden glow and seem to send out burning sparks. Just as gold is the most precious metal, so the justice of rulers is the most excellent of virtues. It sends out sparks of good works to its subjects, which make them glow with love. Second, when things have been put in order, it is necessary to banish any evils that might get in the way. The Virtues do this. They are so named because they fearlessly dare to do anything. They are clothed with very fine white linen, because their power comes from their great purity and their lofty distance from bodily things. (So too in natural bodies we see that the purer and more subtle they are, the greater power they gain.) They bear gems of onyx imitating the color of a human nail because they are the first order who are sent as ministers to those who wish to receive the inheritance of salvation. Because of their dignity, the four higher orders do not descend to lower things, but only act as we have described. They are called assistants, as is written in the book of Daniel the Prophet: 'Thousands of thousands ministered to him, and ten thousand times hundreds of thousands assisted him.'[170] Third, after everything has been set in order and all impediments removed, it is necessary to commit it all to the inferior hierarchy and to order things in detail. This belongs to the Powers, because every power is from the Lord God and whatever is from God is ordered.[171] Their garments have the color of crystal or of water gleaming in the sun, and they are adorned with beryls of the same color. They must have clear knowledge of what is to be set in order, something they receive from the light of the Eternal Son. This is the end of the second hierarchy.

"The third hierarchy executes what the second hierarchy ordains. In carrying this out some spirits are captains and princes of provinces and cities, and so are called Principalities. They are adorned with garments of heavenly color and with sapphires, for just as the starry heaven is the universal cause of everything below, these angels are the captains, that is, the heads of all that is to be governed and accomplished. Some angels take care of individuals. Those to whom the special care of men's souls have been given are the lowest order. (Every soul has a special guardian angel and director.) They glitter with green garments and emeralds that freshen the surrounding air, because they are sent to illuminate those who dwell in the air with strength from on high. They are so filled with strength and vigor that they are able to illuminate human intellects. Between the Principalities and the angels there are some to whom are committed those charged with the common good, such as prelates, preachers, doctors of the Church, and the like. These are called archangels. They reveal greater secrets than do the angels. They shine with a red color and by the splendor of their transparent carbuncles light up the darkness, because they are lit up by charity to disperse the darkness of mortals and reveal secret mysteries. Now you know the orders of all the hierarchies, their ministries and duties.

"Note that their ministries and duties are signified by their various garments. The differences in their works, their wisdom, and their contemplation are shown by the precious stones. You should also know that in this vast multitude each one has his own duty and his own individual characteristics. Because the human mind cannot grasp this, I will leave it out. You should be aware that whatever gifts and powers the lower angels have, the higher have in a more excellent way. Due to the superlative charity that reigns in heaven the higher angels share whatever they have received from God with the lower, according to the latter's capacity. The Glorious Virgin and her Only-Begotten Son, full of all these virtues and precious stones, shine out above all the orders in so splendid a fashion no human ingenuity can grasp it. The light of the three faces that shines down on everything from above represents the majesty of the Most Holy Trinity, which infinitely exceeds all things. With its rays and sweetness it makes heaven supremely bright and happy so that without satiety or stop God is praised, magnified, and glorified forever and ever. Amen."

Having finished his speech, the angel was silent. Do not be surprised that the angel may seem to have departed from current usage in describing the properties and colors of the precious stones. The names of some of the stones may have changed, and angels suit their message to the listener. My angel knew that I had devoted myself to studying the sacred scriptures according to the expositions of the ancient doctors who wrote about these stones in that way and so he explained their qualities thus.[172]

I was utterly astonished upon hearing and seeing such indescribable things, not just from amazement at their greatness, beauty, and order, but even more from the blessed angels' immense love for us, especially when you think of their excellence and our indigence. They do not disdain us; rather they seem to be interested in nothing else besides our salvation, as if they thought it all their concern and their delight to be with the sons of men. Mindful of the scriptures, I was less surprised later on, since it is written of their Lord, "My delight is to be with the sons of men."[173] In my contemplation I saw that all the saints who had appeared in the field around the throne were taken up with great reverence and swiftness into the heavenly orders according to their individual dignity. Only the saints who first accompanied us and the angels who carried the crowns remained. I saw the Virgin's throne so high above that I turned to the holy group and said, "You can ascend to the throne without help, but what can a wretch like me do? The corruptible body weighs down the soul."[174] Amidst these words a ladder from the throne to earth appeared, miraculously prepared by angels' hands. My angel said: "This is the ladder on which you are to ascend, not just in body, but also mentally through the steps of virtue, as is written, 'They go from virtue to virtue; the God of gods will be seen in Sion.' "[175]

I began to go up the ladder by myself. The surrounding holy company also ascended with me, but without the ladder's help. We came to the first choir of angels and hailed them thus: "Praise the Lord, children, praise the name of the Lord." They answered, "May the name of the Lord be blessed, now and forever." We said, "The name of the Lord is to be praised from the rising of the sun to its setting." They responded, "The Lord is high above all the nations, his glory is above the heavens." We said; "Who is there like the Lord Our God, who dwells on high and looks down on the lowly things in heaven and on earth, lifting up the needy man from the earth and raising the poor man from the dungheap to place him among the princes, the princes of his people?" They said, "He makes the barren woman of the house a joyful mother of sons." Finally our "Glory be to the Father and to the Son and to the Holy Spirit" was answered with, "As it was in the beginning, is now, and ever shall be forever and ever. Amen."[176]

The psalm being sung, they asked me what led me here. I answered that I came as the legate of the Florentines to the throne of the Queen of Heaven in order to find out what good news I could bring to this people whose special advocate she was. I showed them the crown, saying that it contained the prayers of the whole people and had also been adorned and confirmed by all the saints of Paradise. I asked if they would deign to add the approval of their prayers to it. Then they asked what we particularly desired from them. I answered: "Will you and the saints who are with us ask God that the Florentines entrusted to you may imitate a holy and angelic life with your aid while still in the body?" Then twelve angels departed from twelve parts of their choir facing the twelve hearts of the first circle of our crown and drew near us. Each carried an emerald in his hand, which he fixed to the bottom of one of the twelve hearts of the first circle so perfectly that it spoiled nothing of the former decoration, but rather increased the beauty and brightness of the arrangement. They said this was the pledge of the prayers we had requested. They sweetly sang the first verse of the nineteenth psalm: "May the Lord hear you on the day of tribulation; may the name of the God of Jacob protect you."[177]

From there we passed to the second choir, whom we saluted like the former, repeating the psalm "Praise the Lord, children," and to whom we also revealed the reasons for the journey. We asked them to intercede with God so that the heads of households, pastors, prelates, and other rulers of Florence to whose care the city is entrusted might be good and holy men and might rule those subject to them with justice. As in the former case, twelve angels from twelve parts of their choir took flight and each fixed a precious carbuncle in the midst of a heart. The name of Jesus wonderfully carved in the middle of each heart shone through the transparency of the carbuncles. They said, "These are the signs of our prayers," and they took up the second verse of the psalm, "May He send you aid from his sanctuary, and may He defend you out of Sion."[178]

We came next to the third choir, that of the Principalities. We acted the same way and asked them to beg with their prayers that God's Spirit so fill the vicars, leaders, prefects, and other public officials of Florence that they might rule the people entrusted to them justly, religiously, and irreproachably. Heeding our request, twelve of them fitted twelve beautiful sapphires to the tops of the hearts in the same way as the others. They sang the third verse of the psalm: "May he be mindful of your every sacrifice, and may your holocaust be a fat one."[179]

We venerated the fourth order in a like way, asking that they obtain for us from God a magistracy like themselves, who would organize everything for the sake of the virtues and for good morals. They graciously promised this, and they appointed ten of their number with ten beryls (the number of hearts in the second crown) to insert one beautiful gem at the bottom of each crown adding the fourth verse, "May he give to you according to your heart, and confirm all your counsel."[180]

Then we went to the fifth choir, reverently saluted the Virtues in the same way, and begged them that those elected magistrates in Florence might be filled with the Holy Spirit to execute justice by zealously and fearlessly correcting and punishing the guilty. Thus the innocent will be able to live in safety. They received the petition with pleasure, and ten of them added ten chosen onyxes to the middle of the crowns while singing the fifth verse: "We will rejoice in your salvation, and we will be magnified in the name of our God."[181]

Going farther, we drew near the sixth choir, the Dominations, and reverently repeated the same message. We asked them to pray that the citizens of Florence become a people from whom wise and just men might be chosen for the Signoria, men who would be first concerned for God's honor and the salvation of souls, and second for the public good of the whole city and its temporal sovereignty. Ten of them confirmed our petition by adding ten chrysolites to the top of each of the hearts of the second crown while saying the sixth verse, "May the Lord fulfill all your petitions; now I have known that the Lord has saved his anointed one."[182] We also saluted the seventh choir and asked them to intercede with God to renew the purity and simplicity of the religious men and women of Florence. Four of them came to us with joyful faces and each fittingly placed a very precious jasper at the bottom of the four hearts of the topmost circle. They sang the seventh verse: "He will hear him from his holy heaven; among the powerful is the salvation of his right hand."[183] Lifted up to the eighth choir, we gave them the customary greeting and veneration and asked that many saints filled with the light of the holy scriptures and true wisdom might be given to Florence so that the Florentine people could have good advice in difficult questions. They approved this and sent four of their number to place four transparent topazes in the middle of the four hearts. They sang the eighth verse, "Some trust in chariots and some in horses, but you will call on the name of the Lord our God."[184]

Finally, we came to the ninth and highest choir, that of the Seraphim completely on fire with divine love. After the accustomed salute and psalm, we begged them to grant to Florence and to the Church Universal perfect prelates, pastors, and preachers filled with the love and fire of the Holy Spirit to enkindle the people with Christ's love. They received our prayers, and four of them joined very red carnelians to the tops of the hearts of the highest crown while singing the ninth verse, "They were bound and have fallen; you have arisen and are raised up."[185]

Although we were still a long way from the throne of the Virgin, who was exalted above all the choirs of angels, we were strengthened by the aid of so many prayers and merits and we sped toward her with great confidence. She saw us coming and called one of the Seraphim to her. She gave him a very splendid small crown artfully constructed of different precious gems and said: "Go and place this on the heart made of many small hearts that sits atop the crown. Say that this is the sign and gift of the prayers I have poured out for the city of Florence." Then she turned to God and said the final verse of the psalm: "Lord, save the king, and hear us on the day in which we call upon you."[186] Our Savior Jesus, who had once been a tiny infant, called out from his mother's lap and summoned the first of the Seraphs. He gave him a single totally red gem brighter than the sun and the most precious of all. He said: "This is the gift of my Passion, which I offered to my coeternal Father so that mercy and grace might be given to the people of Florence. Take it and place it on the crucifix you see standing on the highest heart of the crown, saying 'Glory be to the Father, and to the Son, and to the Holy Spirit. As it was in the beginning, is now, and ever shall be, world without end. Amen.' "

There never was a work so admirable or a gift so tasteful. Strengthened with the aid of so many merits, I was not afraid to ascend the whole ladder and come to the feet of the Queen of the Universe, who was sitting on the highest throne. I was led there and lay prostrate on the ground with the deepest humility and devotion. First of all, I adored the Most Holy Trinity and our Redeemer, the Lord Jesus Christ, and then his Mother. Looking upon her sweet, humble, happy, delightful presence, I began to exult with great jubilation in my whole heart. I was rapt in ecstasy[187] from amazement at such beauty, totally afire with love. Swallowed up by that light, I no longer knew I was mortal. Ardently gazing on that incalculable beauty and light, I was beside myself and broke out with the following words.[188]

"You, Mary, are and will ever be a seal of resemblance, full of wisdom and perfect in beauty, amidst the delights of God's paradise. Every precious stone is your garment—carnelian, topaz and jasper, chrysolite, onyx and beryl, sapphire, carbuncle and emerald. The work of your beauty was gold, and your tabernacles were prepared on the day when you were created. You, Mother and Virgin, were stretched out and protecting like the Cherub whom God placed on his holy mountain. You have walked in the midst of the stones of fire, perfect in your ways from the day of your creation. You are the glory of Jerusalem, you are the joy of Israel, you are the honor of our people. You have acted manfully and your heart is strengthened, therefore the Lord's hand has made you firm and you will be blessed forever. Save us, Queen, Mother of mercy; save us, Life, Sweetness, and Our Hope. Exiled children of Eve, we call out to you; groaning and weeping in this valley of tears, we sigh to you. Ah, our Advocate, turn your merciful eyes toward us, avert the evils we have deserved for our sins, and restore the good things promised us. O merciful, faithful, and sweet Virgin Mary, after this our exile show us the blessed fruit of your womb, Jesus."

When these words were finished, a wondrous harmony came at once from all the hearts in the crown that Lady Simplicity, our companion, carried as they sweetly sang: "Remember, Virgin Mother, when you stand in the sight of God to speak well of us and to avert his wrath from us."[189] With the prayer finished, we offered the crown to the Virgin with all the reverence we could. She received it very graciously with complete courtesy and kindness and placed it on her head. Then she took up her Son in her arms, stood up, and humbly knelt before the Most Holy Trinity. She offered her Son most devoutly and prayed in this way: "Look down, we beseech you, O Lord, upon this family of yours for which my Son, the Lord Jesus Christ, has not hesitated to be delivered into the hands of enemies and to undergo the torment of the cross."[190] Then a devout voice came sweetly from the hearts of the crown, "Have mercy on us, O Lord, have mercy on us, for we are greatly filled with contempt. Because our soul is greatly filled, we are a reproach to the rich and contempt to the proud."[191] All the angels and saints also humbly prayed along with her that the appeals of so many prayers might be heard. A voice spoke to the Virgin from the three faces that represented the Holy Trinity, "Be it done as you wish." The Virgin most mild accepted this response and then sat again on her throne. We all looked at her with complete attention. Filled with immense joy, we said, "Now it is in your power, Mary; our whole salvation is in you alone."

With a smile she prepared to reply. Silence was ordered and we all hung upon her words. She gave an official pronouncement in a high clear voice to the ears of the whole heavenly court. "Florence, dear to Our God and the Lord Jesus Christ, my Son, and also to me, hold fast to the faith, be constant in prayer, and firm in patience. Through these means you will gain glory with men and eternal salvation with God." She did not say any more, but fixed her eyes on me. I confidently said to her: "Virgin Mother, these are general words. We need you to pour out your kindness with a more generous hand." Then she spoke to me in the vernacular so agreeably and gracefully that I was struck with amazement. I do not think it possible to give you exactly what she said, but I will give the full sense.

She said: "Go and take this response to my beloved people. They certainly are sinners who merit every ill because of their iniquities, especially because of the infidelity of the many who refused to believe what you had foretold for years when my Only-Begotten Son had shown them so many signs that they could have no further excuse for unbelief. Even though faith is God's gift, had they not been of such evil and perverse mind, but rather walked rightly before God, my Son would have enlightened them with so much light that they would easily have believed it all. Reprove them so that they will now put away their hardness of heart lest God be further angered. Despite their sins, he has granted me all power because of the constant prayers of the saints in heaven and the just on earth. And so they are now restored the graces originally promised them by God. May the city of Florence become more glorious, more powerful, and richer than it has ever been before. May it stretch its wings farther than it ever has done before, and much farther than many might think. May it fully recover whatever it had, if this was partly lost. May it acquire things that till now have never come within its power. Woe to subjects who rebel against it; they will be gravely punished. It is now four years since you told the Pisans under the inspiration of the same divine light through which you prophesy everything that they would seek their freedom in the tribulation that is now upon us, and that this would be the cause of their ruin. And so it will be."[192]

Then I spoke again. "I beg you not to put it down to rashness, My Lady, if I ask you for some clarifications so that I can more fully satisfy those who delegated me. I would like to know if our city will suffer tribulations before these consolations." She answered, "Son, you have preached the renewal of the Church for many years. It is indeed to come, and soon. By the illumination of the Holy Spirit you have also foretold that the conversion of the infidels, that is, the Turks, Moors, and others, will follow soon after so that many who are now alive will witness it. This renovation and enlargement of the Church cannot take place, as you have predicted, without many afflictions and the sword, particularly in Italy because of the haughtiness, pride, and countless hateful sins of her princes and captains, the cause of all these evils. So it ought not seem hard to you if your city of Florence and your children suffer some troubles. You will be less harmed than other cities."

In the midst of these words she reached out her right hand and presented to my angel a large sphere containing the whole of Italy. The angel took it and opened it. Suddenly I saw Italy in disturbance and many of her major cities torn by great tribulations I was forbidden to mention. Some that did not have outside agitations and wars were shaken by internal crises. I saw Florence disturbed, but much less than the others. Then the Blessed Virgin handed me a smaller sphere on which her first brief response was written in Latin. When that sphere was unlocked I saw the whole of Florence blossoming with lilies that spread far and wide through the battlements and turrets outside the walls. The guardian angels on the walls protected her on all sides. I was glad and said, "My Lady, quite rightly have the small lilies come together with the larger ones that are now beginning to stretch out their branches."[193] She did not respond to this, but added, "My son, if the neighbors of the Florentines who now rejoice in Florence's evils and tribulations were to understand that evils will come upon them they would not be happy at another's misfortune but would weep over their own peril. They will be afflicted with much greater trials than Florence."

I said, "O Glorious Lady, though I am dust and ashes I will still speak a few words. If my people ask whether these promises are absolute (that is, will happen no matter what) or conditional (that is, will or will not happen according to their good or bad works), what am I to say?" She answered, "You know, my son, that they are granted in an absolute and certain manner. They will surely happen. Without doubt God will procure and produce all the means by which these promised graces will gain their goal. Say to the incredulous, those who wish to believe only what they can see and touch, that not a jot or iota will perish, but that it all will take place. Let Florence's wicked citizens and unjust men do whatever evil they can dream up; it cannot prevent so great a good. They will not share in it, but will suffer grave punishment unless they are converted. Say to the good and the just 'that it is well, for they will eat the fruits of their endeavors.'[194] They will be afflicted more or less, depending on how they enforce the holy laws and punish the wicked, the impious, blasphemers, gamblers, gamesters, and especially those who commit the licentious and unspeakable crime against nature. It will also depend on how well they remove the bilge of so many crimes that are the cause of their troubles, and how much they live as Christians by exalting virtue and supressing vice."[195]

I said, "O Humble and Merciful Queen, do not think me

rude if I still ask one more thing. If I am queried, 'When will these things happen?' what am I to say?" She answered: "Quick and soon."[196] But say that just as from the beginning, when you started to foretell Italy's scourges five years ago (though you had begun preaching more than ten years ago in other places), whenever you threatened 'quick and soon' you used to add, 'I do not say this year, nor in two years, nor four, nor eight,' and so never exceeded ten years even though the scourges came more quickly than they had believed, so too you are now to say, 'I tell you quick and soon, but I do not fix the present month of April, nor July, August, or September; nor one year, nor two, nor six, nor any determined time, but only quick and soon.' They will happen more quickly than you may think." After she said this, I was dismissed.

I was so aflame with love and so beside myself from the incomparably beautiful vision of heaven that I had completely forgotten I was mortal and did not wish to leave. When I heard that I was dismissed, I said: "So many ministers wait on you, O Glorious Virgin, that I beg you to delegate one of them to report these responses to the people of Florence. I want to rest a bit since I am quite worn out now by the many labors undertaken in their behalf over several years." My words provoked laughter in the whole heavenly court at my simplicity. The Queen herself smiled, and then to console me she said: "You still have a long way to go, but trust in the Lord and be strong, because the Lord is with you. If you persevere to the end, you will be saved. We all will help you, so do not fear your enemies, but rather rejoice in adversity. You will soon be lifted up into our company where, after many labors, you will receive the crown of life that God has promised to those who love him."[197]

Then I arose and, with all the humility and devotion I had, gave thanks to the indivisible Trinity and to Our Savior Jesus Christ, commending myself, the city, and my fellow Dominicans to his mercy. I also thanked the Most Glorious Virgin Mother and left my heart in her hands, asking that she be our perpetual advocate and sweet refuge in calamities. I thanked the whole court of heaven, who had supported us in gaining so many benefits. Then, after a due act of reverence, I began to descend the ladder along with my companions. As I came first to the choir of the Seraphim I began to sing in a high voice: "Let us praise the Lord for he is good, for his mercy is forever." The angels answered, "Now let Israel say that he is good, for his mercy is forever." Throughout the descent we sang the one-hundred-seventeenth psalm in alternating verses as far as the verse "Open to me the gates of justice." The angels responded after each of our verses, "For he is good, for his mercy is forever."[198]

When I approached the gates, I sang the verse "Open to me the gates of justice." After embraces, thanksgiving, and acts of homage, I again adored the Eternal Majesty and then left the threshold behind, continuing the psalm along with my companions, that is "I give you praise because you have heard me."[199] When it was finished, everything vanished.

After this sermon, in my other talks I often publicly affirmed that the King of France had been chosen by God as a minister of divine justice, and that if the whole world opposed him he would still gain victory and success. It is true, as I said and wrote to him privately, that he would fall into many tribulations, both because he needed to learn humility and also because he did not forbid the evil deeds of his servants, particularly when they mistreated the city of Florence. God will make his people revolt and rebel. He will bring many adversaries and serious difficulties against him, because he wants him to be the friend and supporter of Florence, the city he chose as the beginning of the reformation of Italy and the Church. If he does not freely want to be the friend of Florence, he will be made so by force. But since he is destined to be the minister of God's justice, if he humbles himself and acknowledges his election, he will not be overwhelmed by tribulations. Rather, he will rise up to greater victory after he has been made more humble and pure. Although men will think him dead, he will go forth as a victor and gain a vast empire by following God's commands. If he acts differently and follows a path that does not please God, he could go so far along it that like Saul, the first King of Israel, he would be rejected and another would replace him for this ministry, just as David was elected in Saul's place. The promises and graces granted to the King of France are conditional, not absolute like the prophecy of the reformation of the Church and the graces promised the Florentines.

So that everybody can understand what is a conditional prophecy and what an absolute one, you should note that God knows things to come in two ways. In the first, he knows them as they are always present to his Eternity, in the other, as they proceed from the order of their causes. Although God always knows them at the same time by both ways, because an effect does not receive the whole power of its cause, especially when the cause is as completely superior as God, prophets do not always receive knowledge of things to come under both forms together, but sometimes in the first way (then prophetic knowledge is called prescience or predestination), and sometimes in the second (then such prophetic knowledge is called conditional prophecy of warning or promise).[200] You should understand that things foretold in this way will happen if the order of causes on which they depend is not changed. In this way Jonah said, "Forty days more and Nineveh will be destroyed."[201] These words were not false. They were to be understood in this way—that the sins of Nineveh merited the city's destruction after forty days. Likewise Isaiah said to Ezekiel, the King of Jerusalem, "Set your house in order, because you will die and not live."[202] These words were to be understood as meaning that the disposition of his body was such that his death was preordained and could not be avoided by natural means. The prophet then learns from God. He ought simply to obey God and to announce the future in the way in which God commands him to. Otherwise, he will incur a sin, as Jonah did who was punished for his disobedience, as is written in his prophecy.[203] Hence under God's inspiration I say that if the King of France does what we have said, he will

271

doubtless gain victory and acquire a vast empire. If he does not do it, his cause will be in great danger, and unless he is aided by the prayers of the just he will be rejected by God himself.

I have also often said in public that anyone who attacks Florence will feel God's judgment. I have given another reason for this, besides the authority of the divine light: that this new city and people who have recently been freed after a change of the old regime and form of government have not yet injured or provoked anyone unjustly. So whoever injures or offends them acts unjustly and is subject to God's wrath. I have also openly preached and affirmed by divine inspiration that if any citizen of Florence privately or publicly tries to usurp for himself the commanding role in the city or to harm the new regime, God will gravely punish him, his whole house, and all those who conspired with him, and will finally send him to a miserable end.

On the basis of the same light I have openly revealed before the whole people and have always repeated that the good things divinely promised for Florence and foretold through me would surely have their effect even if the whole world were opposed. If the people pursued and deepened the good way of life they had begun, they would first of all remove a large part of the tribulations to come before the time of prosperity. They would also speed up the gift of graces that had been promised; and, finally, both they and their children would joyfully receive these graces, though the children would have more than the parents. Although all these things were promised to the city absolutely and irrevocably, they were not promised to each person individually. If wicked citizens do not repent, they will not share in these goods. I told the people they should note down the unbelievers and scoffers on one page of a book and the believers on another. I said that of the eight parts of the coming tribulations seven would soon be seen to strike those unbelievers and scoffers. I am exhorting all to believe and to manifest their faith in good works. This can harm nobody, but can be of great profit to all, as well as giving praise and glory to Our Savior Jesus Christ, who with the Father and Holy Spirit is blessed God forever and ever. Amen.

I know that many unspiritual men who do not have the experience of this kind of knowledge will mock me and say that these are contrivances of human devising and poetic fictions rather than visions and prophecies. Let them read the prophets, especially Ezekiel, Daniel, and Zechariah, and they will find that the Holy Spirit formed similar things in them. They too described these things with veils of mystery, and the prophecies were later interpreted by the efforts of the holy doctors. These scoffers should note that much more was revealed to the prophets (and with infinite detail) than what they wrote down. In order to console the elect and to destroy the lies of adversaries I decided to write down only this vision and its explanation, even though I originally thought I would suppress it. As I said, I was compelled to write it down. Whatever I have written is true; not one iota will pass away until it all is accomplished. Though I have tried to describe everything clearly, I believe that many will have various doubts, just as there are doubts concerning the Gospels, which seem so clear, and many more about the prophets, in whom there are many contradictions that the holy doctors harmonize only with the greatest difficulty. Heretics and malefactors were trapped and blinded by them, as the apostle says to the Corinthians: "If our Gospel is hidden, it is hidden for those who are perishing, those whose faithless minds the god of this world has blinded so that the illumination of the Gospel of the glory of Christ, who is God's image, does not blaze forth."[204] If this little work of ours raises doubts in some, it is no surprise. I hope, though, that whoever reads it with the right heart will easily find the solution to every doubt. If someone cannot find it by himself, since the author is still alive, let him go to him, or, when he dies, to his friends and disciples in order to be fully satisfied. If he does otherwise, he will show that he does not love the truth, but is his brother's false accuser. He will provoke the Eternal Judge against him, who will say:

Your mouth has abounded in evil and your tongue has produced frauds. You have sat down and spoken against

273

your brother and placed a scandal against your mother's son. You have done this and I have been silent. In your evil you have thought that I was like you. I will reprove you and stand before your face.[205]

Men trust in merchants' account books, and in the public tables and ancient documents of notaries. They even trust in other men, of whom it is written, "Every man is a liar,"[206] and in the tricks of astrologers and the lies of demons—those fathers and masters of lies whom the powerful so frequently consult. With how much more sincere faith ought they receive our predictions! They have already seen no small part of them fulfilled, and they have never caught me in a lie. With many proofs and signs God has shown that they come from him and not from human invention. I ask God's chosen ones not to be disturbed at such a contradiction, but rather to be strengthened in faith the more they see our predictions become like the teaching of Christ, the prophets, the apostles, and other saints, that is, both in proving to be true and in being persecuted. I have often shown this through the holy scriptures. Thanks be to God who has granted them enough light so that they can see the truth that comes from him. Why wonder that many do not believe and many persecute us? Christ preached to the Jewish people with much greater power than we do and he confirmed his teaching with great and wonderful miracles. Nevertheless, few believed in him and many persecuted him. In his Passion all abandoned him and perfect faith remained only in the Virgin Mother. No one ought to think that God's elect will perish, for as the apostle says:

> God's firm foundation stands, having this seal, "The Lord knows his own," and, "Let everyone who invokes the name of the Lord depart from iniquity." In a great house there are not only vessels of gold and silver, but also of wood and clay. Some are made for honor, some for dishonor. If anyone shall cleanse himself from those things, he will be a

vessel made for honor, sanctified and useful to the Lord, prepared for every good work.[207]

To the immortal King of the ages, invisible and only God, be honor and glory forever and ever. Amen.

Notes

INTRODUCTION

1. A Chinese proverb cited by Alvin Toffler, *Future Shock* (New York, 1970), p. 7.

2. E.g., Hal Lindsey, *The Late Great Planet Earth* (Grand Rapids, 1970) and idem, *There's a New World Coming* (Irvine, 1973).

3. See Frank Kermode, *The Sense of an Ending. Studies in the Theory of Fiction* (Oxford, 1966), chap. 1, especially p.28.

4. J. V. Schall, "Apocalypse as a Secular Enterprise," *Scottish Journal of Theology* 29 (1976): 357.

5. New York, 1974. See Schall, pp. 357–73, for numerous examples.

6. See, for example, E. Käsemann, "The Beginnings of Christian Theology," *Journal for Theology and the Church, vol. 6. Apocalypticism* (New York, 1969), pp. 17–46; W. Pannenberg et al., *Revelation as History* (London, 1969); K. Rahner, "The Hermeneutics of Eschatological Assertions," *Theological Investigations* 4 (London, 1966): 323–46; and J. Moltmann, *The Theology of Hope* (New York, 1967).

7. H. Mottu, *La manifestation de l'Esprit selon Joachim de Fiore* (Neuchatel-Paris, 1977).

8. For the medieval period see my *Visions of the End: Apocalyptic Traditions in the Middle Ages* (New York, 1979).

9. The *Oxford English Dictionary* of 1933 does not note the word "apocalypticism," but the *Supplement to the Oxford English Dictionary* (1972) cites both "apocalyptic" and "apocalypticism," the latter defined as: "An apocalyptic doctrine of belief, esp. one based on an expectation of the imminent end of the present world order."

10. G. Ahlström, "Prophecy," *The Encyclopaedia Britannica. Macropaedia* 15 (Chicago, 1976), p. 62.

11. Prophetism, both in the Old Testament and in its various Christian revivals, at least, tends to be an affair of preaching—the prophet speaks his message to an audience, though it may be written down at a later date.

NOTES

Apocalypticism, on the other hand, is essentially a scribal phenomenon in the sense that the seer writes his message down in a book or finds it already written down.

12. There is no real agreement on a single essential chracteristic, though it is interesting to note that some German investigators, such as G. von Rad and W. Schmithals, stress the distinction between the two ages or aeons, the present evil one and the perfect one to come, while some Anglo-American authors cited below have emphasized the triumph over death, frequently in the form of a bodily resurrection.

13. A number of the early Jewish apocalypses contain no explicit review of world history, and the later Christian writings that are formally similar to Jewish apocalypses show little interest in history, but concentrate on the mysteries of the afterlife. I would understand the latter as belonging to vision literature rather than the apocalyptic tradition.

14. This is one weakness of the stimulating work of W. Schmithals, *The Apocalyptic Movement* (Nashville, 1975).

15. *Interpretation* 25 (1971): 436–53.

16. Ibid., p. 447.

17. Ibid., pp. 440–44.

18. Schmithals, *The Apocalyptic Movement*, p. 148.

19. J. G. A. Pocock, *Politics, Language and Time* (New York, 1971), p. 25.

20. Adela Collins has pointed out that there are three models or types of resistance found in Jewish and Early Christian apocalyptic texts, a revolutionary model, a purely passive model, and a passive synergistic model. See "The Political Perspective of the Revelation of John," *Journal of Biblical Literature* 96 (1977): 241–56.

21. For a more detailed treatment along with accompanying texts, see *Visions of the End*.

22. R. Bultmann, *History and Eschatology: The Presence of Eternity* (New York, 1962), p. 31; and Schmithals, *The Apocalyptic Movement*, pp. 37–39, both note the individual moralism present in Jewish apocalypticism.

23. Kermode, *The Sense of an Ending*, p. 22.

24. *Cosmos and History: The Myth of the Eternal Return* (New York, 1959), chap. 4.

25. Kermode, *The Sense of an Ending*, p. 8.

26. Schmithals, *The Apocalyptic Movement*, p. 35.

27. See George Caird, "Eschatology and Politics," *Biblical Studies in Honour of William Barclay* (London, 1976), p. 84; and the remarks in D. S. Russell, *Apocalyptic Ancient and Modern* (Philadelphia, 1978), p. 24. Caird invokes the distinction only in terms of the future hopes of the Jewish apocalypticists, while I am using it to include a sense of the relation of the present and the future.

28. See Part Three, Selection D.

29. John J. Collins, "The Symbolism of Transcendence in Jewish Apocalyptic," *Biblical Research* 19 (1974): 7. See also his "Apocalyptic Eschatol-

278

NOTES

ogy as the Transcendence of Death," *Catholic Biblical Quarterly* 36 (1974), esp. pp. 41–43.

30. D. S. Russell, *The Method and Message of Jewish Apocalyptic* (Philadelphia, 1964), chap. 14; and Russell, *Apocalyptic Ancient and Modern*, pp. 38–40.

31. Kermode, *The Sense of an Ending*, pp. 24–31.

32. Paul Ricoeur, *The Symbolism of Evil* (New York, 1967), p. 352. See the whole "Conclusion: The Symbol Gives Rise to Thought."

PART I: LACTANTIUS

1. *Lactance. Étude sur le mouvement philosophique et religieux sous le regne de Constantin* (Paris: Hachette, 1901), p. vii. This work is still indispensable for the study of Lactantius's Classical sources.

2. *Lattanzio nelle Storia del Linguaggio e del Pensiero teologico Pre-Niceno* (Zurich: Pas-Verlag, 1970), p. xiii. An important study of Lactantius's thought.

3. The best survey is J. Stevenson, "The Life and Literary Activity of Lactantius," *Studia Patristica* I, 1 (*Texte und Untersuchunge* 63. Berlin, 1957), pp. 661–77.

4. *Lattanzio*, pp. 198, 274–78.

5. Ernst Käsemann, "The Beginnings of Christian Theology," in ed. R. W. Funk, *Journal for Theology and the Church. 6. Apocalypticism*, (N.Y.: Herder and Herder, 1969), p. 40.

6. Martin Werner, *The Formation of Christian Dogma* (Boston: Beacon, 1957), pp. 21–6, 115–16.

7. John Gager, *Kingdom and Community. The Social World of Early Christianity* (Englewood Cliffs, N.J.: Prentice-Hall, 1975), chap. 3.

8. As Gager does, e.g., p. 45.

9. Irenaeus, *Against Heresies* 5:25–35.

10. Hippolytus, *Comm. on Dan.* 4.23–24.

11. P. Vielhauer in ed. E. Hennecke and W. Schneemelcher, *New Testament Apocrypha II*, (Philadelphia: Westminster, 1965), p. 600.

12. B. Thompson, "Patristic Use of the Sibylline Oracles," *Review of Religion* 16 (1952): 115–16. Pichon (212) says: "...les idées et les images des Sibyllins hantent pérpetuellement la pensée de Lactance."

13. E.g., Hippolytus, *Comm. on Dan.* 4.18–19, speaks of such movements at the beginning of the century, and works probably dating from the middle of the century, such as *The Testament of the Lord* and the poems of Commodian, also suggest the same.

14. For the history of these speculations, see A. Luneau, *L'histoire du salut chez les Pères de l'Eglise. La doctrine des âges du monde* (Paris: Beauchesne, 1964).

15. The best account in English remains W. Bousset, *The Antichrist Legend* (London: Hutchinson, 1896).

16. Edited by J. Haussleiter in *CSEL* 49 (1916).

279

NOTES

17. See L. Atzberger, *Geschichte der christlichen Eschatologie innerhalb der vornicänischen Zeit* (Freiberg: Herder, 1896), pp. 583–611; Luneau, 220–21, 229–34; and Loi, 247–52. I have not seen H.W.A. Van Rooijen-Dijkman, *De vita beata. Het zevende Boek van de Div. Instit. van Lactantius. Analyse en Bronnenonderzoek* (Assen, 1967).

18. For these traditions and their history in the fourth and early fifth centuries, see B. Kötting, "Endzeitprognosen zwischen Lactantius und Augustinus," *Historisches Jahrbuch* 77 (1957): 125–39.

19. See Bousset, *The Antichrist Legend*, pp. 184–88.

20. The best study of early Christian chiliastic traditions is J. Daniélou's *The Theology of Jewish Christianity* (Chicago: Regnery, 1964), chap. 14. See pp. 393–95, 400, for Lactantius.

21. The Asclepius is one of the Greek treatises written in Egypt in the third century and ascribed to Hermes Trismegistus, "Thrice-Great Hermes." Aside from the fragments cited by Lactantius and others, it survives only in a fourth-century Latin translation. The text contains an apocalyptic section in chapters 24–26 that has affinities with earlier Egyptian apocalypses, such as the "Prophecies of a Potter."

22. See J. Hinnells, "The Zoroastrian Doctrine of Salvation in the Roman World. A study of the Oracle of Hystaspes," *Man and His Salvation: Studies in Memory of S.G.F. Brandon* (Manchester: Manchester University Press, 1973), pp. 125–48.

23. The translation that follows has been made from the edition of S. Brandt in CSEL 19.1 (Vienna, 1890), pp. 580–672.

LACTANTIUS: THE BLESSED LIFE

1. Cicero, *Pro Murena* 6.14.

2. These goals summarize the contents of the first six books of the *Institutes.*

3. *Timaeus* 37 cd, as known through the discussion in Cicero, *Academica* 2.37.118. Concerning the doctrines of creation discussed in these early chapters, see Book 2.9–12, and the treatment of C. Loi, chap. 3.

4. Aristotle as discussed in *Academica* 2.38.119.

5. *Phaedo* 80c.

6. Many of the writings of Epicurus of Samos (341–270 B.C.) have perished. This is fragment 304 in the standard edition of H. Usener, *Epicurea* (Stuttgart, 1956).

7. Vergil, Georgics 3.244.

8. Apparently a classical proverb.

9. The Brandt edition (585, 1.20) reads "ad eos consolandos." I follow "ad eos confundendos" with PL 6.738B, which the sense demands.

10. The Golden Age, a commonplace of classical theories of history, will be discussed in chap. 24 below.

NOTES

11. Terence, *Phormio* 5.11, 780.

12. *Disputationes Tusculanae* 1.41.99, depending on Plato, *Apology* 42a.

13. For basic Stoic cosmology, see S. Sambursky, *Physics of the Stoics* (London, 1959).

14. Aeneid 6.726–27. On the Christian use of these verses from the speech of Anchises, see P. Courcelle, "Les pères de l'église devant les enfers virgiliens," *Archives d'histoire doctrinale et littéraire du moyen âge* 22 (1955): 37–44.

15. See Sallust, *Bellum Catilinum* 20.11, and Ovid, *Metamorphoses* 1.138–40.

16. Fragment 371.

17. *De rerum natura* 5.156–57, 165–67. Lucretius (94–55 B.C.) was greatly influenced by Epicurus. He was one of Lactantius's most important sources.

18. See Cicero, *Academica* 2.37.118.

19. Epicurus, fragment 382.

20. Hermes Trismegistus, *Asclepius.*

21. A foreshadowing of Augustine's teaching on use and enjoyment, see *De doctrina christiana* 1.3–5, 22.

22. Cicero, *Academica* 2.38.120.

23. In dependence on Classical sources, other Christian authors have developed similar arguments; see Origen, *Against Celsus*, 4.75 sqq., and Gregory of Nyssa, *The Creation of Man*, 7.

24. Asclepiades was a contemporary Christian author whom Jerome mentions as the recipient of two lost works of Lactantius.

25. Fragment 371.

26. Ibid.

27. Lactantius apparently held that God could have created men's souls through the angels as intermediaries, but chose to create them directly instead. There was considerable debate among the Fathers over the question of whether or not the angels could share in the work of creation.

28. 2.9 sqq.

29. The erect stature of man as a sign of his heavenly origin and destiny is a commonplace that goes back to Plato, *Timaeus* 90a.

30. These words about baptism recall 1 Cor. 13.11, and Eph. 4.13.

31. A number of mss. contain a lengthy addition here, clearly not from the pen of Lactantius.

32. In chaps. 6 and 7 *summa* is used both for a summary statement regarding the nature of the universe and for the "sum of all things," the universe itself.

33. *Timaeus* 28c–30b.

34. The coherence of the prophetic and Sibylline traditions is a key theme of the *Institutes*. In 1.6 Lactantius gives a summary of traditional lore about these female seers.

35. Probably Ariston of Ceos, Peripatetic philosopher of the third century B.C.

NOTES

36. Aristippus, the grandson of a companion of Socrates, taught that pleasure was the only goal of action.

37. Pherecydes of Syros (fl. c. 550 B.C.), an early cosmologist, was mentioned by Aristotle.

38. Democritus (c. 460–c. 370 B.C.), the well-known Atomist philosopher, denied immortality, as did Dicaearchus (fl. c. 326–296 B.C.).

39. Zeno (335–263 B.C.) was the founder of Stoicism.

40. Fragment 341. This teaching is presented at greater length in Lucretius, *De rerum natura* 3.978–1023.

41. This implies that, strictly speaking, there are no mysteries peculiar to the Christian religion, though one wonders if Lactanius, who does not show much interest in theoretical questions, would have been willing to go that far in explicit statements.

42. *Phaedrus* 245c, as translated by Cicero in *Tusc.* 1.23.53.

43. A free rendition of the translation in *Tusc.* 1.27.66, taking up arguments from Cicero's lost work *De consolatione* as well. Lactantius does not distinguish between what belongs to Plato and what to Cicero in his rendering.

44. *Tusc.* 1.16.38.

45. *Tusc.* 1.11.23.

46. Cicero, fragment 11, from an unknown work.

47. *De legibus* 1.8.24–25.

48. The exact source of this Hermetic reference is doubtful; some mss. read *theorian* rather than *theoptian*.

49. The role of fire as a source of all life is a Stoic doctrine; see Sambursky, 1–7.

50. *Tusc.* 1.46.110.

51. Probably referring to *Tusc.* 1.30.72. For the scriptural basis, see Matt. 10:28.

52. *Pro Marcello* 4.11.

53. Lucretius's long discussion of the mortality of the soul begins at 3.417. See especially 445–46 for this notion.

54. *Phaedo* 80d.

55. 2.999–1001.

56. 3.447–58.

57. On the theme of the body as the prison of the soul, see P. Courcelle, "Le corps-tombeau," *Revue des études anciennes* 68 (1966): 101–22.

58. Cicero, *De senectute* 8.26.

59. *De sen.* 7.21.

60. 3.459–86.

61. See Books 3.12 and 7.9.

62. Books 3.19 and 7.11.

63. 3.487–525.

64. 3.548–79.

65. 3.526–47.

66. On the relation between blood and the soul, see R. B. Onians, *The*

NOTES

Origins of European Thought about the Body, the Mind, the Soul, the World, Time and Fate (Cambridge, 1951) pp. 44–65.

67. 3.612–14.

68. This passage, a fragment of the Greek original of the *Asclepius*, corresponds to parts of chaps. 31 and 8 in the surviving Latin translation. The notion of man as a being of mixed mortal and immortal natures placed in the middle of the universe goes back to Plato, e.g., *Timaeus*, 41 B.C.

69. Verses also quoted by the Neoplatonic philosopher Porphyry in his *De philosophia ex oraculis* 3.310–15 (ed. G. Wolff, pp. 177–78).

70. Cicero, *Tusc.* 1.22.4.1 and 51.

71. This marks the transition to the properly apocalyptic part of Book 7.

72. *De divinatione* 1.19.36.

73. "Calculation" translates *ratio*. It is possible that Lactantius is using the word in the more general sense of "account" or "matter," but the stress on the number of years suggests a more mathematical emphasis. On contemporary attempts to determine the length of the final age, see B. Kötting, "Endzeitprognosen zwischen Lactantius and Augustinus," *Historisches Jahrbuch* 77 (1957): 125–39.

74. The earliest Christian appearance of the equation of the seven days of creation with seven millennia of world history is found in the *Epistle of Barnabas*, ch. 15 (c. A.D. 140). This *topos* was repeated by many Christian authors, notably Irenaeus, *Against Heresies* 5.28, and Hippolytus, *Comm. on Dan.* 4.

75. Lactantius's desire to show the concord between scriptural and nonscriptural prophecies of the last events is one of the distinctive marks of his apocalypticism, as discussed in the Introduction.

76. Gen. 42 sqq.

77. Probably based on *Oracula Sibyllina* 5.54 sqq.

78. *Orac. Sib.* 3.316–17.

79. The scriptural warrant for this theme of the destruction of Roman power is found especially in Apoc. 17. It was developed by Irenaeus, *Against Heresies* 5.26, and Hippolytus, *On the Antichrist* 25 and 54.

80. *Orac. Sib.* 3.159–61, and 8.6–10.

81. There is some question whether this enumeration of ages comes from Seneca the philosopher or from a Christian author of the same name.

82. E.g., *Orac. Sib.* 8. 139–73.

83. On Hystaspes, see the Introduction.

84. The ten kings are found in Dan. 7.2–8 and 23–25, and in Apoc. 13 and 17. They were discussed by Irenaeus, *Adv. haer.*, 5.26, and Hippolytus, *Comm. on Dan.* 2 and *On the Antichrist* 27.

85. The first Antichrist of the Patristic double-Antichrist tradition. See Introduction. Compare Irenaeus, *Against Heresies* 5.26, Hippolytus, *On the Antichrist*, 51–52, and Commodian, *Song of the Two Peoples*, 933–35. The destruction of the kings appears to be a rabbinical tradition based on Dan. 7.8

and 11.43. Some Christian authors identified this first Antichrist with the returning Nero. Lactantius criticizes this view in his work *On the Deaths of the Persecutors*, 2.

86. Many of the woes set forth in this paragraph are based, directly or indirectly, on the Sibylline Oracles. Elements also reflect the Synoptic "Little Apocalypse" of Mark 13.

87. *Orac. Sib.* 8.239.

88. *Orac. Sib.* 7.123.

89. *Orac. Sib.* 3.544.

90. The great prophet is Elias, more usually seen as coming in the company of Enoch, thus being identified with the two witnesses of Apoc. 11. Lactantius's adherence to the older Jewish tradition of a single witness is probably influenced by Mal. 4:1 and *Orac. Sib.* 2.187.

91. The final, or Eastern, Antichrist, usually held to be of Jewish origin. There was considerable debate over whether he would have a human father or would be born of the devil himself, as claimed here. On these questions, see W. Bousset, *The Antichrist Legend*, pp. 138–43.

92. Apoc. 11:7–12.

93. 2 Thess. 2.4. Discussed in Irenaeus, *Against Heresies*, 5.30, and Hippolytus, *On the Antichrist*, 53 and 63.

94. On the Antichrist's miraculous powers, see Bousset, *The Antichrist Legend*, pp. 175–82.

95. Matt. 24:21.

96. The standard biblical length for the Antichrist's reign, see Dan. 7:25, 8:14; Apoc. 13:5.

97. For the tradition of the flight of the just and the destruction of Antichrist's army, Bousset, *The Antichrist Legend*, pp. 212–21.

98. This important fragment of the *Oracle of Hystaspes* has been studied by J. W. Hinnels, pp. 142–45, who emphasizes that Lactantius's remarks are to be taken not as indication of the lack of a Savior figure in the *Oracle*, but as a criticism of the omission of his role in judgment.

99. *Asclepius* 26.

100. *Orac. Sib.* 5.107–10.

101. *Orac. Sib.* 3.652–53.

102. *Orac. Sib.* 8.326–28.

103. *Orac. Sib.* fragment 6.

104. An allusion to the Easter Vigil. Loi, p. 248, holds that Lactantius was here inspired by a Western liturgical tradition with a strong apocalyptic emphasis.

105. *Orac. Sib.* 8.224.

106. *Orac. Sib.* 3.618.

107. *Orac. Sib.* 3.741–43.

108. *Orac. Sib.* 8.241–42.

109. *Orac. Sib.* 8.413–16.

110. Ps. 1:5.

NOTES

111. Aen. 6.735–40.

112. Ibid., 6.702.

113. According to legend, Tityus was punished in Hades by a vulture that gnawed on his liver that was each day restored. Aen. 6.595–600.

114. See *Orac. Sib.* 2.253–55.

115. Aen. 6.266.

116. Aen. 6.748–51.

117. Lactantius's explanation of metempsychosis as a confused reminiscence of Christian chiliasm is a good example of his syncretizing apologetic technique.

118. Aen. 6.719–21.

119. *Phaedo* 73a, as known through Cicero, *Tusc.* 1.24.57–58.

120. *Academica* 2.24.75.

121. Fragment 14 (ed. A. Gercke, *Chrysippea*, p. 20).

122. *Orac. Sib.* 4.40–43, 187, 46.

123. *Orac. Sib.* 8.81–83.

124. The millennium of Apoc. 20:1–6 is the basis for this key chapter.

125. *Orac. Sib.* fragment 4.

126. The idea that the just in the millennial kingdom would bear prodigious numbers of children was a part of the "Asiatic" tradition most objectionable to anti-apocalyptic Christians. It appears in such earlier writers as Commodian. On this question, see J. Daniélou, *The Theology of Jewish Christianity* (Chicago: Regnery, 1964), chap. 14, especially pp. 384, 394–96.

127. *Orac. Sib.* 5.420–21.

128. This description of the millennial kingdom incorporates many elements from Isa. 30:26, 11:6–8, 65:25. It also uses *Orac. Sib.* 3.619–23.

129. Vergil, Eclogue 4, in rearranged order (lines 38–41, 28–30, 42–45, 21–23).

130. *Orac. Sib.* 3.788–91, 794.

131. Ibid, 3.619–22.

132. Ibid., 5.281–83.

133. Lactantius does not adhere to any specific determination and appears not to look forward to the end as happening in his own lifetime. This would fit with the chronological scheme of such Christian authors as Hippolytus and others. See Kötting, "Endzeitprognosen . . . ," 128 sqq.

134. There is a play on words in the original between *Roma* and the Greek *rume* (street) dependent on *Orac. Sib.* 3.364 and 8.165.

135. The identification of Rome with the force restraining the Antichrist of 2 Thess. 2:6–7 was common among the Fathers. See Tertullian, *Apologetic Work*, 32.

136. Ezech. 38:20–22.

137. Cf. Apoc. 6:15.

138. Ezech. 39:9–10.

139. A final period of peace on earth—here seven years, but more frequently only four days—is found among a number of Patristic authors. See.

NOTES

R. E. Lerner, "The Refreshment of the Saints: The Time after Antichrist as a Station for Earthly Progress in Medieval Thought," *Traditio* 23 (1976): 97–144; he begins his study with Jerome.

140. Apoc. 20:12–15.

141. Some mss. add an address to the Emperor at this point, but Brandt does not print this as part of the original text. Stevenson, pp. 671–72, thinks that it is probably authentic and uses it as a key to date Book VII to the year 313.

142. *Phormio* 2, line 249.

143. *De rerum natura* 6.24–28.

144. Cf. John 6:35; Matt. 11:5.

145. Aen. 4.336.

PART II: ADSO OF MONTIER-EN-DER

1. For a brief survey of the role of Antichrist in patristic thought, see B. McGinn, *Visions of the End*, pp. 16–17, 22–24.

2. Especially 1 John 2:18–19, as well as the reference to false Christs and false prophets in the Little Apocalypse of the Synoptic Gospels (e.g., Matt. 24:24).

3. Sulpicius Severus, *Dialogues* 1:41.

4. *Secret History*, 8 and 12.

5. The illustrated versions of the Beatus commentary make it one of the key monuments of apocalyptic iconography. The most extensive study remains that of W. Neuss, *Die Apokalypse des hl. Johannes in der Altspanischen und Altchristlichen Bibel-Illustrationen*, 2 vols. (Münster: Spanishe Forschungen der Görresgesellschaft, 1931).

6. *Letter on Jewish Superstitions* 27 (PL 40:100).

7. See B. Rosenwein and L. K. Little, "Social Meaning in the Monastic and Mendicant Spiritualities," *Past and Present* 63 (1974): 4–16, on the role of patience in tenth-century monasticism.

8. *Apology* 32.

9. For a more extended treatment, see the discussions and texts in *Visions of the End*, Part One, sections one and seven.

10. On the history of this text, see P.J. Alexander, "Byzantium and the Migration of Literary Works and Motifs: The Legend of the Last Roman Emperor," *Mediaevalia et Humanistica*, N.S. 2 (1971): 47–68.

11. The Last Emperor is not found in the sixth-century Greek version of the text, the "Oracle of Baalbek," but is present in the later Latin versions (eleventh and twelfth centuries), the so-called Tiburtine Sibyl. P. J. Alexander argued that the Tiburtine Sibyl took it over from the Pseudo-Methodius (art. cit., note 35); others have not been so sure. See, e.g., M. Rangheri, "La 'Epistola ad Gerbergam reginam de ortu et tempore Antichristi' di Adsone di Montier-en-Der e le sue fonti," *Studi Medievali*, 3 ser. 14, 2 (1973): 708–10.

12. Mohammed is sometimes referred to as an Antichrist, but these ref-

NOTES

erences are generally late. See P. Alphandéry, "Mahomet-Antichrist dans le Moyen Age Latin," *Mélanges Hartwig Derenbourg* (Paris, 1909), pp. 261–77.

13. Trans. from the Latin translation ed. by E. Sackur, *Sibyllinische Texte und Forschungen* (Halle, 1898), pp. 89–90.

14. The fullest treatment of the history of this legend is to be found in A. R. Anderson, *Alexander's Gate, Gog and Magog, and the Inclosed Nations* (Cambridge, Mass.: The Mediaeval Academy of America, 1932).

15. The best discussion of the political background and implications of the text is that of R. Konrad, *De ortu et tempore Antichristi: Antichristvorstellung und Geschichtsbild des Abtes Adso von Montier-en-Der* (Munich: Kallmunz, 1964).

16. Rangheri, "La 'Epistola ad Gerbergam'"; and D. Verhelst, "La préhistoire des conceptions d'Adson concernant L'Antichrist," *Recherches de théologie ancienne et médiévale* 40 (1973): 52–103.

17. Konrad, *De ortu et tempore Antichristi*, pp. 114–15.

18. The text was first edited in modern times by E. Sackur in *Sibyllinische Texte und Forschungen*, pp. 104–13. Verhelst's edition is *Adso Dervensis: De Ortu et Tempore Antichristi* (Corpus Christianorum. Continuatio Mediaevalis XLV. Turnhout: Brepols, 1976), pp. 20–30.

ADSO OF MONTIER-EN-DER: LETTER ON THE ORIGIN AND TIME OF THE ANTICHRIST

1. Probably an allusion to the political problems and weakness of Louis IV.

2. The terms of this petition are based on the Prayer for the Sixteenth Sunday after Pentecost.

3. Rorico, Bishop of Laon from 949 to 976, was a natural brother of Louis and formerly imperial chancellor.

4. This etymology is found in a number of patristic and early medieval authors, e.g., Isidore of Seville, *Etymologies* 8:9 (PL 82:316B); Bede, *Commentary on 1 John* 2 (PL 93:94A); and Adso's most popular source, Haymo of Auxerre, *Exposition on 2 Thessalonians* (PL 117;779d).

5. Another commonplace; see Jerome, *Commentary on Daniel* 4:11 (CC 75A, p. 920); and Paulus Alvarus, *Luminous Letter* 21 (PL 121:535B).

6. See Isidore, *Sentences* 25:1 (PL 83:592B); and Bede, *Commentary on 1 John* 2 (PL 93:95A).

7. Gen. 49:17. The identification of the tribe of Dan with the source of the Antichrist appears to go back to intertestamental Judaism (see W. Bousset, *The Antichrist Legend*, pp. 170–74). The earliest surviving Christian witness is Irenaeus, *Against the Heresies* 5, 30, 2. Adso's immediate sources include Jerome, *Commentary on Daniel* 4:11 (p. 920); Gregory the Great, *Moral Commentary on Job* 31:24 (PL 76:596CD); Bede, *Explanation of the Apocalypse* 1:7 (PL 93:150C); and Alcuin, *Questions and Responses on Genesis* (PL 100:564D).

8. The tradition that the Antichrist would be born of a virgin in blasphemous parallel to Christ was apparently once widespread. It survives in a

few still-extant texts, such as the Pseudo-Hippolytan Homily discussed by Bousset, *The Antichrist Legend*, pp. 140–41.

9. These last two sentences are based on Haymo, *Commentary in 2 Thess.* 2 (PL 117:781D, 779D).

10. Babylon as the place of the origin of the Antichrist is a very ancient tradition. Adso's proximate source may well be Haymo (PL 117:780A).

11. Based on Bede, *The Reckoning of Times* (PL 90:574C).

12. The rebuilding of the Temple by Antichrist is mentioned as early as Hippolytus at the beginning of the third century, *The Antichrist* 6, 5, 11. It is found in Haymo (780B). On this theme, see Bousset, *The Antichrist Legend*, pp. 160–63.

13. Speculation about the miracles that the Antichrist would perform formed a long tradition by Adso's time. For a summary, see Bousset, *The Antichrist Legend*, pp. 175–82, who notes the dispute about whether or not the Antichrist would actually have the power to raise the dead or would only seem to.

14. See Alcuin, *The Faith of the Holy Trinity* 3:19 (PL 101:51C); and Haymo of Auxerre, *Exposition on the Apocalypse* (PL 117:1073AB).

15. The list of ways in which the Antichrist would progressively gain control over the world was later to play an important part in the dramatic organization of the *Play of Antichrist*.

16. The tradition that interprets the "falling-away" as the end of the Roman Empire is an ancient one among the Christian Fathers. Adso found it in Haymo, *Commentary in 2 Thess.* 2 (PL 117:779D, 780D).

17. There has been considerable speculation about who the "learned men" (*doctores nostri*) are that Adso is referring to. Most authorities today hold that it refers to Carolingian authors among whom the legend of the Last Emperor was already found, rather than patristic writers.

18. All accounts of the Last Emperor culminate his career in Jerusalem, but there is some difference of opinion about the locale of his act of deposition. For the Pseudo-Methodius, the deposition will take place on Golgotha, the Tiburtine Sibyl does not mention a place, and the *Play of Antichrist* has it happen in the Temple. This variety indicates the presence of diverse oral and written traditions no longer fully extant.

19. In the *Play of Antichrist* the Emperor survives his act of deposition to continue on as the King of the Germans.

20. Based on Haymo (779D).

21. A parallel to the fullness of virtue ascribed to Christ in Col. 2:3. The corporeal dwelling of evil in the Antichrist is found in Bede, *Explanation of the Apocalypse* 2:13 (PL 93:172), and Haymo (780B).

22. The exegesis of 2 Thess. 2:4 in this paragraph is heavily dependent on that of Haymo (779D–800B).

23. Adso's teaching on the two witnesses of Apoc. 11 depends on Bede, *The Reckoning of Times* 69 (PL 90:574A).

24. From Bede, ibid.

NOTES

25. From Bede, *The Reckoning of Times* (574B).

26. Both Bede, *The Reckoning of Times* (574C), and Haymo (781C) allow for either possibility. The notion that Michael was to slay the Antichrist was considered by Bousset as a survival of an early Jewish tradition (*The Antichrist Legend*, pp. 227–31).

27. Jerome, *Commentary on Daniel* (p. 933), and Haymo (781D) both mention the Mount of Olives.

28. This period of penance after the destruction of the Antichrist originated with Jerome's attempt to try to harmonize two different reckonings of the days of the Antichrist given in Dan. 12:11–12. Both Bede and Haymo witness to this tradition, which has been studied in detail by R. Lerner, "The Refreshment of the Saints: The Time after Antichrist as a Station for Earthly Progress in Medieval Thought," *Traditio* 23 (1976): 97–144 (see 106–08 for Haymo and Adso).

PART III: JOACHIM OF FIORE

1. Joachim began work on the three in 1183. The Testamentary Letter prefixed to the *Exposition* says that the only work he had finished revising and sent to the Pope was the *Book of Concordance*.

2. The fullest account of Joachim's life together with an edition of two primary sources is to be found in H. Grundmann, "Zur Biographie Joachims von Fiore und Rainers von Ponza," *Deutsches Archiv für Erforschung des Mittelalters* 16 (1960): 437–546.

3. For the context of this meeting between Joachim and the pope, see B. McGinn, "Joachim and the Sibyl," *Cîteaux* 34 (1973): 97–138.

4. On these interviews, see M. Reeves, *Prophecy in the Later Middle Ages: A Study in Joachimism* (Oxford, 1969), pp. 3–15.

5. The third authentic surviving letter is the "Testament" mentioned above.

6. On Joachim's visions, see Reeves, *Prophecy*, pp. 21–25.

7. *Exposition on the Apocalypse* (Venice, 1527), f. 39v.

8. *Literal Commentary on Genesis* 12:7 and following, especially 14 and 25 for its infallible character.

9. *Literal Commentary* 12:26 speaks of the visions of Isaiah and of John in the Apocalypse as belonging to the spiritual type.

10. *Ten-Stringed Psaltery* (Venice, 1527), Preface, f. 227r–v.

11. See M. Reeves and B. Hirsch-Reich, *The Figurae of Joachim of Fiore* (Oxford, 1972), pp. 20–74.

12. Tradition ascribed to Joachim a revelation of the meaning of scripture given on Mt. Tabor when he was on pilgrimage. See Reeves, *Prophecy*, pp. 21–22.

13. As recounted by Ralph of Coggeshall, *English Chronicle* (Rolls Series 66), p. 68.

NOTES

14. On the history of the exegesis of the Apocalypse, see W. Kamlah, *Apokalypse und Geschichtstheologie* (Berlin, 1935).

15. H. Grundmann, *Studien über Joachim von Fiore* (Leipzig, 1927), chap. 1; H. De Lubac, *Exégèse médiévale* (Paris, 1959–1964), vol. I, part 2, pp. 437–558; and H. Mottu, *La manifestation de l'Esprit selon Joachim de Fiore* (Neuchatel-Paris, 1977), chaps. 1–3.

16. Especially chap. 1, pp. 77–123.

17. The fullest study is De Lubac, *Exégèse médiévale*.

18. See chaps. 2–4 of the translation.

19. Mottu, *La manifestation*, pp. 101–12. Mottu also mentions a fourth, less crucial, component of the *typicus intellectus*, that of compensation (pp. 112–13).

20. *Prophecy*, pp. 19–27.

21. M. Reeves, "The *Liber Figurarum* of Joachim of Fiore," *Mediaeval and Renaissance Studies* 2 (1950): 65.

22. See my forthcoming paper "Symbolism in the Thought of Joachim of Fiore."

23. Reeves and Hirsch-Reich, *The Figurae*, p. x.

24. The facsimile edition of L. Tondelli, M. Reeves, and B. Hirsch-Reich, *Il Libro delle Figure dell'Abate Gioachino da Fiore* (Turin, 1953), vol. II, contains twenty-three figures, but some of these are doubles.

25. *Il Libro*, Tavola XXII, reproduced here as Plate 3. For a discussion see Reeves and Hirsch-Reich, *The Figurae*, pp. 170–73.

26. Joachim's notion of the Tetragrammation as IEUE with its various combinations (clearly visible in the *figura*) is based upon the tract entitled *Clerical Instruction* of the converted Jew Petrus Alphonsi; see Reeves and Hirsch-Reich, *The Figurae*, 40–6.

27. For a more detailed analysis of the figure, see Reeves and Hirsch-Reich, *The Figurae*, 192–8.

28. Tondelli was the first to prove the connection. For studies in English see Reeves and Hirsch-Reich, *The Figurae*, 324–5; and P. Dronke, "Tradition and Innovation in Medieval Western Colour-Imagery," *Eranos Jahrbuch* 41(1972), 98–106. The translation used here is that of Dorothy Sayers.

29. *Il Libro*, Tavola XIV, reproduced here as Plate 6.

30. *Il Libro*, Tavola XXIII, reproduced here as Plate 5.

31. See Reeves, *Prophecy*, pp. 505–08.

32. E.g., *Exposition*, ff. 175v–176r.

33. For a detailed study of these hopes, see Reeves, *Prophecy*, Part Two.

34. *Il Libro*, Tavola XII, reproduced here as Plate 7.

35. H. Grundmann, *Neue Forschungen über Joachim von Fiore* (Marburg, 1950), pp. 85–121; Reeves and Hirsch-Reich, *The Figurae*, pp. 232–48.

36. E.g., *Book of Concordance* (Venice, 1519), f. 56r.

37. *De articulis fidei di Gioacchino da Fiore*, ed. E. Buonaiuti (Rome, 1936), pp. 43–44.

NOTES

SELECTION A: LETTER TO ALL THE FAITHFUL

1. This letter was one of Joachim's more popular works to judge by the number of ms. copies that survive. M. Reeves, *The Influence of Prophecy*, p. 516, lists a dozen. The translation is based on the edition of J. Bignami-Odier in "Notes sur deux manuscrits de la Bibliothèque du Vatican," *Mélanges d'archéologie et de la histoire* 54 (1937): 220–23. Bignami-Odier made use of the text as found in Vat. lat. 3822, f. 1r–v, which contains two illegible places. I have filled these in by a comparison with Milan, Bibl. Ambros. H. 15, inf., ff. 47–48. In addition, I have corrected one misreading in Bignami-Odier's transcription.

2. Ezech. 3:17. The role of the watchman (*speculator*) as the one who interprets the coming fulfillment of prophecy to the faithful was also emphasized by Pope Gregory I, who ascribed it primarily to the bishops. See R. Manselli, *La "Lectura super Apocalypsim" di Pietro di Giovanni Olivi* (Rome: Instituto Storico Italiano per il Medio Evo, 1955), pp. 12–13.

3. This fundamental principle of Christian scriptural exegesis (e.g., 1 Cor. 10:11) was the basis for Joachim's literal concordances of events in the Old Testament with those in the time of the Church.

4. Among Joachim's other short works is a brief treatise on predestination, the *Dialogue on God's Foreknowledge and on the Predestination of the Elect.*

5. In Gen. 19, Lot leaves for the mountains when he departs from Sodom. To ascend a mountain is always a symbol of the contemplative life for Joachim.

6. The city of Segor (Gen. 19:20-23), the first stage of Lot's journey to the mountain, was spared by his intercession from the fate of Sodom and Gomorrah.

7. The coming era of peace, the messianic third *status*, is briefly proclaimed.

SELECTION B: LETTER TO THE ABBOT OF VALDONA

1. This translation is made from the edition of J. Bignami-Odier, "Notes sur deux manuscrits de la Bibliothèque du Vatican," *Mélanges d'archéologie et de histoire* 54 (1937): 226–27, based on Vat. lat. ms. 3822, f. 4r, though in five places I have preferred the alternate readings given from Paris, Bibl. nat. ms. lat. 3595, f.34.

2. Valdona is most likely the Cistercian house of Barona in the diocese of Milan where interest in the persecuting German empire and its fate would have been strong in the late twelfth century.

3. Joachim means that he finds it impossible to pen a joyful message.

4. An obscure sentence that may mean that the Calabrian's doleful message came at a time when there was no overt persecution, and thus seemed less convincing.

NOTES

5. Joachim's practice is to identify Babylon with the persecuting German empire.

6. The reference to the increasing opposition to his ideas and the dissemination of some of his works seem to argue to a date toward the end of the Abbot's life.

7. Joachim's mixture of pessimism and optimism concerning the near future is evident.

SELECTION C: THE BOOK OF CONCORDANCE

1. The final sentence of Chapter 1 of Part 1 serves as an introduction to the terms used here: "Because some people understand *concordia* as that spiritual understanding which ought properly to be defined as *allegoria*, we must first show how *concordia* and *allegoria* differ, so that when we come to treat individual cases in their context, having cleared the streambeds so that both rivers may flow freely, unobstructed by any hindrance, we may hasten to finish this work." Neither typology nor allegory in its various meanings translates Joachim's *concordia* and *allegoria*. Because, therefore, the English terms would tend to mislead the reader, the Latin terms have been retained. For the same reason, I have retained the Latin *status* and *tempus* (pl. *tempora*), translation of which would in my opinion be misleading, because neither necessarily means a historical age or period in our sense of those terms.

2. Latin: Concordiam proprie esse dicimus similitudinem eque proportionis novi ac veteris testamenti.

3. Latin *virtus*. *Virtus* here has its classical meaning of strength.

4. Latin *similitudo mysterii*. *Mysterium* appears to be closely related to *concordia*, *allegoria* and *spiritualis intellectus* or *intelligentia*. Both *concordia* and *allegoria* are keys to the understanding of that *mysterium* or hidden significance which God has implanted in scripture and in history while *spiritualis intellectus* or spiritual understanding is the state of knowing this meaning.

5. Matt. 3:17 conflated with Luke 3:22.

6. By others Joachim means all of those people whom John baptized except Christ.

7. Latin: velud quoddam itinerarium.

8. Ps. 80:11 (Vulgate 79:12).

9. Latin *stationes suas*.

10. See Marjorie Reeves, *Joachim of Fiore and the Prophetic Future* (New York, 1977), pp. 6–7: "History is, in one sense, completed in its two parts, but hovering over each there is a third development, a new quality of life rather than a third set of institutions, a quasimystical state rather than a new age. It is notable that Joachim never uses the word *etas* or *tempus* when he is thinking in terms of the pattern of threes: for this he always uses *status*. Thus 'third age' is really incorrect." Professor Reeves is correct in saying that Joachim usually or almost invariably uses *status* for the pattern of threes and *tempus* or *etas* for other schemes but this passage is crucial for the meaning of *status*.

NOTES

When Joachim says that he ought better to say *status* than *tempus*, does he mean simply that it will be less confusing if he uses *status* for this particular pattern and *tempus* in other patterns or does he mean that *status* is a more accurate description than *tempus*? In chapter 11, this threefold pattern will be described as the *prima diffinitio*, symbolized by *alpha*. The other key pattern is the twofold, symbolized by omega, which will be introduced in chapter 8 below.

11. Joachim is referring to the forty-second generation after the birth of Christ, which, using his approximation of thirty years to a generation, means roughly the years 1230–1260, A.D.

12. Normally Joachim speaks of *status* or *status mundi. Status seculi* means *status* of the age but it is possible that he means *mundi* here, i.e., *status* of the world.

13. See below chapter nine.

14. See below chapter nine.

15. Joachim means that there ought to be parallels between persons, orders, etc., in the third as well as in the first and second *status.*

16. John 5:17.

17. Rom. 8:29.

18. Acts 1:25.

19. Joel 2:28.

20. Augustine, *The City of God* 3:3–5. Joachim appears to believe that the father of Romulus and Remus was named Moechus, i.e., Adulterer. Roman tradition named Mars as their father.

21. 2 Cor. 12:4.

22. Eph. 4:13. The use of this text here may suggest that Joachim envisioned the third *status* as the fulfillment of the Body of Christ.

23. Matt. 10:5; 1 Cor. 7:1–2.

24. A number of manuscripts but not all read "the third to the Holy Spirit alone," which sharpens but does not change the meaning of the text.

25. Joachim means by this that the Trinity in itself is one and indivisible so that all three persons always work simultaneously, but in the historical unfolding of the Trinity, there are real distinctions between the work of the persons.

26. John 14:16–17.

27. John 1:33.

28. John 20:22.

29. Ibid.

30. Joachim wrote a commentary on the Life and Rule of Saint Benedict, *Tractatus de Vita S. Benedicti et de Officio divino secundum eius doctrinam*, ed. C. Baraut, *Analecta sacra tarraconensia* 24 (1951): 42–118.

31. Joachim took up the Trinity at much greater length in the *Psalterium decem chordarum* (Venice, 1527).

32. Ps. 103:24; Ps. 110:2.

33. In the printed edition of the *Liber de concordia* (Venice, 1519), this is

NOTES

part of chapter 10, but in the manuscripts it appears correctly as a separate chapter. I have translated *diffinitio* as pattern.

34. Cf. John 2:6.
35. Augustine, *The City of God* 22:30.
36. Lev. 25:22.

SELECTION D: BOOK OF FIGURES

1. The most complete study of this figure is to be found in M. Reeves and B. Hirsch-Reich, *The Figurae of Joachim of Fiore*, pp. 146–52. The authors point out one important fact for understanding some of the complications of the figure, i.e., that the seven-headed dragon of Apocalypse 12 always implies for Joachim both the four beasts from the seventh chapter of Daniel (the fourth of whom has ten horns and then a smaller eleventh growing in their midst) and the beast from the sea with seven heads and ten horns of Apoc. 13 and 17.

2. The essential message of the diagram is found in the identification of the kings and their respective persecutions inscribed above the dragon's heads and between the necks. Very similar lists are found in two other sources: the Introductory Book to the *Exposition on the Apocalypse*, ff. 10r–11r, where the kings are Herod, Nero, Constantius, Chosroes (whose kingdom was conquered by the sect of Mohammed), one of the kings of Babylon, and Saladin; and in the account of Joachim's interview with Richard the Lion-hearted in Messina in 1190 where the heads are Herod, Nero, Constantius, Mohammed, Melsemutus, and Saladin. For the background on Joachim's views on the role of Islam in the apocalyptic crisis of his time, see E. R. Daniel, "Apocalyptic Conversion: The Joachite Alternative to the Crusades," *Traditio* 25 (1969): 127–39.

3. Reeves and Hirsch-Reich, *The Figurae*, pp. 149–50, note that passages in the *Exposition on the Apocalypse* also involve concordances of different orders of the Church raised up to overcome various persecutions. Ideally, this would be extended to include the order of the spiritual men for the time of the double persecution of the sixth age, though Joachim nowhere makes this explicit.

4. Constantius II (337–61), the persecuting Arian emperor.

5. The *Exposition on the Apocalypse*, f. 134va, says that the *Mauri* are popularly called *Meselmuti*, so Joachim seems to have had some north African Moorish ruler in mind here. See Reeves and Hirsch-Reich, *The Figurae*, pp. 87–88.

6. Other texts in the *Exposition* and in the early *Commentary on an Unknown Prophecy* identify the fifth head with a persecution of the King of Babylon, that is, a German Emperor.

7. That is, clerics attached to collegiate churches.

8. This is inscribed at the dragon's tail.

9. The Commentary is in two parts: *A*, a reflection on Apoc. 12:3–4,

294

giving further details on the sixth and seventh heads of the dragon; and *B*, a defense of Joachim's unusual doubling of the final Antichrist made necessary by his belief in a coming third state of history after the defeat of the seventh head of the dragon.

10. One of the most common patterns of history found in Joachim's writings, both early and late, is the parallel between the seven persecutions of the people of Israel in the time of the Old Testament and the seven persecutions of the Church in the era of the New. This is most frequently symbolized by the seven seals of the Apocalypse and their respective openings. See M. Reeves and B. Hirsh-Reich, "The Seven Seals in the Writings of Joachim of Fiore," *Recherches de théologie ancienne et médiévale* 21 (1954): 211–47.

11. Speculation over the identity of the ten kings portrayed in the ten horns of the beast goes back to the patristic period when they were generally seen as ten rulers who would destroy the Roman Empire. Joachim sees them as kings who will be gathered by the sixth head (Saladin) and who will unwittingly serve God's design by slaying Christians.

12. As E.R. Daniel points out in "Apocalyptic Conversion," pp. 132–34, this passage is intelligible only if written before the death of Saladin in 1193. It is possible that Joachim expected a temporary victory over Islam from the Third Crusade (1189–1192), though it is clear that he later abandoned this view.

13. The belief in two Antichrists, one from the East and one from the West, common among patristic authors, may be echoed here, but a more likely background is to be found in Joachim's fears of an alliance between Western Patarene heretics and Moslems (see, e.g., *Exposition on the Apocalypse*, f. 134). The Simon Magus of Acts 8:9–24 became the subject of later legends in which he served as Nero's wonder-working adviser who was eventually destroyed by Saint Peter.

14. Forty-two months, or three and a half years, the traditional extent of the reign of the Antichrist.

15. Reeves and Hirsch-Reich, *The Figurae*, p. 150, show that the doubling of the persecution in the sixth age is a necessity in Joachim's thought so that the seventh age may be one of complete peace.

16. In a typical concordance, the abbot parallels the victory of Cyrus over Babylon in the sixth age of the Old Testament with the coming defeat of the German Empire at the hands of the revived sixth head allied with the seventh. Compare this with the "Letter to the Abbot Valdona" and the "Letter to All the Faithful," which also expect the destruction of the empire.

17. The conversion of the Jews was always an important theme in Joachim's apocalyptic. See B. Hirsch-Reich, "Joachim von Fiore und das Judentum," *Miscellanea Mediaevalia* IV (Cologne, 1966), pp. 228–63.

18. Joachim is notably chary of speculating on the length of the coming *status* of peace.

19. The term *maximus* or *magnus Antichristus*, later popularized by Peter Olivi in his *Postil on the Apocalypse*, seems to have originated with Joachim.

NOTES

20. In the words of Reeves and Hirsch-Reich: "This is the programme of the Last Things which is Joachim's unique contribution to this subject. Unlike the traditional view he places his 'age of gold' after, not before, the great manifestation of the Antichrist, but, contrary to what is often understood as Joachimism, he sees this third *status* itself as ending on a note of final tribulation" (*The Figurae*, p. 152).

SELECTION E: THE TWELFTH TABLE

1. The suggestion for translating *novus ordo* as the "New People of God" was made by J. Ratzinger, *The Theology of History of St. Bonaventure* (Chicago: Franciscan Herald Press, 1971), p. 39.

2. Two summaries of scriptural texts frame the top of the diagram to the left and the right and highlight the organic and harmonious order of the various divisions of Joachim's monastic utopia that forms the Mystical Body of the Contemplative Church.

3. M. Reeves and B. Hirsch-Reich point out that the five central oratories to which two more are added produce a pattern of five and seven that is characteristic of Joachim's number symbolism (*The Figurae*, pp. 234–36).

4. Each oratory is associated with a patron saint, an allegorical animal, a gift of the Holy Spirit, and a part of the body suggesting the function of the oratory. In this case the nose appears to suggest the discretion necessary for the administration of the whole.

5. The Spiritual Father whose command and authority all obey is to be almost certainly identified with the "new leader who will ascend from Babylon, namely a universal Pontiff of the New Jerusalem, that is, of Holy Mother the Church," of the *Book of Concordance*, f. 56r. Joachim never envisaged the end of the papacy in the third *status*, but its transformation to a more spiritual and monastic way of life.

6. The four monastic oratories around the central one housing the Spiritual Father have as their identifying animals the tetramorph, or four beasts, of Apoc. 4:6–9, which Christian tradition interpreted as symbols of the four evangelists. While the order of the beasts moves counterclockwise, the order of importance of the oratories moves clockwise and hence we start at the top with the virginal contemplatives symbolized by the eagle of John.

7. Scapulars were originally cords worn around the shoulders to hoist up monastic tunics for manual labor. Both scapulars and hoods are mentioned in Regula 55 of Benedict's *Rule*.

8. This group sounds very much like Cistercian *conversi* or working lay-brothers. Indeed the cape (*cappa*) was the distinctive garb of the *conversi*.

9. The specification of distances and the careful details of community life indicate that Joachim had a concrete historical realization in mind.

10. The mention of the poor implies what will become clearer below, that is, the existence of other persons outside the ideal community in the coming *status*.

NOTES

11. A *stadium* was an eighth of a Roman mile.

12. This communistic sharing of goods has not gone unremarked. Marxist philosopher Ernst Bloch has claimed that "Joachim was cogently the spirit of *revolutionary Christian social utopianism*. . . . He was the first to set a date for the kingdom of God, for the communistic kingdom, and to demand its observance." See *Man on His Own* (New York: Herder and Herder, 1971), p. 137.

PART IV: THE FRANCISCAN SPIRITUALS

1. The literature on the Franciscan Spirituals is large. Among the key studies are F. Ehrle, "Die Spiritualen, ihr Verhältnis zum Franciscanerorden und zu den Fraticellen," *Archiv für Literatur-und Kirchengeschichte* 1 (1885): 509–69; 2 (1886): 106–64, 249–336; 3 (1887): 553–623; 4 (1888): 1–190; D. Douie, *The Nature and Effect of the Heresy of the Fraticelli* (Manchester: Manchester Univ. Press, 1932); L. Oliger, "Spirituels," *Dictionnaire de théologie catholique* 14.2 (Paris, 1941), cc. 2522–49; G. Leff, *Heresy in the Later Middle Ages* (New York: Barnes and Noble, 1967), vol. I, part 1; and E. Privat, ed., *Franciscains d'Oc. Les Spirituels ca. 1280–1324* (Toulouse: Cahiers de Fanjeaux 10, 1975).

2. Among the fullest accounts of Angelo's life are Douie, chap. 3; and L. von Auw, *Angelo Clareno et les spirituels franciscains* (Lausanne, 1952). For a study of his spirituality, E.R. Daniel, "Spirituality and Poverty: Angelo da Clareno and Ubertino da Casale," *Medievalia et Humanistica* N.S. 4 (Denton: North Texas State Univ., 1973), pp. 89–98.

3. The *Historia* was partially edited by F. Ehrle in the *Archiv* 2 (1886): 127–55, 256–327. A complete edition was made by P. Alberto Ghinato, *Angelus a Clarino, Chronicon seu Historia septem Tribulationum Ordinis Minorum* (Rome: Sussidi e Testi per la Gioventù Francescana 10, Rome, 1959).

4. This is not to deny the presence of other attitudes toward the end present among the Franciscans, as pointed out by E.R. Daniel, *The Franciscan Concept of Mission in the High Middle Ages* (Lexington: Univ. of Kentucky Press, 1975).

5. See J. Ratzinger, *The Theology of History in St. Bonaventure* (Chicago: Franciscan Herald Press, 1975); and B. McGinn, "The Significance of Bonaventure's Theology of History," *Journal of Religion. Special Supplement. The Medieval Religious Heritage, 1274–1974* (Chicago: Univ. of Chicago, 1978), pp. S564–81.

6. The fullest account of the story of Angelo's group is to be found in A. Frugoni, *Celestiniana* (Rome: Istituto Storico Italiano per il Medio Evo, 1954), pp. 123–67.

7. "Die Papstprophetien des Mittelalters," *Archiv für Kulturgeschichte* 19 (1929): 77–159. Grundmann's arguments have been considered probable, if not quite certain, by the other major study of this literature, M. Reeves, "Some Popular Prophecies from the Fourteenth to the Seventeenth Centur-

NOTES

ies," in G.J. Cuming and D. Baker, *Popular Belief and Practice*, Studies in Church History 8 (Cambridge: Cambridge Univ. Press, 1972), pp. 107–34.

8. See B. McGinn, "Angel Pope and Papal Antichrist," *Church History* 47 (1978): 155–65.

9. Ed. F. Ehrle in *Archiv* 1 (1885): 566–69.

10. For a summary of Angelo's views on the Church, see Frugoni, pp. 164–67.

11. Douie, *Nature and Effect*, p. 133.

12. For this whole question the best account remains M. D. Lambert, *Franciscan Poverty* (London: S.P.C.K., 1961). For Ubertino's writings on the poverty questions, see C. T. Davis, "Le Pape Jean XXII et les spirituels. Ubertino de Casale," *Franciscains d'Oc*, pp. 263–83.

13. The literature on Olivi is large. Besides the general works listed above, I mention only R. Manselli, *La "Lectura super Apocalypsim" di Pietro di Giovanni Olivi* (Rome: Instituto Storico Italiano per il Medio Evo, 1955); and D. Burr, *The Persecution of Peter Olivi*, Transactions of the American Philosophical Society, N.S. 66, 5 (Philadelphia, 1976).

14. *Ecclesia Spiritualis* (Stuttgart: Kohlhammer, 1964) 2, p. 259.

ANGELO OF CLARENO: A LETTER OF DEFENSE TO THE POPE

1. Translated from the edition of F. Ehrle, "Die Spiritualen und ihr Verhältnis zum Franciscanerorden," *Archiv für Literatur-und Kirchengeschichte* 1 (1886): 521–33. The title itself is indicative. *Epistola excusatoria* is a technical term for a letter defending nonattendance at some hearing or function. In the text Angelo usually refers to his enemies as *fratres*, here translated as Franciscans or Friars. His own group are sometimes *fratres*, more frequently *socii*, here translated as brethren or companions.

2. In late 1316 or early 1317, Pope John XXII had summoned the leaders of the Spiritual party to a Consistory in which among other actions he confirmed the sentence of excommunication of Angelo and his group contained in a Bull of Boniface VIII.

3. The observance of the Rule was one of the key issues in the struggle between the Spirituals and the Conventuals.

4. Angelo and such Spiritual leaders as Peter Olivi upheld the legitimacy of Boniface's election; but others, such as Ubertino of Casale, believed that Celestine's resignation had not been lawful and that Boniface's election was invalid.

5. Angelo now begins his historical account with a reference to the first imprisonment of the Spirituals of the Marches about 1278 as a result of the troubles following rumors emanating from the Second Council of Lyons (1274) that the pope was about to compel the Franciscans to accept property.

6. Minister General from 1289–1295, Raymond was favorable to reform and the Spiritual cause.

NOTES

7. This commission appears to have been given in 1290. King Hayton II of Armenia was so favorable to the Order that in 1294 he resigned his throne and joined the Franciscans.

8. The Chapter of Paris was held in 1292.

9. Probably in late 1293. The temporary resting place of the group was the hermitage of S. Maria del Chiarino near Ascoli Piceno. Angelo took his subriquet "da Chiarino" from this spot.

10. Angelo and Liberato now went on ahead to see the pope.

11. Peter of Murrone, Benedictine hermit and monastic reformer, was elected pope on July 5, 1294, and took the name of Celestine V. The interview took place between August and October of the same year. It was the pope who gave the emissaries their new names, Peter of Macerata becoming Fra Liberato and Peter of Fossombrone Fra Angelo. An unfriendly chronicler named Jordan tells us: "The two changed their names, the first called himself Liberato, the second Angelo, because he pretended to have angelic revelations."

12. The Testament of Francis (1226) was a central document for the differences between the two parties. See Introduction.

13. Napoleon Orsini, a cardinal since 1288, became one of the chief protectors of the Spirituals.

14. Angelo has summarized the battery of arguments, some perhaps self-serving, why the excommunication issued by Boniface VIII and Peter of Constantinople in lost Letters probably of 1299 was not binding. The historical buttressing for his claim is given in the following paragraphs.

15. Matt. 10:23.

16. The *finis prefixus* or "end appointed" might be a reference to the coming millennial period, the Franciscan version of Joachim's third *status*, or it might be a reference to the certainty of death.

17. Celestine renounced the papacy on December 13, 1294. Boniface soon showed himself hostile to the Spiritual cause. On April 8, 1295, in the bull "Olim Coelestinus," he annulled all the actions of his predecessor, among which was the approval of the Poor Hermits. In November of the same year he deposed Raymond Gaufridi, the minister favorable to the *zelanti*, and put in his place the anti-Spiritual John of Murrovalle.

18. Probably Trixonia in the mouth of the Gulf of Corinth. This area of Greece was at that time under Frankish rule.

19. This would have been about 1297.

20. Boniface's bull against the Poor Hermits, entitled "Saepe sacram ecclesiam," was written about 1299 to Peter, the Latin Patriarch of Constantinople, and to the Bishops of Athens and Patras. It has not survived.

21. This would have been about 1300. Again, Angelo implicitly claims that he was never officially served the bull of excommunication.

22. Angelo's group fled to Greek territory, the lands of the Sevastocrator of Epirus in southern Thessaly, probably early in 1301.

NOTES

23. Brother Jerome, later Bishop of Kaffa, is the arch-villain for Angelo. *Torquatus*, the surname of an important branch of the Roman Manlii, is apparently being used in the root sense of "twisted," i.e., perverse.

24. On Peter Olivi, the great Provençal Spiritual, see Introduction.

25. The wordplay on *depositio* (deposition, testimony, and witness) is difficult to bring out in English. Wadding's *Annales* under 1311 note the promotion of Brother Jerome to a suffragan bishopric of the Mongol mission.

26. Patriarch Peter died in the middle of 1301.

27. This mission took place in 1302.

28. These legations would have been sent before the death of Boniface on October 11, 1303.

29. Benedict XI was chosen pope on October 22, 1303, at Perugia, where he died on July 7, the following year.

30. I here follow an emendation of the text suggested by the editor.

31. Clement V was elected at Perugia on June 13, 1305, and soon removed to France where he was crowned at Lyons on November 14.

32. Liberato died in the latter half of 1307 at S. Angelo della Vena near Viterbo. Angelo then became the leader of the Poor Hermits.

33. Angelo's return appears to have taken place in early 1305 during the long interregnum between Benedict and Clement. See the Introduction for speculations regarding the activity of his group during this period.

34. The length of the Franciscan habit had been one of the key questions in the debates between the two parties in the order, and papal condemnations of unapproved orders (IV Lateran in 1215, and II Lyons in 1274) allowed immediate action against unusual religious garb.

35. This would have been before September of 1305 when Napoleon departed for southern France with the new pope.

36. Isnard, Archbishop of Thebes, was sent to Rome in 1308 and became Patriarch of Antioch in 1311. The investigation appears to have taken place in 1310.

37. John de Papazuris (1302–1326).

38. Probably a Bishop of Viterbo of this name who died in 1311.

39. Penitentiaries were papal officials given powers to absolve from grave sins. They first appear toward the middle of the thirteenth century.

40. Opened on October 6, 1311.

41. Angelo was to remain at Avignon in the household of Cardinal Jacopo Colonna until the middle of 1318.

42. Cf. Rom. 8:16.

43. Literally, "iudicium subverterunt," "overturned the judgment or trial," thus containing the notions of both ruining the reputation and perverting the judicial process.

44. This list of the earliest martyrs of the Spiritual party forms the second tribulation of the *History of the Seven Tribulations*, that under the Generalate of Elias (1232–1239). Angelo here is giving a *precis* of the stages of his longer, more properly apocalyptic, work. See Introduction.

NOTES

45. The third tribulation that under Crescentius of Jesi (1244–1248).

46. The fourth tribulation, that of John of Parma, the only Spiritual to become General (1247–1257). He was compelled to step down because of his friendship with the Joachite-sympathizing friars who had caused the 1254 "Crisis of the Eternal Gospel," but the stories regarding his punishment by the Conventuals are largely fiction created by the Spirituals.

47. The fifth tribulation of the *History*.

48. Ps. 71:12.

49. Gen. 9:5.

PETER JOHN OLIVI: LETTER TO THE SONS OF CHARLES

1. Translated from the edition of F. Ehrle in *Archiv für Literatur-und Kirchengeschichte* 3 (1887): 534–40.

2. The three sons of Charles II (1285–1309) had been imprisoned in Catalonia since 1288. Louis, the eldest, was later to give up the crown for the Archbishopric of Toulouse and (what was dearer to his heart) the robes of a Franciscan. He died in 1297 and was subsequently canonized. Robert ruled Naples from 1309 to 1343 and was a protector of the Fraticelli descendants of the Spirituals.

3. John 12:24.

4. Aristotle, *On Generation and Corruption*, 1.3.

5. Olivi uses a technical scholastic term here that might be literally rendered as "be subject to his rule in obediential potency."

6. Phil. 4:7.

7. John 12:24.

8. Gal. 4:1.

9. John 16:21.

10. Luke 24:26.

11. Acts 14:21.

12. James 1:2–4.

13. James 5:10–11.

14. Heb. 12:1–3, 6–7.

15. Heb. 12:8.

16. Heb. 12:11.

17. John 15:13.

18. 1 Tim. 6:12.

19. From the hymn "Sanctorum meritis inclyta gaudia," of First Vespers of the Common for Many Martyrs.

20. Eccli. 34:11.

21. Heb. 5:8.

22. John 15:2.

23. Cant. 2:12.

24. Apoc. 6:12.

25. Apoc. 9:14–16.

301

26. Apoc. 16:12–14. As pointed out in the Introduction, Olivi believed that he was living in the midst of the crisis of the overlapping of the Fifth and the Sixth Age, foretold in the Apocalypse under the figures of the sixth seal, the sixth trumpet, and the sixth vial.

27. Apoc. 17:3–17.

28. Apoc. 7:2–17, 10:8–11. R. Manselli in *La "Lectura super Apocalysism" di Pietro de Giovanni Olivi* (Rome: Instituto Storico Italiano per il Medio Evo, 1955), pp. 170–71, rightly points out that many of the specific themes of Olivi's Joachite apocalyptic are not highlighted here. Nevertheless, the concordance between the story of the Deluge and the current crisis foretold in the Apocalypse is typical of Joachite exegesis in general, and the reference to the preaching of evangelical poverty to all indicates that Olivi meant the Angel of the Sixth Seal to be understood as Saint Francis.

29. *Minoratus* in the text.

30. Olivi's experience of persecution as a result of his trial in 1283 speaks here.

31. *Imbeguinari*. The terms *begina* and *beginus* as applied to heretics (probably from *Albigenses*) appear in the late twelfth century. They were the customary terms in the fourteenth century for Olivi's followers.

32. 1 Cor. 4:10.

33. 1 Cor. 3:8.

34. 1 Cor. 1:25.

35. 1 Kings 2:6; Tob. 3:2.

36. Reminiscent of the words with which Angelo later concluded the first part of the sixth tribulation in his *History*: "We pray to be liberated from the six tribulations so that in the seventh he may free us from evil." Here, contrary to Manselli, we find explicit reference to the future hopes of the Spirituals.

37. Brother Peter Scarerii, a friend of Olivi and afterwards Bishop of Rapolla.

38. Phil. 4:7.

PART V: SAVONAROLA

1. "L'Apocalypse en 1500. La fresque de l'Antéchrist à la chapelle Saint-Brice d'Orvieto," *Bibliothèque d'humanisme et renaissance* 14 (1952): 124–40. See Plate 7.

2. For a more detailed treatment of this era, see my *Visions of the End* (New York: Columbia University Press, 1979).

3. Among the most common of these was the widespread acceptance of a double notion of the Antichrist. Many looked forward to both a "Mystical Antichrist," a false pope who would mislead the Church, and a "Great Antichrist," or persecuting ruler.

4. Reeves, *Prophecy*, pp. 310–11 and *passim*.

NOTES

5. See B. McGinn, "Angel Pope and Papal Antichrist," *Church History* 47 (1978): 155–73.

6. See my forthcoming article, "Apocalyptic Consciousness and Group Identification in Thirteenth-Century Religion."

7. See, e.g., E. Garin, "L'Attesa dell'Età Nuova e la 'Renovatio,' " in *L'Attessa dell'Età Nuova nella Spiritualità della Fine del Medioevo* (Convegni del Centro di Studi sulla Spiritualità Medievale. III. Todi: L'Accademia Tudertina, 1962), p. 11:35.

8. The best introduction to these prophets is the articles of G. Tognetti, notably, "Le fortune della pretesa profezia di San Cataldo," *Bollettino dell'Istituto Storico Italiano per il Medio Evo* 80 (1968): 273–317; and "Note sul Profetismo nel Rinascimento e la letteratura relativa," in *Bolletino . . .* 82 (1970): 129–57.

9. R. Ridolfi, *The Life of Girolamo Savonarola* (London: Routledge and Kegan Paul, 1959), p. 22.

10. Translated from the most popular rendition of the earlier version of the text as given in Reeves, *Prophecy*, p. 328.

11. The history of the text has been studied by M. Chaume, "Une prophetie relative à Charles VI," *Revue du moyen âge latin* 3 (1974): 27–42.

12. On this important book to which my account owes much, see the review of S. Camporeale, "Savonarola. Umanesimo e Profezia," *Revista di Storia della Chiesa in Italia* 31 (1977): 508–13.

13. Quoted in Ridolfi, p. 171.

14. E.g., P. Villari, *Life and Times of Girolamo Savonarola* (New York: Scribner's, 1888), pp. 320–24; and Ridolfi, p. 114.

15. See M. Meiss, *Painting in Florence and Siena after the Black Death* (New York: Harper and Row, 1973), chap. 5.

16. E.g., *Prediche sopra Aggeo*, ed. L. Firpo (Rome: A. Belardetti, 1965), XIV, esp. pp. 234–40.

17. *Prediche Italiane ai Fiorentini*, ed. R. Palmarocchi (Florence: La Nuova Italia, 1933), III², p. 313. See also pp. 320 and 528. These texts are discussed in Weinstein, pp. 77, 173–75.

GIROLAMO SAVONAROLA: THE COMPENDIUM OF REVELATIONS

1. Translated from the edition of Angela Crucitti, *Girolamo Savonarola. Compendio di Rivelazioni e Dialogus de veritate prophetica*, Edizione Nazionale delle Opere di Girolamo Savonarola (Rome: A. Berlardetti, 1974). Although it appears that, contrary to his usual practice, Savonarola did not in this case write in Latin first, it does seem that he worked on both versions of the text almost simultaneously (see Crucitti, pp. 379–386). I have translated from the Latin text, but have compared with the Italian throughout. There are many minor verbal differences, but no change of content.

2. Matt. 7:6.

NOTES

3. The vision took place on the night of March 31, 1495.

4. The vernacular text was first published by Francesco Buonaccorsi on August 18, 1495; four other editions followed in less than a year. Buonaccorsi published the Latin text on October 3, and in 1496 Latin editions appeared at Paris and Ulm.

5. The lukewarm friends of whom the Dominican speaks here are priests and monks who opposed him throughout his career. For their opposition at this juncture, see Ridolfi, pp. 114–115.

6. Dan. 12:4.

7. Prov. 3:32.

8. Matt. 11:25.

9. 1 Kings 9:9.

10. This definition is based on Aquinas, *Summa of Theology* (hereafter cited as STh). The following discussion of the charism of prophecy is deeply influenced throughout by St. Thomas's discussion in qq. 171–174 of the IIaIIae.

11. For Aquinas's condemnation of divination, see IIaIIae, q. 95. "Judicial" astronomy is what we would call astrology.

12. Heb. 4:13.

13. Osee 12:10.

14. Dan. 10:1.

15. Dan. 5:25.

16. *Celestial Hierarchy* 4.3.

17. Rom. 13:1.

18. Amos 3:7.

19. For an analysis of the relation between the Florentine situation and Savonarola's prophetic career, the fundamental book is that of D. Weinstein.

20. As Weinstein points out (p. 117), Savonarola's account is better prophecy than history at this point. The Dominican had first been in the city from 1482 to 1487, and was reassigned there in 1490 not 1489. He first began his prophetic preaching in San Gimignano in 1486, not in Florence (Weinstein, pp. 74–76).

21. These three forms of proof are also found in the "Renovation Sermon" preached on January 13, 1495, after the departure of Charles and his army.

22. Gen. 6:16.

23. The invasion of Charles VIII began in late August of 1494.

24. Giovanni Pico della Mirandola (1463–1494), one of the most remarkable Humanists of the day, had known Savanorola since at least 1482 and had been instrumental in his return to Florence (Ridolfi, p. 29). The friar attended the Count's deathbed on November 16, the day before the entrance of Charles into Florence.

25. Weinstein (p. 76) doubts Savonarola's claims for a gradual disclosure of the divine character of his revelations, showing that there is no evidence in the surviving sermons before the critical events of late 1494.

NOTES

26. Although none of the revealed messages are taken directly from scripture, all of them are constructed from scriptural reminiscences. The sword of the Lord is a frequent prophetic image (e.g., Isa. 1:20, Jer. 46:10), and the phrase "swiftly and soon" (*cito et velociter*) occurs in Joel 3:4.

27. Reminiscences of Matt. 5:12, Eccli. 2:11, Apoc. 22:11, and Wisd. 2:9 are found in this passage.

28. Apoc. 19:2. A picture of this vision is found on the obverse of the famous Savonarola medallion, shown here in Plate 10.

29. Cf. Gen. 4:10.

30. Ps. 88:33.

31. Ps. 88:34.

32. Jer. 2:32.

33. Ezech. 5:11.

34. Cf. Ezech. 5:6.

35. Reminiscences of Dan. 4:32, Ezech. 5:13 and 19, Isa. 45:22, Lam. 4:11, and Ezech. 7:25 are found here.

36. Ps. 118:103.

37. Ps. 41:10.

38. Reminiscences of Is. 30:18, Joel 2:13, Ps. 102:6, Isa. 1:15, Job 14:13, and Ps. 74:11 are found in these addresses.

39. Is. 45:1–4.

40. Lorenzo died on April 8, 1492; Innocent on July 25 of the same year.

41. Late October, 1494.

42. The legates were named on Nov. 5. Their meeting with Charles took place in Pisa on Nov. 8.

43. Ps. 24:10.

44. Thomas Aquinas notes that God always rewards more than he should and punishes less than he should; see STh Ia, 21, 4, ad 1.

45. 1 Tim. 6:15–16.

46. Job. 12:17–18.

47. This was an important theme in the traditions about the Last World Emperor.

48. On the change in Savonarola's prophecy from a basically pessimistic message to one of millenarian optimism centered on the city of Florence, see Weinstein, especially chapters four and five.

49. "The Appeal against the Six Beans" was an attempt by Savonarola and others to mitigate the process by which six votes of the aristocratic Council of Eight (cast by white beans) were sufficient to inflict severe criminal sentences and even death. In the interest of reducing party strife, Savonarola argued for the possibility of appeal in such cases to the whole Signoria or the Council of Eighty. A law allowing an appeal to the General Council was passed in March 1495. Savonarola was later criticized for his role in this reform. See Villari, pp. 277–278.

50. 2 Cor. 3:5.

51. Rom. 8:26.

NOTES

52. James 1:4.

53. Rom. 5:3–5.

54. The change in government from the control of the Medici to the dominance of the Signoria took place while Savonarola was on embassy to Charles VIII. His first sermon on his return, probably preached on November 11, shows his immediate support for the new regime. See *Prediche sopra Aggeo* IV, pp. 61–76.

55. This sermon was XIII of the *Prediche sopra Aggeo* (ed. cit., pp. 209–28), given on December 14. It does not appear that Savonarola originated many of the particulars of the new Venetian-style constitution, as he claims here, but he was an early and important supporter of the new forms of government.

56. The reforms were decreed on December 22–23. For a discussion of the Friar's role, see Weinstein, pp. 247–266.

57. Job. 9:13.

58. This doctrine is basically Thomist, cf. STh IIaIIae 2, 1; 4, 8; etc.

59. Prov. 10:9, 3:32.

60. Ps. 5:7.

61. Although a number of authors of the end of the fifteenth century mixed apocalypticism and astrology, such as Johannes Lichtenberger, the court astrologer of Frederick III, and the Dominican Giovanni Nanni of Viterbo, Savonarola, in line with traditional Thomistic teaching, makes his opposition to astrology clear.

62. These two phrases summarizing Aristotle's position are from *Periherm.* 9:19, and *Met.* 5:2.

63. The friar seems to refer to three works attributed to Albert, *The Experiments of Albert*, *The Wonders of the World*, and *The Secrets of Women*.

64. Isa. 47:10.

65. Isa. 47:13–14.

66. Jer. 10:2–3.

67. Isa. 41:25.

68. See STh Ia, 84, 6; IaIIae 9, 5; IIaIIae 95, 5.

69. 1 Cor. 15:8.

70. The source of this saying is unknown.

71. Amos 3:6–7.

72. Acts 1:7. A favorite text for attacking apocalyptic expectations, at least since the time of Saint Augustine; see *City of God* 18:53.

73. Acts 1:6.

74. Gen. 7:4.

75. Jer. 25:11.

76. Dan. 9:24–27.

77. 1 Cor. 12:11.

78. Rom. 9:18–21.

79. Num.24.

80. Matt. 7:22–23.

NOTES

81. *Gratiae gratis datae*, a technical term in the Thomistic theology of grace for special gifts of God given for distinct purposes as distinguished from justifying grace, the *gratia gratum faciens*; see IaIIae, 11, 4.

82. 1 Cor. 13:1.

83. The friar probably has the Sibylline Oracles in mind, as well as the writings of Bridget of Sweden and Catherine of Siena.

84. 1 Thess. 5:20.

85. Rom. 4:17.

86. Heb. 4:13.

87. Innocent III, *Register* 2.141 (PL 214.695–98).

88. Jer. 28:7–9.

89. John 10:41–42.

90. John 1:23.

91. Eccli. 19:4.

92. 1 Cor. 13:7.

93. See Jerome's *Life of Paul* and *Life of Hilarion* (PL 23). Gregory the Great's *Dialogues* contain numerous references to prophecy. It is difficult to know exactly what work of Augustine Savonarola had in mind, but *Catechizing the Young* (e.g., 4.7 and 9, 24.44) and *The Care for the Dead* (e.g., 12.15, 17.21) are possible candidates.

94. 1 John 4:1.

95. STh IIaIIae, 5:4.

96. Ps. 111:4.

97. A frequent theme in Aristotle, if not precisely in these words. E.g., *De Caelo* 1.4, and 2.11.

98. Matt. 11:25, Luke 10–21.

99. 1 Cor. 1:20–21.

100. Isa. 33:18–19.

101. John 9:39.

102. Eccles. 1:15.

103. Matt. 20:16, 22:14.

104. *Epist.* 53 (PL 22.272).

105. Luke 21:15.

106. Acts 6:10.

107. 1 Par. 17:2.

108. Matt. 22:29.

109. 4 Kings 4:27.

110. Gal. 1:10.

111. 1 Cor. 4:10.

112. Wisd. 5:1.

113. Wisd. 5:3–5.

114. Matt. 5:11–12.

115. 1 Kings 16:7.

116. 2 Cor. 5:10.

117. STh Ia, 5:5, etc.

NOTES

118. 1 Cor. 4:4.

119. 2 Cor. 11:17, 12:11.

120. The break with the Lombard Congregation was effected by a papal brief of May 22, 1493. The fullest study of the separation is J. Schnitzer, *Savonarola im Streite mit seinem Orden und seinem Kloster* (Munich: J.F. Lehmann, 1914).

121. Prov. 13:10.

122. 2 Tim. 2:4. It was precisely this scriptural text that had been invoked against Savonarola at a meeting in early 1495 by his fellow Dominican Tommaso da Rieti (Villari, p. 329).

123. *Nic. Ethics* 3:7.

124. While by no means a real democracy (the number of citizens eligible for the Great Council has been calculated as about 3,000), the new republican government represented a considerable expansion of the active political base of the city. See the summary in Weinstein, pp. 255–256.

125. These obscure sentences are clearer in the Italian, whose sense has guided the rendering given here.

126. On Savonarola's messianic concept of Florence, see Weinstein, especially chapters four and five.

127. Matt. 10:24.

128. Apparently a classical proverb.

129. Ps. 59:5–7.

130. Acts 13:48.

131. Cf. Luke 24:17.

132. The exchange is a choral rendition of Isa. 26:1–9. Other examples of the same form will be seen below.

133. Luke 1:68 sq.

134. *Latria, dulia,* and *hyperdulia,* are traditional terms in Latin theology, see STh IIaIIae, 103, 3 and 4.

135. Luke 2:29 sq.

136. John 15:12, 13:35.

137. Acts 4:32.

138. Ps. 121:7–9.

139. The Italian text adds that the pearl signifies a good conscience.

140. 3 Kings 10:18–20.

141. Cf. Ezech. 2:1, 3, 23; 44:4.

142. As pointed out in the Introduction, other passages make it clear that Savonarola believed in a coming holy pope, the *Pastor Angelicus,* who would renew the Church.

143. Isa. 55:1.

144. John 7:37.

145. Apoc. 22:17.

146. John 4:13–14.

147. This theme of a return to the perfection of the early Church complements the future-oriented notion of a more perfect age of the Church on

earth, which Savonarola shared with many other late medieval apocalyptic authors. Similar elements are found in the thought of Joachim.

148. The medieval *Bestiary* stressed the elephant's chastity due to his habit of underwater copulation.

149. See Jerome, *On Hebrew Names* (PL 23,887).

150. Exod. 33:23.

151. There had been an extensive controversy in Latin theology over the question of whether it was possible to have a direct vision of God in this life.

152. Ps. 112:1–2.

153. Zach. 8:5.

154. Ps. 113:14.

155. Ps. 113:15.

156. Matt. 18:3.

157. James 1:17.

158. Apoc. 7:14.

159. 2 Cor. 6:6.

160. Lam. 4:7.

161. Ps. 117:1–2.

162. Heb. 2:16.

163. Ps. 66:2–3.

164. Ps. 66:4–6.

165. Ps. 66:7.

166. The description of the nine choirs of angels that follows is based on a long tradition whose fundamental source is to be found in the Pseudo-Dionysius, *Celestial Hierarchy*, especially chapters 5–10.

167. Ezech. 28:13.

168. Isa. 6:3; Matt. 21:9.

169. Jth. 15:10–11.

170. Dan. 7:10.

171. Rom. 13:1.

172. The Friar here shows his reliance on the tradition of allegorical interpretation of precious gems, especially those mentioned in the scriptures. The most complete study of this tradition is now in process of publication, C. Meier, *Gemma Spiritalis. Methode und Gebrauch der Edelsteinallegorese vom frühen Christentum bis ins 18.Jahrhundert* Teil I (Munich: W. Fink, 1977).

173. Prov. 8:31.

174. Wisd. 9:15.

175. Ps. 83:8.

176. The choral dialogue is taken from Ps. 112:1–9.

177. Ps. 19:1.

178. Ps. 19:2.

179. Ps. 19:3.

180. Ps. 19:4.

181. Ps. 19:5.

182. Ps. 19:6.

183. Ps. 19:7.
184. Ps. 19:8.
185. Ps. 19:9.
186. Ps. 19:10.
187. *Excessus mentis*, a technical term for mystical ecstasy; see the article "Extase," in the *Dictionnaire de spiritualité* 4.2, cc. 2045–2189, *passim*.
188. The following speech to the Virgin is a pastiche based on Ezech. 28:12–15, Jth. 15:9–10, and the well-known Compline hymn *Salve Regina*.
189. The Offertory verse for the Feast of the Seven Sorrows of the Blessed Virgin (Sept. 15).
190. A liturgical prayer in the form of a Collect.
191. Ps. 122:3–4.
192. On November 9, the same day that Florence expelled the Medici, the Pisans cast off the Florentine rule under which they had lived since 1406. Despite Savonarola's continued prophecies of the recovery of this city, it was to remain free until 1509.
193. The lilies are the citizens of Florence. The friar is praising the new form of government in which the lower and upper classes are united in harmony.
194. Isa. 3:10.
195. The celestial warrant for the regulations concerning public morality in the Florentine Republic under Savonarola.
196. Josue 23:16; Joel 3:4.
197. James 1:12.
198. Only verses 1, 2 and 19 are quoted in the Latin; the vernacular gives the whole psalm written out as described.
199. Ps. 117:28.
200. Thomistic doctrine, STh IIaIIae 174, 1.
201. Jon. 3:4.
202. Isa. 38:1.
203. Jon. 1:12–16.
204. 2 Cor. 4:3–4.
205. Ps. 49:19–21.
206. Ps. 115:11; Rom. 3:4.
207. 2 Tim. 2:19–21.

Bibliography

The literature relating to apocalypticism is large and not easily accessible through standard bibliographies. I have tried to give a critical overview of the medieval materials in my article "Apocalypticism in the Middle Ages: An Historiographical Sketch," *Mediaeval Studies* 37(1975): 252-86. The following selective bibliography is divided into three sections for easier use:

A. The Origins of Apocalypticism and Apocalyptic Spirituality.
B. Patristic Apocalypticism (c. A.D. 100-400)
C. Medieval Apocalypticism (c. A.D. 400-1500)

    (1) General Works
    (2) Early period (400-1200 A.D.)
    (3) Late period (1200-1500 A.D.)

A. The Origins of Apocalypticism and Apocalyptic Spirituality in General.

Apocalypticism. Journal for Theology and Church. vol. 6. New York, 1969.
Bousset, Wilhelm. *The Antichrist Legend.* London, 1896.
———. "Beiträge zur Geschichte der Eschatologie." *Zeitschrift für Kirchengeschichte* 20(1899-1900): 103-31, 261-90.
———. *Die Offenbarung Johannis.* Göttingen, 1906.
Bultmann, Rudolf. *History and Eschatology. The Presence of Eternity.* New York, 1962.
Charles, R.H., et al. *The Apocrypha and Pseudepigrapha of the Old Testament in English.* 2 vols. Oxford, 1913.
———. *A Critical and Exegetical Commentary on the Revelation of St. John.* Edinburgh, 1920.
Collins, Adela. "The Political Perspective of the Revelation of John." *The Journal of Biblical Literature* 96(1977): 241-56.

BIBLIOGRAPHY

Collins, John. "Apocalyptic Eschatology as the Transcendence of Death." *Catholic Biblical Quarterly* 36(1974): 21-43.
———. "The Symbolism of Transcendence in Jewish Apocalyptic." *Biblical Research* 19(1974): 5-22.
Eliade, Mircea. *Cosmos and History. The Myth of the Eternal Return.* New York, 1959.
Hanson, Paul D. *The Dawn of Apocalyptic.* Philadelphia, 1975.
Hartman, Lars. *Prophecy Interpreted.* Lund, 1966.
Hennecke, Edgar, et al. *New Testament Apocrypha.* 2 vols. Philadelphia, 1963.
Kermode, Frank. *The Sense of an Ending: Studies in the Theory of Fiction.* Oxford, 1966.
Koch, Klaus. *The Rediscovery of Apocalyptic.* Studies in Biblical Theology. 2nd ser., vol. 22. Napierville, 1970.
Löwith, Karl. *Meaning in History.* Chicago, 1949.
Malvenda, Tomás. *De Antichristo libri undecim.* Rome, 1604.
Moltmann, Jürgen. *The Theology of Hope.* New York, 1967.
Pannenberg, Wolfhart, et al. *Revelation as History.* London, 1969.
Rahner, Karl. "The Hermeneutics of Eschatological Assertions." *Theological Investigations.* London, 1966, Vol. 4:323-46.
Russell, D.S. *Apocalyptic Ancient and Modern.* Philadelphia, 1978.
———. *The Method and Message of Jewish Apocalyptic: 200 B.C.-A.D. 100.* Philadelphia, 1964.
Schall, J.V. "Apocalypse as a Secular Enterprise." *Scottish Journal of Theology* 29(1976): 357-73.
Schmithals, Walter. *The Apocalyptic Movement: Introduction and Interpretation.* Nashville, 1975.
Smith, Jonathan Z. "Wisdom and Apocalyptic." In. B.A. Pearson, ed., *Religious Syncretism in Antiquity.* Missoula, Mont., 1975, pp. 131-56.
Talmon, Yonina. "Pursuit of the Millennium: The Relation between Religious and Social Change." *Archives européenes de sociologie* 3(1962): 125-48.
Wilder, Amos N. "The Rhetoric of Ancient and Modern Apocalyptic." *Interpretation* 25(1971): 436-53.

B. PATRISTIC.

Atzberger, L. *Geschichte der christlichen Eschatologie innerhalb der vornicänischen Zeit.* Freiberg, 1896.
Bietenhard, Hans. "The Millennial Hope in the Early Church." *Scottish Journal of Theology* 6(1953): 12-30.
Daniélou, Jean. *The Theology of Jewish Christianity.* Chicago, 1964.
Hinnells, J.R. "The Zoroastrian Doctrine of Salvation in the Roman World: A Study of the Oracle of Hystaspes." In E.J. Sharpe and J.R. Hinnels, eds., *Man and his Salvation: Studies in Memory of S.G.F. Brandon.* Manchester, 1973, pp. 125-48.

BIBLIOGRAPHY

Kötting, B. "Endzeitprognosen zwischen Lactantius und Augustinus." *Historisches Jahrbuch* 77(1957): 125-39.

Loi, Vincenzo. *Lattanzio nelle Storia del Linguaggio e del Pensiero teologico Pre-Niceno.* Zurich, 1970.

Luneau, Auguste. *L'Histoire du salut chez les Pères de l'Église: La doctrine des âges du monde.* Paris, 1964.

Pelikan, Jaroslav. *The Emergence of the Catholic Tradition (100-600).* Chicago, 1973.

Pichon, René. *Lactance. Étude sur le mouvement philosophique et religieux sous le regne de Constantin.* Paris, 1901.

Schmidt, Roderich. "*Aetates mundi:* Die Weltalter als Gliederungsprinzip der Geschichte." *Zeitschrift für Kirchengeschichte* 67(1955-56): 287-317.

Thompson, B. "Patristic Use of the Sibylline Oracles." *Review of Religion* 16(1952): 115-36.

Weinel, Heinrich. "Die spätere christliche Apokalyptik." In Hans Schmidt, ed., *EUCHARISTERION: Studien zur Religion und Literatur des Alten und Neuen Testaments. Festschrift Hermann Gunkel.* Göttingen, 1923, pp. 141-73.

Werner, Martin. *The Formation of Christian Dogma.* Boston, 1965.

C. MEDIEVAL.

(1) General works.

Alexander, Paul J. "Medieval Apocalypses as Historical Sources." *American Historical Review* 73(1968): 1997-2018.

Anderson, Andrew R. *Alexander's Gate: Gog and Magog and the Enclosed Nations.* Cambridge, Mass., 1932.

Cohn, Norman. *The Pursuit of the Millennium.* New York, 1970.

Kampers, Franz. *Kaiserprophetieen und Kaisersagen im Mittelalter.* Munich, 1895.

Lerner, Robert. "Refreshment of the Saints: The Time after Antichrist as a Station for Earthly Progress in Medieval Thought." *Traditio* 32(1976): 97-144.

McGinn, Bernard. *Visions of the End: Apocalyptic Traditions in the Middle Ages.* New York, 1979.

Manselli, Raoul. *La "Lectura super Apocalypsim" di Pietro di Giovanni Olivi: Richerche sull'escatologismo medioevale.* Rome, 1955.

Töpfer, Bernhard. *Das kommende Reich des Friedens.* Berlin, 1964.

(2) Early Medieval.

Alexander, Paul J. *The Oracle of Baalbek: The Tiburtine Sibyl in Greek Dress.* Washington, D.C., 1967.

———. "Byzantium and the Migration of Literary Works and Motifs: The Legends of the Last Roman Emperor." *Mediaevalia et Humanistica* n.s.2(1971): 47-82.

Alphandéry, Paul. "Mahomet-Antichrist dans le moyen âge latin." In *Mélanges Hartwig Derenbourg.* Paris, 1909, pp. 261-77.

BIBLIOGRAPHY

Bloomfield, Morton W. "Joachim of Flora: A Critical Survey of his Canon, Teachings, Sources, Biography, and Influence." *Traditio* 13(1957): 249-311.

Erdmann, Carl. "Endkaiserglaube und Kreuzzugsgedanke im 11. Jahrhundert." *Zeitschrift für Kirchengeschichte* 51(1932): 384-414.

Grundmann, Herbert, *Neue Forschungen über Joachim von Fiore*. Marburg, 1950.

———. *Studien über Joachim von Fiore*. Leipzig, 1927. Reprint: Darmstadt, 1966.

———. "Kirchenfreiheit und Kaisermach um 1190 in der Sicht Joachims von Fiore." *Deutsches Archiv ür Erforschung des Mittelalters* 19(1963): 353-96.

———. "Zur Biographie Joachims von Fiore und Rainers von Ponza." *Deutsches Archiv für Erforschung des Mittelalters* 16(1960): 437-546.

Kamlah, Wilhelm. *Apokalypse und Geschichtstheologie: Die mittelalterliche Auslegung der Apokalypse vor Joachim von Fiore*. Berlin, 1935.

Kmosko, Michael. "Das Rätsel des Pseudomethodius." *Byzantion* 6(1931): 273-96.

Konrad, Robert. *De ortu et tempore Antichristi: Antichristvorstellung und Geschichtsbild des Abtes Adso von Montier-en-Der*. Munich, 1964.

McGinn, Bernard. "Joachim and the Sibyl." *Cîteaux* 34(1973): 97-138.

———. "Symbolism in the Thought of Joachim of Fiore." In a forthcoming Festschrift for Marjorie Reeves.

Mottu, Henri. *La manifestation de l'esprit selon Joachim de Fiore*. Neuchatel and Paris, 1977.

Rangheri, Maurizio. "La *Epistola ad Gerbergam reginam de ortu et tempore Antichristi* di Adsone di Montier-en-Der e le sue fonti." *Studi Medievali* 3rd ser. 14(1973): 677-732.

Rauh, Horst-Dieter. *Das Bild des Antichrist im Mittelalter: Von Tyconius zum Deutschen Symbolismus*. Münster, 1973.

Reeves, Marjorie. "History and Prophecy in Medieval Thought." *Mediaevalia et Humanistica* n.s.5(1974): 51-75.

———. "The Abbot Joachim's Sense of History." In *1274: Année charnière. Mutations et continuités*. Paris, 1977, pp. 781-96.

———, and B. Hirsch-Reich. *The Figurae of Joachim of Fiore*. Oxford, 1972.

Sackur, Ernst. *Sibyllinische Texte und Forschungen*. Halle, 1898.

Verhelst, D. "La préhistoire des conceptions d'Adson concernant l'Antichrist." *Recherches de théologie ancienne et médiévale* 40(1973): 52-103.

(3) Late Medieval.

L'Attesa dell'Età nuova nella Spiritualità della Fine del Medioevo. Convegni del Centro di Studi sulla Spiritualità Medievale III. Todi, 1962.

Benz, Ernst. *Ecclesia Spiritualis*. Stuttgart, 1934.

Bignami-Odier, Jeanne. *Études sur Jean de Roquetaillade*. Paris, 1952.

Bloomfield, M., and M. Reeves, "The Penetration of Joachimism into Northern Europe." *Speculum* 29(1954): 772-93.

Burr, David. *The Persecution of Peter Olivi*. Transactions of the American Philosophical Society, vol. 66, part 5. Philadelphia, 1976.

BIBLIOGRAPHY

Daniel, E. Randolph. *The Franciscan Concept of Mission in the High Middle Ages.* Lexington, 1975.

———. "Apocalyptic Conversion: The Joachite Alternative to the Crusades." *Traditio* 25(1969): 127-54.

———. "Spirituality and Poverty: Angelo da Clareno and Ubertino da Casale." *Mediaevalia et Humanistica* n.s.4(1973): 89-98.

Douie, Decima L. *The Nature and Effect of the Heresy of the Fraticelli.* Manchester, 1932.

Ehrle, Franz. "Petrus Johannis Olivi, sein Leben und seine Schriften." *Archiv für Literatur-und Kirchengeschichte des Mittelalters* 3(1887): 409-552.

———. "Die Spiritualen, ihr Verhältnis zum Franciscanerorden und zu den Fraticellen." *Archiv für Literatur-und Kirchengeschichte* 1(1885): 509-69; 2(1886): 106-64, 249-336; 3(1887):553-623; 4(1888): 1-190.

Franciscains d'Oc. Cahiers de Fanjeaux, vol. 10. Toulouse, 1975.

Frugoni, Arsenio. *Celestiniana.* Rome, 1953.

Grundmann, H. "Die Papstprophetien des Mittelalters." *Archiv für Kulturgeschichte* 19(1929): 77-138.

Holder-Egger, O. "Italienische Prophetieen des 13.Jahrhunderts." *Neues Archiv der Gesellschaft für ältere Deutsche Geschichtskunde* 15(1890):143-78; 30(1905):322-86; 33(1908):96-187.

Kaminsky, Howard. *A History of the Hussite Revolution.* Berkeley and Los Angeles, 1967.

Kurze, Dietrich. "Nationale Regungen in der spätmittelalterliche Prophetie." *Historische Zeitschrift* 202(1966): 1-23.

Lambert, Malcolm D. *Franciscan Poverty.* London, 1961.

Leff, Gordon. *Heresy in the Later Middle Ages.* 2 vols. New York, 1967.

Lerner, Robert. "Medieval Prophecy and Religious Dissent." *Past and Present* 72(1976): 3-24.

McGinn, B. "The Abbot and the Doctors: Scholastic Reactions to the Radical Eschatology of Joachim of Fiore." *Church History* 40(1971): 30-47.

———. "Angel Pope and Papal Antichrist." *Church History* 47(1978): 155-73.

———. "The Significance of Bonaventure's Theology of History." In David Tracy, ed., *Celebrating the Medieval Heritage. Journal of Religion. Supplement* 58(1978): s64-s81.

Oliger, Livarius. "Spirituels." *Dictionnaire de théologie catholique.* Paris, 1923-50. Vol.14:2522-49.

Partee, Carter. "Peter John Olivi: Historical and Doctrinal Study." *Franciscan Studies* 20(1960): 215-60.

Ratzinger, Joseph. *The Theology of History in St. Bonaventure.* Chicago, 1971.

Reeves, M. *The Influence of Prophecy in the Later Middle Ages: A Study in Joachimism.* Oxford, 1969.

———. *Joachim of Fiore and the Prophetic Future.* London and New York, 1976.

———. "Some Popular Prophecies from the Fourteenth to the Seventeenth Centuries." In *Studies in Church History. Vol. 8: Popular Belief and Practice.* Cambridge, 1972, pp. 107-34.

BIBLIOGRAPHY

Ricerche sull'Influenza della Prophezia nel Basso Medioevo. Bullettino dell'Istituto Storico Italiano per il Medio Evo 82(1970): 1-128.

Rohr, J. "Die Prophetie im letzten Jahrhundert vor der Reformation." *Historisches Jahrbuch* 19(1898): 29-56, 447-466.

Weinstein, Donald. *Savonarola and Florence.* Princeton, 1970.

Werner, Ernst. "Popular Ideologies in Late Medieval Europe: Taborite Chiliasm and its Antecedents." *Comparative Studies in Society and History* 2(1959-60): 344-63.

West, Delno C., ed. *Joachim of Fiore in Christian Thought: Essays on the Influence of the Calabrian Prophet.* 2 vols. New York, 1975.

Index to Foreword, Preface, Introductions and Notes

318

319

Faith, xv.
Fall, xiv.
Father, xv, xvi, 103, 104.
Fathers of the Church, 17, 23, 82, 83, 84, 281, 283, 285, 288, 295.
Ficino, Marsilio, xviii, 183.
Firpo, L., 303.
St. Francis, xvii, 150, 151, 152, 155, 156, 157, 299, 302.
Franciscans, xvii, 108, 150, 151, 152, 153, 157, 186, 189; Conventuals, 150, 155, 298, 301; Sprituals, xii, 12, 149–151, 154, 155, 157, 297–303.
Fraticelli, xvii, 10, 154, 301.
Frederick II, 11.
Frederick III, 306.
Frugoni, A., 297, 298.
Funk, R.W., 279.

Gager, John, 20, 279.
Galatians, 1:10, 307; 4:1, 301.
Garin, E., 303.
Gaufridi, Raymond, 298, 299.
Genesis, 4:10, 305; 6:16, 304; 7:4, 306; 9:5, 301; 19, 291; 19:20–23, 291; 42 sq., 283; 49:17, 287.
Gercke, A., 285.
Gerberga, Queen, 82, 83, 87.
Ghinato, P. Alberto, 297.
Giovanni Nanni of Viterbo, 306.
Girolamo, Fra, 188.
Gnosticism, 20.
God, and creation, xiv; as judge, 8; as lovable, 112; plan of, 6, 7, 13, 22, 104, 154, 295; revelations of, xv; seeking of, 7; as terrifying, 112, worship of, 19.
Gog, 86.

Gregory I, Pope, 291.
Gregory of Nyssa, 281.
Gregory the Great, 287, 307.
Grundmann, Herbert, 101, 111, 153, 289, 290, 297.
Guilloche of Bordeaux, 187.

Ham, 104.
Haussleiter, J., 279.
Haymo of Auxerre, 87, 287, 288, 289.
Hayton II, King of Armenia, 299.
Hebrews, 2:16, 309; 4:13, 307; 5:8, 301; 11:31, 112; 12:1–3, 301; 12:6–7, 301; 12:8, 301; 12:11, 301; 13:1, 304.
Heilbroner, Robert, 2.
Hennecke, E., 279.
Heresy, 10, 20, 154, 295, 302.
Hermes Trismegistus, 280, 281.
Herod, 294.
Hinnells, J., 280, 284.
Hippolytus, 21, 22, 88, 100, 279, 283, 284, 285, 288.
Hippolytus, Pseudo-, 288.
Hirsch-Reich, B., 103, 289, 290, 294, 295, 296.
History, end of, xii, 1, 5, 10, 12, 21, 157; and Incarnation, xv; lineal concept of, xiii; perfection of 13; process of, xv, 9, 12, 13, 14, 22, 85; and redemption, xv; sacred, 85; stages of, xvi, xvii, 102, 104, 106, 107, 108, 111, 151, 156, 185, 191, 283, 292, 293, 295; terror of, 13; theology of, 101, 103, 108, 112, 150, 152, 156, 158; triumph of, xvi.
Hollerich, Michael, 16.

320

Holy Spirit, xvi, 99, 100, 102, 104, 107, 108, 185, 293, 296.

Hope, for future, 7, 83, 103, 107, 185, 188; and history, xii; of renewal, 87, 108, 185, 186, 188, 191, 308; for return of Christ, 19, 99; for salvation, 6, 15; in suffering, 8, 12, 14.

Hussites, 11.

Illumination, xvi, xvii, 12, 99.

Incarnation, xv.

Innocent VIII, 305.

Irenaeus, xiv, 20, 21, 279, 283, 284, 287.

Issac, 107.

Isaiah, 1:15, 305; 1:20, 305; 3:10, 310; 6:3, 309; 11:6–8, 285; 26:1–9, 308; 30:18, 305; 30:26, 285; 33:18–19, 307; 38:1, 310; 41:25, 306; 45:1–4, 305; 45:22, 305; 47:10, 306; 47:13–14, 306; 55:1, 308; 65:25, 285.

Ishmael, 107.

Isidore of Seville, 287.

Islam, xv, 10, 83, 85, 86, 294, 295.

Isnard, 300.

Jacopone da Todi, 155.

Jacob, 107.

James, 1:2–4, 301; 1:4, 306; 1:12, 310; 1:17, 309; 5:10–11, 301.

Japeth, 104.

Jeremiah, 10:2–3, 306; 25:11, 306; 28:7–9, 307; 46:10, 305.

Jerome, 17, 281, 286, 287, 289, 307, 309.

Jerome, Brother, 300.

Jerusalem, 86, 106, 185, 289; New, xiv, 296.

Joachim of Fiore, xii, xvi, xvii, xviii, 3, 8, 12, 14, 150, 153, 157, 183, 185, 191, 289–297, 309; figures of, 103, 104, 106, 111, 290; hermeneutics of, 100–102, 106; importance of, 97–98; life of, 97–99, 289; visions of, 99–100, 289; *Book of Concordance*, 16, 97, 101, 102, 289, 290, 292–294, 296; *Book of Figures*, 103, 104, 106, 107, 290, 294–296; *Exposition on the Apocalypse*, 97, 289, 290, 294; *Ten-Stringed Psaltery*, 97, 289, 293; *Treatise on the Life of St. Benedict*, 107, 293.

Joachim, Pseudo-, 150, 151.

Job, 9:13, 306; 12:17–18, 305; 14:13, 305.

Joel, 2:13, 305; 2:28, 293; 3:4, 310.

John, xiv, 1, 84, 98, 100, 101, 278, 296.

John, 1:23, 307; 1:33, 293; 2:6, 294; 4:13–14, 308; 5:17, 293; 6:35, 286; 7:37, 308; 9:39, 307; 10:41–42, 307; 12:24, 301; 13:35, 308; 14:16–17, 293; 15:2, 301; 15:12, 308; 15:13, 301; 16:21, 301; 20:22, 293.

1 John, 2:18–19, 286; 4:1, 307.

John XXII, Pope, 149, 152, 153, 154, 155, 156, 157, 298.

John Climacus, 153.

John of Murrovalle, 299.

John de Papazuris, 300.

John of Parma, 152, 301.

John the Baptist, 292.

Jonas, 1:12–16, 310; 3:4, 310.

Joseph, 107.

Josiah, 102.

Josua, 23:16, 310.

Judaism, xiii, xiv, xv, xvi, 7, 9, 23, 82, 104, 107, 287, 289, 295.
Judgement, Day of, xvii; imminent, 6, 7, 12, 19, 21, 23.
Judith, 15:9–10, 310; 15:10–11, 309.
Justin Martyr, 21, 24.
Justinian, 83.

Kamlah, W., 290.
Käsemann, Ernst, 3, 19, 277, 279.
Kermode, Frank, 13, 15, 277, 278, 279.
Kingdom, 19, 20, 23, 188, 285, 297.
1 Kings, 2:6, 302; 9:9, 304; 16:7, 307.
3 Kings, 10:18–20, 308.
4 Kings, 4:27, 307.
Konrad, R., 87, 287.
Kötting, B., 280, 283, 285.

Lactantius, xiii, xiv, xv, 14, 81, 82, 98, 279–286; apocalypticism of, 18–24; importance of, 17; life of, 17–18; *Divine Institutes*, xi, 12, 18, 22.
Lambert, M.D., 298.
Lamentations, 4:7, 309; 4:11, 305.
Last World Emperor, xv, 10, 11, 85–88, 185, 187–188, 286, 288, 305.
Leff, G., 297.
Lerner, R.E., 286–287.
Leviticus, 25:22, 294.
Liberato, Fra, 152, 299, 300.
Lichtenberger, Johannes, 306.
Lindsey, Hal, 1, 2, 277.
Little, L.K., 286.
Loi, Vincenzo, 17, 18, 280, 284.

Lord, return of, xi, xiii; Risen, 19; servants of, xvi.
Lot, 291.
Louis IV, 87, 287.
Louis the Pious, 83.
Lucius III, Pope, 98.
Lucretius, 281, 282, 286.
Luke, 1:68 sq., 308; 2:29 sq., 308; 3:22, 292; 10:21, 307; 21:15, 307; 24:17, 308; 24:26, 301.
Luneau, A., 279, 280.
Lyons, Second Council of, 298.

Magog, 86.
Magyars, 83.
Malachy, 4:1, 284.
Man of Perdition, 87.
Manasses, 107.
Manselli, R., 291, 298, 302.
Mark, 13, 284.
Martin of Tours, 82.
Matthew, 3:17, 292; 5:11–12, 307; 5:12, 305; 7:6, 303; 7:22–23, 306; 10:5, 293; 10:23, 299; 10:24, 308; 10:28, 282; 11:5, 286; 11:25, 304, 307; 18:3, 309; 20:16, 307; 21:9, 309; 22:14, 307; 22:29, 307; 24:21, 284; 24:24, 286.
McGinn, B., 277, 278, 286, 289, 297, 298, 302, 303.
Medici, Lorenzo de, 186, 305.
Medici, Piero de, 187.
Meier, C., 309.
Meiss, M., 303.
Melsemutus, 294.
Messianism, 4, 5, 10, 11.
Methodius, Pseudo-, xv, 85, 86, 286, 288.
Michael, 289.

Michael of Cesena, 155.
Millenarianism, 4, 5, 7, 19, 20, 99, 107, 185, 188, 305.
Millenium, age of, xi, 14, 23, 107, 150, 152, 157, 183, 186, 188, 191, 285; visions of, xiv, xv.
Mohammed, 286, 294.
Moltmann, Jürgen, 3, 15, 277.
Mongols, 10.
Monti, Dominic, 16.
Morality, and apocalypticism, 12, 23; crisis of, 7; roots of, xiii; of waiting, xiv, xv.
Moran, James, 16.
Moses, 108.
Mottu, H., 3, 101, 102, 277, 290.
Mystical Body, xvii, 184, 293, 296.
Mysticism, xviii.

Nero, 11, 82, 284, 294, 295.
Nesi, Giovanni, 183.
Neuss, W., 286.
New Testament, xi, 3, 19, 82, 99, 100, 102, 103, 104, 106, 107, 295.
Noah, 104.
Numbers, 24, 306.

Old Testament, xv, 5, 22, 98, 99, 102, 103, 104, 107, 291, 295.
Oliger, L., 297.
Olivi, Peter John, xii, 295, 298; and Spirituals, 156–158, 300, 302; *Lecture on the Apocalypse*, 156, 157; *Letters to the Sons of Charles II*, 12, 157, 301–302.
Onians, R.B., 282.
Oracle of Apollo, 24.
Oracle of Hystaspes, 24.
Oracula Sibyllina, 282–285; cf.

also Sibylline Oracles.
Origen, 281.
Orsini, Napoleon Cardinal, 155, 299.
Osee, 12:10, 304.
Otto the Saxon, 87.
Ovid, 281.

Palmarocchi, R., 303.
Pannenberg, Wolhart, 3, 15, 277.
Papacy, 10, 11, 111, 153, 184, 185, 191, 296.
1 Paralipomenon, 17:2, 307.
Parousia, 19, 20.
Paul, xiv, 112.
Paulus Alvarus, 287.
Payne, Richard, 16.
Persecution, xvii, 7, 8, 9, 12, 83, 84, 86, 98, 111, 152, 157, 186, 191, 291, 292, 294; of Church, 23, 106, 295; of Diocletian, 17; of Jews, 7, 295.
Peter, 295.
Peter of Constantinople, 299, 300.
Peter of Fossombrone, 149, 299; cf. Angelo of Clareno.
Peter of Macerata, 299; cf. Liberato, Fra.
Peter of Murrone, 299; cf. also Celestine V.
Petrus Alphonsi, 290.
Pherecydes of Syros, 282.
Philip of Majorca, 154.
Philippians, 4:7, 301, 302.
Piagnoni, the, xviii, 189.
Pichon, René, 17.
Pico della Mirandola, 17, 304.
Plato, 282; *Apology*, 281, 286; *Phaedo*, 280, 282, 285; *Phaedrus*,

Weinstein, Donald, 188, 190, 304, 305, 306, 308.
Werner, Martin, 19, 279.
Whore of Babylon, 84.
Wilder, Amos N., 7.
Wisdom, 2:9, 305; 5:1, 307; 5:3–5, 307; 9:15, 309.

Wolff, G., 283.
World, ages of, 22; end of, 102, 103; transformation of, 14.

Zachariah, 8:5, 309.
Zeno, 282.

Index to Text

328

Genesis, 197; 6:12, 114; 6:13, 114; 18:26 ff., 116; 19:20, 117.

Gentiles, 128, 214.

Gerberga, Queen, 89.

God, abandoning of, 115; belief in, 27, 208; commands of, 27, 56, 77, 178, 198, 204, 222, 245, 246, 270, 271; as Creator, 29, 31, 32, 33, 63, 126, 129, 243; denial of, 33, 44, 92; goodness of, 204, 209, 211, 253, 270; knowledge of, 45, 114, 115, 194, 196, 212, 249, 271; love for, 45, 246, 253; mercy of, 89, 198, 200, 202, 204, 206, 207, 209, 218, 232, 244, 245, 254, 264, 269, 270; new people of, 142; people of, 73, 77, 92, 94, 96, 117, 119, 125; perfection of, 28, 44; promises of, 211, 244, 269; providence of, 28, 30, 31, 33, 35, 36, 40, 44, 96; rule of, 28, 173, 258; Spirit of, 51; teaching of, 25–28, 41, 56, 123, 124, 145, 193, 239; will of, 119, 137, 197, 207, 210, 219, 227, 235, 236; works of, 28, 32, 35, 36, 44, 56, 72, 173, 204, 226, 233, 241; and world, 29–31; worship of, 25, 35, 36, 38, 39, 49, 53, 61, 71; wrath of, 61, 76, 77, 119, 201, 207, 246, 265, 272.

Gods, 39, 40, 45, 48.

Gog, 136, 140, 141.

Gomorrah, 115.

Good, earthly, 25, 38, 39, 46, 48, 79, 80, 232–234, 248; and evil, 34, 36, 37, 38; heavenly, 39, 46, 71, 78; highest, 38, 42, 43, 79; of soul, 38.

Grace, 89, 121, 122, 128, 142, 173, 175, 176, 204, 207, 211, 218, 219, 235, 239, 244, 245, 248, 251, 268, 271.

Gregory XI, Pope, 237.

Gregory, Saint, *Dialogues*, 225.

Heaven, gates of, 241, 246; King of, 176; Kingdom of, 73, 89, 174, 201, 206, 250; rewards of, 25, 39; and virtue, 27, 39; visions of, 198, 247–270.

Hebrews, 10:31, 116.

Hell, 66, 204.

Hercules, 94.

Heresy, 159, 161, 166, 168, 171, 172, 223, 224, 273.

Hermes, 33, 53; *The Perfect Treatise*, 63.

Herod, 136, 250.

Holofernes, 138.

Holy Spirit, 74, 75, 90, 91, 209, 263; and baptism, 121, 122, 126, 127, 132; and *concordia*, 120, 123, 125; gifts of, 128, 129, 132, 219, 228, 244; and inspiration, 192, 201; and revelation, 127, 202, 213, 229, 267, 273; and Trinity, 126, 129–133, 243.

Hystaspes, 59, 63.

Illumination, 257; and prophecy, 195, 207, 225, 267; and truth, 193, 195, 217, 229.

Innocent III, 202.

Inquisitors, 168, 169, 170.

Inspiration, from God, 197, 201, 204, 209, 223, 235, 236, 272; and Holy Spirit, 192, 201, 213; and predictions, 192.

Isaac, 120, 121, 123, 125, 129, 131, 133.

Nature, and body, 47, 215; of man, 36, 38, 42, 53, 141; of soul, 45, 67; and Stoics, 29.

New Testament, 146, 208, 217, 221, 225, 228, 248, 249, 253; and *concordia*, 120, 122, 127, 128, 132, 133, 134.

Numbers, 219.

Old Testament, 146, 208, 217, 220, 225, 228, 248, 249, 253; and *concordia*, 120, 122, 127, 128, 132, 133, 134.

Olivi, Peter John, 167, 171, 173.

Oratory, of Abraham, 147–148; of John the Baptist, 146–147; of John the Evangelist, 144; of Mother of God, 144; of Paul, 144–145; of Peter, 145–146; of Stephan, 145.

Osee, 194; 4:1–2, 114.

Papacy, 160, 166.

Paraclete, 131.

Patriarchs, 120, 121, 253.

Paul, 92, 93, 96, 113, 126, 130, 139, 142, 175, 177, 209, 216, 218, 219, 231, 234, 237; Oratory of, 144–145.

Paul, Brother, 169.

Persecution, 218, 222, 228, 231, 274; of Angelo, 161, 165; of Antichrist, 89, 91, 92, 94, 96, 136, 140; seven, 136, 137, 139.

Peter, 116, 128, 218; Oratory of, 145–146.

2 Peter, 2:7, 116.

Peter de Capocci, 170.

Peter, Patriarch of Constantinople, 159, 167.

Phanuel, 251.

Pharisees, 239.

Pherecydes, 42, 43.

Philippians, 1:8, 118.

Plato, 25, 26, 29, 31, 42, 43, 44, 49, 53, 55, 71, 217.

Pico della Mirandola, 197.

Polites, 53.

Poor Hermits, 160.

Predictions, of future, 192, 194, 195, 197, 201, 215, 216, 219, 220, 221, 223, 226, 228, 229, 231, 235, 239, 240, 266, 267, 271, 272, 274; proof of, 192, 221, 223, 239, 240.

Prophecy, cf. also Savonarola; and Antichrist, 138, 141; discernment of, 195, 213–240, 273; at the end, 61, 94, 178; and end of world, 57, 59, 69, 72, 74, 75; and God's teaching, 25, 271; light of, 193, 194, 195, 213, 215, 216, 226, 228, 232, 272; and the Sibyl, 42, 54, 59, 61, 63, 65, 66, 72, 73, 75, 76; and scripture, 56, 121.

Proverbs, 2:14, 116.

Psalms, 7:3, 117; 13:3, 114; 22:3, 90; 29:5, 118; 48:2, 115; 50:7, 90; 67:19, 142; 67:24, 146; 71:8, 92, 139; 89:4, 56; 94:7–8, 147; 105:38, 137; 105:38–39, 114; 136:1, 118; 136:3, 118.

Punic War, 59.

Punishment, 125; eternal, 28, 39, 55, 68, 69, 77; of God, 116, 117, 175; and judgment, 27.

Pythagoras, 43, 53, 71.

Radamanthus, 69.

Raymond Berengar, Lord, 173.

Raymond, Brother, 162, 163.

Red Sea, 174.

Redemption, 89, 123, 126, 173, 176, 264.
Religion, false, 25, 74; secrets of, 42, 77; true, 25, 48, 71, 77, 78, 206.
Remus, 128.
Resurrection, 69, 70, 71, 72, 77.
Robert, Lord, 173.
Romulus, 59, 128.
Rorico, Don, 89.
Revelation, from God, 26, 29, 44, 126, 194, 197, 221; and Holy Spirit, 127, 202, 213, 229, 267, 273; prophetic, 193, 217; of Savonarola, 192, 202, 206; of wrath, 113.
Reward, eternal, 25, 39, 46, 78, 206; for vice, 25, 38, 39, 55; for virtue, 25, 27, 36, 37, 38, 39, 46, 55, 66.
Romans, 9:27, 94; 14:16, 90.

Saladin, 136, 137.
Salvation, 89, 121, 122, 192, 195, 205, 217, 254, 258, 260, 263, 266; of souls, 213, 237, 240, 244.
Samaria, 122.
Samuel, 232.
Sara, 120, 122.
Saracens, 138.
Satan, 90, 137, 140, 141, 147, 241.
Saturn, 73.
Saul, 180, 271.
Savonarola, *Compendium*, 192, 193; predictions of, 192, 201, 202, 206, 207, 213–240; revelations of, 192, 202, 206; visions of, 192, 196, 201, 207, 215, 219, 247–270.
Scribes, 239.
Scriptures, 42, 47, 55, 56, 68, 76,

89, 94, 113, 192, 194, 196, 197, 198, 209, 212, 214, 215, 217, 223, 224, 228, 230, 248, 260, 274.
Seal, 177.
Sebastian, Saint, 252.
Segor, 117.
Sevastocrator, 167.
Sibyl, 42, 54, 59, 61, 63, 65, 66, 72, 73, 75, 76.
Signs, 43, 141, 178, 214; and Antichrist, 92, 141; and *concordia*, 123; of end, 57–65, 177; and prophecy, 221, 223, 224, 227, 266, 274.
Simon Magus, 138.
Simon of Assisi, 171.
Simon of Comitissa, 171.
Sin, 209, 215; and Antichrist, 90, 93; and cleansing, 195; forgiveness of, 244, 254; penance for, 96, 113, 175, 200, 202, 246; punishment for, 28, 48, 55, 67, 68, 69, 77, 118, 139, 198, 203, 265, 266, 268, 271.
Sion, 118, 241, 261, 262.
Socrates, 29.
Sodom, 114, 116.
Solomon, 91, 194, 212, 247.
Son of God, 142, 248, 259, 266; and *concordia*, 120, 123, 128; at end of world, 62–66, 69, 72; and redemption, 123, 173; reign of, 72–75, 77; Passion of, 201, 264; and Trinity, 126, 129–133, 243.
Son of Perdition, 91, 93.
Soul, and body, 34, 38, 39, 40, 49, 50, 51, 260; death of, 38, 48, 51; immortality of, 40–55, 67, 68; numbers of, 36, 37;

peace of, 47; rewards of, 28;
works of, 48.
Status, 123, 124, 125, 126, 127,
130, 131, 133, 134, 142.
Stephan,
of, 145
Stoics, 29

DATE DUE

Tarquin,
Temple,
Temptati
Tempter,
Tempus,
133, 13
Terence,
2 Thessal
94, 13
Thomas,
Thomas
Thomas
Time, to
contin
55, 61,
114, 11
140, 17
124, 13
tribula
1 Timotl
2 Timotl
Titus, 1:1
Tityus, 6
Torquatı
Trinity,
132, 13
260, 264, 205, 206, 209.
Trismegistus, 45.
Trojans, 59.
Truth, 25; denial of, 27; and
God, 198, 213; and
illumination, 193, 194; and
prophecy, 75, 193, 231;
understanding of, 26, 28, 41.

Vergil, 30, 69, 70, 71, 74.
Vice, and Antichrist, 90; man
drawn to, 26, 27;
overthrowing of, 205, 239, 268;
39;
, 222.
242–245,
274.
; and
36, 39, 48;
mortality,
sition to,
of, 27, 205,
, 25, 36, 37,
08; way of,
, 262.
aradise,
, 194, 196,
192, 196,
247–270;
, 273.
hristian, 77,
f God, 28,
of man, 29,
30, 200, 202,
227, 228,
, 26, 28, 263;
233.
5, 29–37,
of, 44,
115, 124,
ıal, 25, 31,
--, ...-, --, -5; order of,
28; slavery of, 57; structure of,
25.

Zachariah, 249, 273.
Zachary, 120, 122, 123, 124, 125,
133, 251.
Zeno, 42.
Zenobius, Saint, 252.